# SELECTED LETTERS OF P. T. BARNUM

P. T. BARNUM AT HIS DESK. A lithograph by Charles Baugniet made in 1844 while Barnum was on his first trip to Europe with Tom Thumb.

SELECTED LETTERS

of P. T. BARNUM

EDITED AND INTRODUCED BY A. H. SAXON

"All praise to Him for permitting me always
to look upon the bright side of things"

*P. T. Barnum*

New York    COLUMBIA UNIVERSITY PRESS    1983

Library of Congress Cataloging in Publication Data

Barnum, P. T. (Phineas Taylor), 1810–1891.
  Selected letters of P. T. Barnum.

  Includes index.
  1. Barnum, P. T. (Phineas Taylor), 1810–
1891.  2. Circus owners—United States—
Biography.  3. Circus owners—United States—
Correspondence.  I. Saxon, A. H.  II. Title.
GV1811.B3A4  1982  338.4′77913′0973    82-12843
ISBN 0-231-05412-2


Columbia University Press
New York    Guildford, Surrey

Copyright © 1983 A. H. Saxon
All rights reserved
Printed in the United States of America

for

**L.-R. DAUVEN**

friend

# ❧CONTENTS❧

[vii]

# ⚜ILLUSTRATIONS⚜

[ix]

# ❦INTRODUCTION❧

**P. T. BARNUM HAS** the paradoxical distinction of being one of America's best known, least understood phenomena. To the average person in the street his name is synonymous with "circus," blatant self-advertisement, and the apocryphal statement "There's a sucker born every minute." More knowledgeable individuals also associate his name with the introduction of "jumbo" and "white elephant" to the language and recall that he once wrote a rather notorious autobiography. This last contribution, first published in 1854, in its day alternately damned as the confessions of a confidence man and hailed as a perfect pattern-book for would-be Yankees and "cute" businessmen, was translated into several languages and sold, in various editions, over a million copies during Barnum's lifetime. Its complacent author continued to augment and fiddle with it during the last quarter century of his life (on his deathbed he ordered his wife to write the account of his final days and funeral, which came to be titled *The Last Chapter*), and since then it has rarely been out of print. For better or worse, today it is regarded as an authentic piece of Americana.

There were three enduring passions in Barnum's life: his autobiography, his American Museum in New York City, and his adopted city of Bridgeport, Connecticut. The second of these, acquired by the budding showman toward the end of 1841, was a hugely popular institution attended by over forty-one million visitors during Barnum's association with it, the basis of his fortune and reputation as America's premier showman, and, until its second and final conflagration in 1868, renowned the world over as one of America's preeminent "sights." Here, for the modest sum of 25 cents (children half price), one could spend the better part of a day contemplating a hodgepodge of thousands of curiosities both living and dead, natural and unnatural, comprising animals and freaks, minerals and models, wild Indians, wax figures, and automatons, not to mention such questionable acquisitions as the "Fejee Mermaid." Visitors often brought lunches which they consumed on the premises; and eventually, at no extra charge, some three thousand of them at a time could also profitably amuse themselves in a large "lecture room" (actually a well-equipped theatre), where they were entertained by "scientific" demonstrations and skits by Tom Thumb, magic shows, harangues by Barnum, ballets and spectacles, and such edifying dramas as *Uncle Tom's Cabin* and W. H. Smith's *The Drunkard*— all in an atmosphere, as the proprietor promised, free from the noxious fumes of "segars" and rum, and with no "improper" characters let in to mingle with the innocent and genteel.

Almost until his death in 1891 Barnum was frequently preoccupied with the idea of reviving his museum, at one time enlisting support for a grand national "free" museum (a novel but unannounced feature of which was to be a "paying" museum next door— the showman believing, no doubt correctly, that visitors attracted to the one establishment could easily be induced to part with a quarter to enter the other), later projecting a chain of museums in conjunction with his circus partner James A. Bailey, and always on the lookout for "curiosities," whether animate or inanimate. Meanwhile, he lent his support to such recently founded institutions as the Smithsonian in Washington, the American Museum of Natural History in New York City, and the Barnum Museum at Tufts College in Medford, Massachusetts. The last repository, as might be expected, was named after its chief benefactor, who looked upon it as his "pet" project and not only provided the money and endowment for the building itself, but thereafter also insured a steady flow of exhibition and study materials, often the remains of circus animals, including the mounted hide of the great Jumbo himself, who was destined to become the school mascot. Even after he had launched the concern that shortly became world-renowned as "Barnum & Bailey," he continued to think not so much as a "circus," but as a "museum" man. Indeed, the freak shows, illusions, menagerie, and other exhibits that traveled with the "Greatest Show on Earth" were all extensions of his earlier interest.

Not the least curious of these traveling exhibits was Barnum himself, who visited the show whenever he could and never missed an opportunity to ride round the hippodrome track in a horse-drawn carriage and address a few words of greeting to his cheering patrons. Many of these last, in fact, considered the aging showman the greatest attraction of all. By the 1880s Americans and foreigners alike had long been familiar with the history of the tall, portly, genial-looking gentleman with the Yankee twang—if not from personal experience, then from reading about it, chiefly in Barnum's autobiography, cheap editions of which were sold "on the show."

Barnum himself, as he grew older, came increasingly to realize, and at times regret, the curious dilemma he had got himself into. On the one hand was the image he had fostered, even gloried in, during his early career when he was making his way at the American Museum and professed not to care what newspapers and the public said about him, so long as they said something. This was the period that included such outright frauds as the Fejee Mermaid and the Woolly Horse, following his earlier exploitation of the decrepit black slave Joice Heth, whom Barnum had brazenly advertised as the 161-year-old nurse of George Washington; the same period he then wrote about—more accurately, crowed over—in the first edition of his autobiography, which confirmed his claim to the title "Prince of Humbugs." And on the other hand, from around 1850 on, was the more solid, respectable image he wished to project to his fellow citizens and the world in general—the period that included his management of the morally irreproachable, "legitimate" attraction Jenny Lind, his involvement with the temperance movement and Universalist church, his career in Connecticut politics and his bid for Congress, and in time the founding of the "Greatest Show on Earth," which Barnum always looked upon as a grand moral and educational institution, blending instruction with wholesome amusement in the best Horatian tradition. Yet the earlier image of humbug and clamorous self-promotion continued to dog him, and Barnum, although he never repudiated the title of "showman," was more than once defensive about his chosen profession in later life.

From 1846, the year in which he purchased the land on which to erect his garish Moorish-style residence Iranistan, until his death in 1891, that life was increasingly centered on the city of Bridgeport. Barnum's energy and influence there extended to a broad spectrum of public improvements—an impressive record, indeed, when one considers the scope of his activities elsewhere. He served one term as mayor of the city and creditably represented his district four times in the Connecticut legislature, where he vigorously opposed the powerful railroad interests in the state and was a leader in the movement to grant Negroes the right to vote. He was president of the local hospital and water company; president and one of the original directors of the Pequonnock Bank, which today continues as the Connecticut National, the largest in the state; an active member of the parks commission; a supporter of and the first to be issued a card by the public library; and the donor of the lot and building that today constitute the Barnum Museum. Besides the four successive mansions he built in Bridgeport, Barnum soon became one of the city's largest property owners. In partnership with William H. Noble, he developed the section of the city known as East Bridgeport, inducing people to settle there by selling them land for the same price he had paid for it and even advancing them the money with which to build their homes. It was Barnum, too, who conceived and carried through the plan to establish Seaside Park on Long Island Sound and who donated considerable land and money to this project. The handsome Mountain Grove Cemetery to the west of the city, today the one remaining truly beautiful locale in all Bridgeport, is another example of his civic spirit and liberality. And both money and land were freely given to a variety of other worthwhile causes.

Yet it would be erroneous to assume that all these improvements sprang from a spirit of pure disinterestedness. Barnum himself frequently described his activities *pro bono publico* as "profitable philanthropy," and there can be little doubt that a good many of these projects did indeed prove profitable for him. His development of East Bridgeport provides a spectacular case in point. Although residents and industries were originally attracted to the new area by the highly advantageous terms already mentioned, and although Barnum and Noble enhanced this attraction by laying out a public park and erecting bridges to connect the area with central Bridgeport, the two partners readily foresaw that one result of such generosity would be a rapid rise in the value of their real estate. With this in mind they shrewdly reserved every other lot for sale at a later date. Less than forty years later, as Barnum informs us in his autobiography, land which originally had cost him $200 an acre was valued as high as $3000 and $4000 per acre.

Similarly, his contributions toward the establishment of Mountain Grove Cemetery were not entirely altruistic, since in the process he managed to acquire for development the land on which the city's earlier cemetery had stood—land that, unlike that occupied by the new cemetery, was in the very heart of the city. Even Seaside Park, perhaps the least profitable of his "philanthropies," was not without some tangible benefit to the donor. In presenting to the city a tract of land for inclusion in the park, Barnum kept back an adjacent area. And it was here that he built his third and fourth Bridgeport homes, Waldemere and Marina, set off by the beauties of the park and Long Island Sound. Only vestiges of these residences remain today, but in the park itself, now defiled by an ever-increasing mound of garbage dumped on its western flank by the City of Bridgeport, a monumental seated figure of the showman gazes pensively out to sea.

Those who have written about Barnum have all been indebted to the autobiography, and a number of these authors have consulted little else. Others, among whom the late Harvey Root and, more recently, Neil Harris deserve to be singled out for particular commendation, have patiently searched out previously untapped primary sources and have contributed much that is new to our understanding of Barnum. The present writer has himself, in numerous ways, been involved with the history of Barnum for more than a decade, in the course of which he has often had the opportunity to examine original documents, memorabilia, and other materials pertaining to the showman's career. Among these have been a great many letters, whose style and contents are often worthy of attention. Only a few have been published to date, and it was in the belief that they would prove equally interesting to others curious about Barnum and his activities that the present work was conceived. At one time, too, the editor considered arranging the letters by subject matter, but eventually rejected this plan as unfeasible. The chronological approach has its advantages, not the least of them being the revealing of the gradual expansion of Barnum's interests and circle of acquaintances. Those choosing to read the letters in conjunction with the autobiography will no doubt find this arrangement better, too. A chronology of Barnum's life is included as an additional aid.

At the outset it should be pointed out that those who come to this volume in search of sensational material or passages revelatory of new facets of Barnum's personality will probably be disappointed. For Barnum, in his letters, at least, appears to have been very much the same in private as he was in public life, and introspection and self-doubt were not a part of his character. "All praise to Him for permitting me always to look upon the bright side of things," as he wrote to a friend shortly after his bankruptcy in 1856. What does emerge from a reading of his letters is an appreciation of the surprising range of his interests and activities, his depth of involvement in many of these, and the ease and assurance with which he addressed his correspondents, from friends and business associates to the President of the United States. Such supreme self-confidence was only to be expected, perhaps, since Barnum himself, from early middle age on, was one of America's, if not the world's, most celebrated figures. He liked to boast of how letters from abroad addressed simply "P. T. Barnum, America" reached him without difficulty, and the truth of this statement, like so many of his claims, can be documented in extant sources. A large part of his daily existence was unabashedly devoted to manipulating the press and public opinion so as to acquire and maintain for himself and his enterprises what he was pleased to term "notoriety." As will be seen in the following letters, this obsession did not abate with increasing age.

A major hurdle facing anyone working with Barnum manuscript materials is the often near-illegibility of the handwriting itself, particularly in regard to obscure proper names that cannot be inferred from the manuscripts' contents. One is almost tempted to attribute this to some congenital defect, for in his autobiography Barnum describes his grandfather Taylor's chirography as being so wretched that "he himself could not read it half the time." Understandably, then, those who have consulted such materials and written on Barnum have sometimes introduced interpretative errors into their works, and the problem has not always been avoided by authors who have relied on transcriptions furnished by libraries and collections. While making no claim to infallibility, the editor has over the past several years become fairly well acquainted with the peculiarities of Barnum's handwriting. He has, moreover, as a matter of policy, worked almost exclusively from original manuscripts or their photostats—the only exceptions (and these are clearly indicated) being a few letters whose originals could not be located, but whose transcriptions were deemed of sufficient interest to merit their inclusion, even if in an imperfect state.

This said, it must be acknowledged that Barnum could, whenever he wished to or occasion demanded it, write a decent, easily followed hand. He sometimes employed an amanuensis, and toward the end of his life he occasionally experimented with a typist. The greater part of his voluminous correspondence, however, was scrawled in his own hand at top speed across the strikingly engraved stationery that so impressed such recipients as Jenny Lind, and by his own admission not much attention was paid to organization.

He seems to have written incessantly. Almost to the day of his death he continued to pour forth his thoughts, advice, directions, and requests: to his partners and business associates; to editors, scientists, and eminent divines; to strangers seeking his autograph or trying to tempt him into investing in hare-brained schemes; to his neighbors, friends, and many relations; even to the youngest of his great-grandchildren, who doubtless needed help in interpreting what "Grandpop" Barnum had to say. When at home with his family, it was his custom to leave notes lying about for his wife and daughters to discover. The telephone, fortunately, was still in its infancy during his final years. In Bridgeport, where his residence was among the first to have one installed, he used it to keep in touch with his office uptown and to summon weary relatives to play cards with him.

The bulk of this correspondence, as Professor Harris claims in his study of Barnum, has probably been destroyed or lost. Yet a formidable amount of material remains, not only in public institutions such as libraries and universities, but in business and municipal archives and private collections. The present edition is based on an examination of over three thousand letters, plus several hundred letters written to Barnum, and hardly a week goes by without some augmenting of this mass. Judging by a recent auction at the Waldorf-Astoria and a swelling flow of letters onto the market, the resur-

[xix]

gence of interest in Barnum owing to the Broadway musical purportedly founded on his life has led some individuals to take stock of their family scrapbooks. Letters that a generation ago could be picked up for five or ten dollars today go for at least ten times those figures—in some instances as high as several hundred dollars.

In selecting the letters for inclusion in this volume, the editor has been guided by several considerations, among them (1) the desire to give, so far as is possible, a representative sampling of letters written over Barnum's lifetime; (2) the intrinsic interest of the letters themselves, not only in regard to such well-known aspects of Barnum's career as his management of Jenny Lind and the acquisition and death of the great elephant Jumbo, but also as concerns such lesser known aspects as his sympathy for the woman's rights movement and his relations with family and friends; (3) in some instances the stature of the persons addressed; and (4), admittedly largely a subjective criterion, the humor, at times unintentional, or oddness of some of these epistles.

The editor has also, in order to present readers with as full a selection as possible, excised a fair number of passages of minor interest, in every case indicating such deletions by the use of the ellipsis. Four spaced periods following a signature indicates the omission of postscript material. No attempt has been made to distinguish between printed and written dates or places in the headings of letters, and usually only so much of the latter is given as to establish the cities or towns in which the letters were written. The style of dating has been made consistent and follows the day-month-year form; and Barnum's own occasional, often incomplete identifications of recipients that precede the salutations have been replaced by the information at the top of each letter. In the salutations themselves, the common abbreviation "Dr" for "Dear" has been silently expanded so as not to conflict with the many "Doctors" Barnum wrote to. Closings, too, of which "Truly Yours"—often abbreviated "Truly Yrs," "Trly Yrs," or even "TY"—is by far the most common, have been expanded without comment. Some space and, the editor hopes, confusion have been spared owing to the system of annotation employed. In place of the usual welter of burdensome notes that recommence with each successive letter, here supernumerals and footnotes are entirely dispensed with, and all explanatory material has been subsumed into a series of commentaries that immediately precede or follow their respective letters.

Within the texts of the letters themselves, editorial interpretations and occasional expansions of Barnum's abbreviations are bounded by brackets. Bracketed conjectural words are *preceded* by question marks; the editor's own comments, rarely necessary, are both bracketed and italicized. Capitalization, when not obviously used for emphasis, has been regularized; and with the few exceptions where Barnum is indicating some typographical feature he wishes followed in a bill or other publication, no distinction is made between single, double, and triple underlining—all of which the exuberant writer employed in abundance. In deference to modern readers, punctuation has been freely altered, run-on sentences have occasionally been pointed, and the original paragraphing has sometimes been lengthened or shortened. Words that were broken or hyphenated in Barnum's day have been joined to give them their modern appearance, but alternate spellings ("expense/expence," "traveled/travelled," "marvelous/marvellous," etc.) have been preserved. Genuine misspellings, rare in any case, have also been let stand—although as the astute reader will have surmised from the qualifying adjective, questions sometimes arise concerning these, owing to the difficulty, already noted, of deciphering Barnum's handwriting. The apostrophe was a mark virtually unknown to him, and especially when writing in haste he was wont to omit letters or entire syllables from words that posed no difficulty for him at other times ("goverment" vs. "government," e.g.). It is sometimes impossible to deduce just which letters are missing (in his letter of 7 October 1832 to Gideon Welles, for instance, "beginning" is written "beginng"), and these deficiencies have generally been made good without editorial comment.

While preparing this edition of Barnum's letters, the editor was assisted and encouraged by numerous individuals. The residual heirs and descendants of Barnum, besides giving their initial consent to the project, provided many family anecdotes and clues to the personality of their illustrious ancestor and generously supplied copies of materials in their possession. Here the editor is especially indebted to Mrs. Alvin C. Breul, the "Mildred" of Barnum's letters and the last of the proud showman's "baby double-grands"; to her son Alvin C. Breul Jr., Esq.; to the late Mr. Paul T. Rennell and Mrs. John D. Upton; to Miss Mary Upton; to Mrs. Herbert Barnum Seeley Jr.; and to Mrs. Augustine W. Tucker Jr.

Librarians, curators, and archivists and their able assistants at the over one hundred institutions visited or contacted were most helpful and generous with their time. Those deserving special commendation include Miss Dahlia Armon, Mrs. Lucy B. Burgess, Mr. James B. Casey, Mr. William Cox, Dr. W. H. Crain, Mr. Thomas Dunnings, Miss Diana Haskell, Mr. Paul T. Heffron, Miss Mary Ann Jensen, Mr. Robert Johnson-Lally, Mr. Karl Kabelac, Miss Heather McCallum, Dr. Russell E. Miller, Mr. Stephen Nonack, Mr. Benjamin Ortiz, Mr. Louis A. Rachow, Miss Diana Royce, Rev. Alan Seaburg, Mr. Carl Seaburg, Mr. Irwin Sexton, Mr. Robert Sokan, Miss Barbara Strong, and Mr. Alexander D. Wainwright.

A goodly number of private individuals and collectors—among them some who wish to remain anonymous, and therefore cannot be named—have been most helpful, in particular Messrs. Fred D. Pfening Jr. and his son Fred D. Pfening III; Mr. William C. Gamble and Mr. Henry F. Barbeau, chairman of the board and president, respectively, of Ward's Scientific Establishment; Dr. Miriam Blank and Raymond E. Blank, Esq.; Miss Nancy Marchand and Mr. Gilbert Cates; Mr. Edward Cameron Cridlebaugh Jr.; Mrs. Kermit S. Edgar; Dr. Laurence Senelick; Dr. D. Barton Stevens and Mr. Donald L. Stevens; Dr. Robert R. Smith; Mr. Cyril B. Mills; and Mr. Stuart Thayer.

As in the past, the editor has received much aid and advice from his worthy friends and neighbors Messrs. Robert Pelton and David W. Palmquist, curator of the Barnum Museum and head of Historical Collections at the Bridgeport Public Library, respectively. The editor also takes pleasure in acknowledging the stimulation and often telling insights of his students at Yale University, where he was privileged to conduct a seminar on Barnum while the book was in its final stages of preparation.

The initial research and collecting of materials were supported in part by a grant from the American Philosophical Society, whose aid is gratefully acknowledged.

To these and any other individuals or institutions inadvertently overlooked, the editor tenders his warmest thanks.

*Fairfield, Connecticut*
*New Year's Day, 1982*

# ☙CHRONOLOGY❧

1810     PHINEAS TAYLOR BARNUM BORN 5 July at Bethel, Connecticut, the first child of Philo Barnum by his second wife Irene (or Irena) Taylor. "Taylor" joins four surviving children by his father's first marriage to Polly Fairchild.

1810–26     RECEIVES SPORADIC EDUCATION while shirking work on the family farm. From around age ten clerks in father's country store, and between the ages of twelve and sixteen manages lotteries on his own. Father farms, keeps village tavern and small livery stable, runs a freight service between Bethel and Norwalk, and sires four more children.

1826     PHILO BARNUM DIES insolvent on 7 September (the autobiography erroneously gives 1825 as the year of his death; his headstone in the Bethel churchyard records 1828; probate records establish the correct date). "Taylor" chooses his uncle Alanson Taylor as his guardian and now clerks in a store in Grassy Plain, a mile from Bethel, where he meets the tailoress Charity ("Chairy") Hallett. He shortly travels to Brooklyn to clerk in a grocery store, and afterwards works in porterhouses. Attends theatre frequently.

1828    RETURNS TO BETHEL to open his own fruit, confectionery, oyster, and toy store. Becomes lottery agent on a grand scale in partnership with his uncle Alanson.

1829    MARRIES CHARITY HALLETT in New York City on 8 November.

1830    BUILDS HOUSE in Bethel.

1831    OPENS THE "YELLOW STORE" in Bethel in partnership with his uncle Alanson. Busies himself with religious controversy and politics, and on 19 October publishes the first issue of the *Herald of Freedom and Gospel Witness*.

1832    IN OCTOBER is fined $100 and sentenced to sixty days in the Danbury jail for libel.

1833    BUSINESS INTERESTS BEGIN to falter and he sells out his share in the "Yellow Store." First daughter, Caroline, born 27 May.

1834    CONNECTICUT LOTTERIES PROHIBITED after 3 June. Gives up the *Herald of Freedom* after publishing the 160th issue on 5 November and moves his family to New York City.

1835    AFTER SEVERAL MONTHS of unemployment, briefly runs a boarding house and grocery store. In August buys Joice Heth, the "nurse" of George Washington, and enters upon his career as a showman. While exhibiting her, meets and engages the Italian juggler Signor Antonio, whom Barnum renames "Signor Vivalla."

1836    JOICE HETH DIES on 19 February. Stages fake competitions between Vivalla and circus juggler Roberts. In April Barnum becomes secretary, treasurer, and ticket-seller with Aaron Turner's traveling circus and takes Vivalla with him. When his engagement with Turner ends in October, forms his own small troupe, which becomes known as Barnum's Grand Scientific and Musical Theatre, and tours the South.

1837　COMPANY DISBANDS in May, and Vivalla leaves Barnum at this time. After a brief trip home, in July Barnum forms a new company in Kentucky. Troupe later travels to New Orleans on boat he buys.

1838　COMPANY DISBANDS and Barnum returns to New York. Enters into partnership with Proler, a manufacturer of boot-blacking, who eventually swindles him and runs off.

1839　SIGNS CONTRACT with John Diamond's father for his son's services as "negro dancer" and begins touring with this attraction.

1840　MANAGES VARIETY PERFORMANCES in the saloon of New York's Vauxhall Garden, then tours again. Second daughter, Helen, born 18 April.

1841　MASTER DIAMOND ABSCONDS while they are touring the South. Barnum arrives back in New York in April and becomes U.S. agent for *Sears' Pictorial Illustrations of the Bible,* a speculation that lasts around six months. Gets up a summer season at the Vauxhall saloon. Writes advertisements for the Bowery Amphitheatre and articles for the newspapers. On 27 December becomes proprietor of the American Museum, formerly Scudder's, with a ten-year lease on the building and an agreement to purchase the Museum's collections from his landlord, which he does within a year.

1842　HIRES THE FEJEE MERMAID from Moses Kimball of the Boston Museum and carefully engineers publicity for this fraud. In November meets Tom Thumb (Charles S. Stratton), then four years old, and begins exhibiting him at the Museum in December. Third daughter, Frances, born 1 May.

1843　BUYS PEALE'S New York Museum for $7000 and runs it as a "rival" establishment for some six months before incorporating its collections into the American Museum's. In August stages a buffalo hunt in Hoboken and later repeats it at Camden.

[xxvii]

1844　LEAVES FOR EUROPE with Tom Thumb and entourage on 18 January. After a successful opening campaign in London, they tour, over the next three years, France, Belgium, the English provinces, Scotland, and Ireland. Meanwhile, Barnum engages in other speculations, writes a series of articles on his experiences abroad for the *New York Atlas,* and occasionally returns to the U.S. Daughter Frances dies on 11 April.

1845　ACQUIRES THE BALTIMORE MUSEUM, which is managed by Uncle Alanson until his death in 1846, after which Barnum sells it.

1846　BUYS SEVENTEEN ACRES of land in Fairfield, Connecticut, adjacent to Bridgeport, for the first of his famous mansions, Iranistan. Fourth daughter, Pauline, born 1 March.

1847　IN FEBRUARY ARRIVES back in New York with Tom Thumb and takes him on an extensive tour of the U.S. and Cuba. Renews the lease of the American Museum for 25 years. Around this time begins thinking about temperance and becomes a teetotaler.

1848　GIVES UP TOURING with Tom Thumb and returns to New York in the spring. Is elected president of the Fairfield County Agricultural Society and continues in this office until 1854. Throws a big housewarming at Iranistan on 14 November.

1849　OPENS PHILADELPHIA MUSEUM in Dr. Swain's building at Chestnut and 7th Street. Exhibits "Colonel Frémont's Woolly Horse." Mountain Grove Cemetery established in Bridgeport. Conceives and sets going plan to bring Jenny Lind to America.

1850　BUYS PEALE'S Philadelphia museum collection and divides it with Moses Kimball. The American Museum undergoes extensive renovation and reopens 17 June. Sends out expedition to capture elephants in Ceylon. Jenny Lind arrives in New York on 1 September and gives her first concert at Castle Garden on 11 September. Following her New York debut, Barnum takes her on tour.

1851    CONTINUES TO TOUR with Jenny Lind, visiting Cuba and the southern states and arriving back in New York in May. In June breaks with her after managing 95 concerts. Sells his Philadelphia museum, which later burns. In the spring, in partnership with Seth B. Howes and Sherwood Stratton (Tom Thumb's father), sends out Barnum's Great Asiatic Caravan, Museum, and Menagerie. The show travels for nearly four years and features Tom Thumb. Becomes a trustee of Tufts College, a founder and first president of the Pequonnock Bank of Bridgeport, and the American agent for Phillips' Fire Annihilator, which fails a public demonstration. In partnership with William H. Noble, buys extensive property in East Bridgeport and begins developing it. Lectures on temperance during the winter of 1851–52.

1852    JENNY LIND DEPARTS America in May. Barnum's daughter Caroline marries David W. Thompson on 19 October. The ceremony is marred by a fire at Iranistan.

1853    *THE ILLUSTRATED NEWS,* in which Barnum is a partner, publishes its first issue on 1 January and is sold to *Gleason's Pictorial* at the end of the year.

1854    IS COERCED into becoming president of the faltering New York Crystal Palace Company. Resigns after three months. In December Redfield publishes *The Life of P. T. Barnum,* the first edition of the autobiography, with an 1855 imprint.

1855    SELLS THE COLLECTIONS of the American Museum to John Greenwood Jr. and Henry D. Butler, with the lease on the building retained in Charity's name.

1856    EARLY IN THE YEAR Barnum is commonly known to be bankrupt through his East Bridgeport speculations and dealings with the Jerome Clock Co. of New Haven. Assigns Iranistan and other Bridgeport property and removes with his family first to Long Island, then to New York City. At end of year sails for England with Tom Thumb and the Howard family, of *Uncle Tom's Cabin* fame, to retrieve his fortune.

1857    FOLLOWING A SEASON in London, tours with Tom Thumb in Germany and Holland before returning to England. Resigns trusteeship of Tufts College. In August returns to Bridgeport, where his daughter Helen marries Samuel H. Hurd on 20 October. Iranistan burns during the night of 17–18 December.

1858    BACK IN ENGLAND, meets John Fish, his future father-in-law, and prepares lecture "The Art of Money-Getting."

1859    CONTINUES TO LECTURE while touring the English provinces. Returns to U.S.

1860    ON 24 MARCH BUYS back the American Museum collections from Greenwood and Butler and announces his solvency from the stage of the Museum. Builds Lindencroft, his second Bridgeport mansion, and switches to the Republican party. Prince of Wales, traveling incognito, visits American Museum on 13 October.

1861    IMPORTS WHITE WHALES and exhibits the first hippopotamus in the U.S. In December engages the midget Commodore Nutt.

1862    TOURS WITH NUTT and calls on President Lincoln at the White House. Sends out expeditions to the tropics to fill the Museum's aquaria and runs the Aquarial Gardens in Boston around this time. Engages the midget Mercy Lavinia Warren Bump, whose name he shortens to Lavinia Warren.

1863    AFTER EXHIBITING themselves at the Museum, Tom Thumb and Lavinia Warren are married on 10 February, then leave on a triumphal honeymoon tour.

1864    IN JANUARY PAYS for three volunteers from Bridgeport to fight in the Civil War. Busies himself building the Museum's collections and writes a series of "letters" on humbugs for the *New York Weekly Mercury.*

1865    REPRESENTS FAIRFIELD in the Connecticut legislature, where on 26 May he delivers a much publicized speech in favor of enfranchising Negroes. The American

Museum burns on 13 July. Opens his new American Museum on 6 September. Seaside Park established. Carleton publishes *The Humbugs of the World,* based on the articles originally written for the *Mercury.*

1866    SERVES A SECOND TERM in the Connecticut legislature. Becomes partner and president of the Barnum and Van Amburgh Museum and Menagerie Company, a touring show that winters its animals at the Museum. Daughter Pauline marries Nathan Seeley on 1 March. In autumn Barnum makes a tour of the western states lecturing on "Success in Life."

1867    RUNS FOR U.S. CONGRESS and loses. Sells Lindencroft on 1 July, moves into an interim house in Bridgeport, and buys a mansion at 438 Fifth Avenue in New York for use as a winter residence.

1868    THE AMERICAN MUSEUM burns again during the night of 2–3 March. Barnum dissolves his partnership with the Barnum and Van Amburgh Company and "retires." His mother dies on 14 March.

1869    IN JUNE MOVES into Waldemere, the third of his Bridgeport mansions. Forms a company that includes Mr. and Mrs. Tom Thumb, Commodore Nutt, and Lavinia's sister Minnie Warren and sends it on a three-year trip around the world. *Struggles and Triumphs,* a reworking and expansion of the 1855 autobiography, first published by Burr.

1870    TRAVELS TO CALIFORNIA with a party that includes John Fish and his daughter Nancy. Lays plans for a circus with W. C. Coup and Dan Castello. Friendship with Mark Twain, then living in Hartford, begins around this time.

1871    P. T. BARNUM'S MUSEUM, Menagerie, and Circus opens under canvas in Brooklyn on 10 April. At the end of the touring season the show moves into the Empire Rink in New York City.

1872    THE CIRCUS MOVES on rails this season, at the end of which a second company is formed to tour the South during the winter months. In August buys the Hippotheatron at 14th Street in New York City, where the main body of the show opens on 18 November. In October pays a visit to Colorado and a cattle ranch of which he is part owner. Around this time also speculates in Denver real estate, eventually making over some of his Colorado holdings to his daughter Helen, who settles in Denver with her second husband. Hippotheatron burns on 24 December.

1873    IN THE AUTUMN attends the International Exhibition at Vienna and visits several European cities. While Barnum is in Hamburg, Charity dies in New York on 19 November.

1874    BARNUM'S ROMAN HIPPODROME opens in New York in April and tours under canvas during the summer. On 25 June the citizens of Bridgeport give a "complimentary" dinner in his honor. In September Barnum is a delegate to the Universalist convention in New York City and there marries Nancy Fish, daughter of his English friend John Fish, on 16 September.

1875    ELECTED MAYOR of Bridgeport on 5 April. The Roman Hippodrome again takes to the road, and Professor Donaldson, the aeronaut, disappears with his balloon over Lake Michigan after taking off from the show on 15 July. In November the show properties and animals are auctioned off in preparation for a new Centennial spectacle. During the autumn Barnum travels and lectures for the Redpath Bureau on "The World and How to Live in It."

1876    THE CENTENNIAL circus tours the country with new managers, and Barnum gets up an exhibition for the Centennial celebration in Philadelphia. He is relieved when his term as mayor of Bridgeport expires on 3 April.

1877    DAUGHTER PAULINE DIES on 11 April. Barnum spends the summer in England, where he occasionally lectures. In November is elected to represent Bridgeport in the Connecticut General Assembly.

1878    BUSIES HIMSELF with improvements to Seaside Park while serving in the legislature.

1879    REPRESENTS BRIDGEPORT a second term in the General Assembly.

1880    RUNS FOR the Connecticut senate and loses. Erects a business building in Bridgeport, where his real estate interests remain considerable. Enters into partnership with James A. Bailey and James L. Hutchinson to form a combined circus. During the winter of 1880–81 suffers a near-fatal illness and recuperates in Florida.

1881    THE BARNUM & LONDON Circus opens at Madison Square Garden on 28 March with three rings and electric lighting. Barnum presents an ornamental fountain to his home town of Bethel. On 12 November the combined circus ends its first season and returns to its new winter quarters in Bridgeport.

1882    THE ELEPHANT "Baby Bridgeport" is born at winter quarters on 2 February. Jumbo arrives in America on 9 April and joins the circus at Madison Square Garden.

1883    TOM THUMB DIES on 15 July. In November Matthew Arnold visits Bridgeport and is Barnum's guest.

1884    THE CIRCUS FEATURES an ethnological exhibition called "The Grand Congress of Nations." Barnum's disappointing white elephant arrives in New York on 28 March. On 18 June the Barnum Museum of Natural History is officially opened at Tufts College. On 11 November the Bridgeport Hospital opens with Barnum as its first president. He also establishes prizes of gold medals for the best orations in the Bridgeport schools.

1885    JUMBO IS KILLED by a train on 15 September while the circus is at St. Thomas, Ontario. Bailey, on the verge of a breakdown, retires from the show and a new concern is formed with Barnum, Hutchinson, James E. Cooper, and W. W. Cole as partners.

[xxxiii]

1886    THE CIRCUS OPENS at Madison Square Garden on 1 April with the "double Jumbo" and his "widow," Alice. "Baby Bridgeport" dies on 12 April.

1887    AT THE END of the season on 22 October, Hutchinson, Cooper, and Cole withdraw and James A. Bailey becomes Barnum's equal partner in Barnum & Bailey. Jenny Lind dies on 2 November. On 20 November fire destroys the Bridgeport winter quarters and a large part of the menagerie.

1888    THE WINTER QUARTERS are rebuilt, and Barnum presents a lot in Bridgeport for the Barnum Institute of Science and History, whose building he also finances. Builds Marina, his fourth and last Bridgeport mansion.

1889    DURING THE TOUR this season, one of the trains is wrecked on the way to Montreal, killing 33 horses and 2 camels. At the end of the season the entire show embarks for England and a season at London's Olympia during the winter of 1889–90. On 9 November a banquet is given in Barnum's honor at London's Hotel Victoria. Toward the end of the tour a recording of his voice is made.

1890    IN MARCH RETURNS to the U.S. in time for the show's opening in New York, leaving his sick wife in London. In the autumn he and Nancy journey to Colorado to visit Barnum's daughter Helen. With Bailey and Cooper, acquires Adam Forepaugh's circus and runs it as a separate show. On 6 November is stricken with his final illness, "congestion of the brain," aggravated by a weakening of the heart. At Thanksgiving gives a parsonage to Bridgeport's Universalist Church of the Redeemer.

1891    APPROVES PLANS and signs contract for the Barnum Institute building, today the Barnum Museum, on 16 March. Dies at 6:34 P.M. on 7 April. Funeral and burial in Mountain Grove Cemetery on 10 April.

1893    THE BARNUM INSTITUTE of Science and History officially opens on 18 February. Thomas Ball's monumental statue of Barnum is unveiled in Seaside Park on 4 July.

1906     JAMES A. BAILEY DIES on 11 April, and the following year the circus is bought by Ringling Brothers.

1929     NANCY FISH BARNUM, having left Bridgeport and twice married since Barnum's death, dies at Cannes on 23 June.

1877. **P. T. BARNUM'S** 1877.

NEW AND ONLY

# Greatest Show on Earth

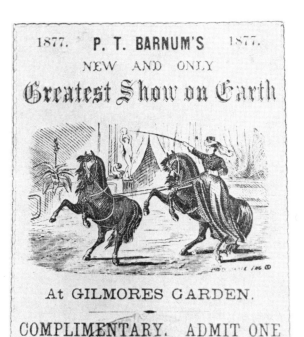

At GILMORES GARDEN.

COMPLIMENTARY. ADMIT ONE

*Agent*

# {1}

## TO GIDEON WELLES

In October 1831 Barnum became editor and publisher of the *Herald of Freedom and Gospel Witness,* a weekly paper he ran for the next three years. His object in founding the paper, as he tells us in his autobiography, was to oppose the religious fanaticism that was then sweeping New England and to combat what he and his Democratic friends believed to be the threat of the country's being taken over by a "great religious coalition." The youthful editor's outspokenness on these and other topics soon landed him in difficulties, and on three occasions he was prosecuted for libel. The most sensational of these trials was caused by Barnum's accusing Seth Seelye (or Seeley), a prominent Bethel citizen, of usury, and was heard before the eminent jurist and Yale law professor David Daggett (1764–1851).

Editor Barnum was convicted and, as he wrote to his good friend Gideon Welles (1802–78), then editor of the *Hartford Times* and a member of the Connecticut legislature, spent the next sixty days in the Danbury jail. His "suffering for daring to tell the truth," however, does not appear to have been all that intense. His cell, where he received his many friends and supporters, was papered and carpeted in anticipation of his stay; and from within these "gloomy walls" he continued to edit the *Herald of Freedom,* whose subscription list was now swelled by several hundred names. On 5 December, the day of his release, Barnum was fêted with a banquet, ode, and oration in the very courtroom where he had been sentenced, and was then conveyed the three miles to his home in Bethel in the midst of a triumphal procession of some forty horsemen and sixty carriages, accompanied by a band, the discharging of cannon, and the cheers of "several hundred citizens who did not join in the procession."

Barnum's reference to his legal difficulties with his uncle Alanson Taylor, with whom he had frequent business dealings both before and after this date, is unexplained. Sellick Osborn (1782–1826), the editor of a Democratic paper in Litchfield, Connecticut, had been sued and imprisoned for libel during his journalistic career. Zalmon Wildman (1775–1835), another prominent Democrat, later to serve in the U.S. Congress, was one of the "Officers of the Day" in charge of the celebrations upon

[1]

Barnum's release from jail; and John Milton Niles (1787–1856), at this time the Hartford postmaster, was later a U.S. Senator and Postmaster General.

Danbury Common Jail, 7 October 1832

Dear Sir,

I am by the unhallowed decree of that lump of superstition, David Daggett, sent within these gloomy walls *sixty days* for daring to tell the truth!! My trial with Alanson Taylor did not come on this term on account of the absence of witnesses, but my trial with Seth Seelye has come and the best counsel in the county were employed against me. Seelye testified in his own defence, and in his testimony he contradicted four unimpeachable witnesses. Daggett charged the jury in such a manner that many intelligent men who were present remarked that he was the best lawyer that had plead in behalf of the state. The bar and seat of the judge was filled with *priests,* there being no less than eight present. Brother Holly of the *Sentinel* will report the case at length, and I hope you will take the trouble to read the trial and then make such remarks as justice demands. The excitement in this and the neighboring towns is very great, and it will have a grand effect. *Public opinion* is greatly in my favor. After the judge had given his cursed *charge,* I was advised by many to forfeit the bonds, which were but $100, but I chose to go to prison, thinking that such a step would be the means of opening many eyes, as it no doubt will. A number of the Presbyterians in this town have declared it to be oppression and are begin[ni]ng to raise their voices against it. The same spirit gove[r]ns my enemies that imprisoned Sellick Osborn and burnt to death Michael Servetus by order of John Calvin. But the *people* are more enlightened than in the days of Calvin, and they will upon reading my trial express their indignation at such oppression and persecution.

You will observe that the Democrats in this county have a convention at Bridgeport on Thursday next. I am constantly writing to our friends in different parts of the county, urging upon them the importance of attending this meeting, and I think it will be well attended and be the means of helping our

[2]

party very much in this county. Judge Wildman is so lame with the rheumatics that he cannot walk, but he declares he will attend the convention if he is obliged to hire men to carry him in their arms. He is a man of spirit and sense. It is a great pity we had not about twenty men like him in this county. You will observe in my paper of last week that I have engaged the services of our friend Andrews; if you can give him a compliment you would much oblige me, as by my copying it into my colu[m]ns it might prove of much service to my paper. Please accept my warmest thanks and those of my wife for your assistance in recovering the lost shawl. It came safe, and my wife was thrown into ecstacies [*sic*] as an offset for the tears which (womanlike) she had shed over the loss of it. Lest I might tire your patience too much, I will draw to a close. Please give my respects to Judge Niles and the rest of our friends, tell them that I am suffering for daring to tell the truth, but that the kindness of *friends* keeps my spirits buoyed up in this day of trial. Let me hear from you when opportunity shall offer, and believe this to be from your obedient servant in good spirits,

P. T. Barnum

## TO ZALMON WILDMAN

Although Barnum claimed he never had any taste for politics, this and the following letter, detailing his activities during a Democratic caucus, would seem to indicate otherwise. Benjamin Hoyt, along with Wildman, had served as an "Officer of the Day" upon Barnum's release from prison. Judge Daggett, not yet seventy, continued to serve on the bench until the end of the following year, at which time he was compelled to retire on account of his age.

Hartford, 14 May 1833

Dear Sir,

I arrived here this morning at 10 o'clock, and since that time I have been very busy. I find many more acquaintances here than I expected and have no doubt but I shall spend the

BARNUM'S FIRST WIFE, the pretty tailoress "CHAIRY" HALLETT.
OIL PORTRAIT. PRIVATE COLLECTION.

[4]

week agre[e]ably and I hope *usefully*. From what I have learned thus far I think there is no doubt but you will be nominated instead of Beers at the county meeting, which meets tomorrow evening immediately after the adjournment of the House. . . . Our prospects so far as the offices of county court & probate judge are concerned are, I think, highly flattering, and I cannot but hope that a good arrangement will be made concerning our justices. I have hardly broached this subject yet, but shall attend to it this evening. I may be home on Saturday, but I think it doubtful whether I get there before Monday.

If you should be at Bethel, please say to our people that you have heard from me, and especially tell Esqr. Hoyt that all will be done that can be, but it is by no means best for him to flatter himself too much, for it is not certain that any movement can be made concerning our present justices. It would do my soul good to see the old Esqr. reinstated and I shall strain every nerve to effect it, but after all, the case is a doubtful one.

My much esteemed friend *Judge Daggett* is here and will try the state prison mutine[e]rs tomorrow. I intend to get an opportunity to speak with him and return him my thanks for his kindness in helping me to 1000 subscribers. Mr. Smith, a member from Berlin, has just been introduced to me by G. Welles, and he says he will be one of ten to pay my expences to Attleborough and back for the purpose of learning whether or not Daggett is over 70 yrs. of age.

I have also for the first time been introduced to Brother Barber of the *N[ew] H[aven] Register*. "Ah," says he (slapping me on the shoulder), "I would have had a day of rejoicing and a night of illumination if we could have elected old Judge Wildman to Congress." I told him if you had been put onto the ticket from Fairfield Co. and Loomis from Hartford Co., the whole ticket would have been elected, and so said he.

Yours &c. very respectfully,

P. T. Barnum

[5]

. . . I have just opened this letter to inform you that after much debate a law has just passed the House abolishing the act relating to thanksgivings and fasts. . . . I sincerely thank God for this act of our Democratic legislature. I hope you will spread the glorious news.

P. T. B.

## TO ZALMON WILDMAN

Hartford, 15 May [1833]

Respected Sir,

A meeting of the members from Fairfield County has just broken up and I hasten to give you the result of their deliberations. The appointment of judge of the county court has been reconsidered and the name of *Zalmon Wildman* substituted for that of *Jacob Beers*!! So that matter of course is sealed, and I would thank heaven if I could say the same by the office of probate judge, but this is not the fact. They *would not* reconsider their former nomination of R. Booth, so that now my whole attention will be paid to getting the subject properly brought before the House. Smith and Sanford and the whole possee of them are about half *afraid* to take the requisite measures to crush the *intriguer,* but if I do not make them "toe the mark" and move tomorrow morning before the House to erase the name of *Reuben* and substitute that of *Thomas,* I am mistaken. All that *can* be done by me *will* be, and I have still good hopes that the intriguing serpent will have his head bruised by the heel of Jackson Democracy.

As respects our justices, I cannot learn that a word has been said in the county meeting concerning them, and I greatly fear we shall not make out much in that particular; however, after the probate office is disposed of (which, by the by, I consider of infinitely the most importance), I shall pay my undivided attention to a removal of some of our Federals and fools and substituting in their places good, honest Democrats who know "B from Bull's foot," and that is more than Tim Hickok knows.

As I before said, it is doubtful what course our friends will take concerning the justices, for it seems to be hard to make them understand the necessity of removing any of them; but still I shall talk longer, and stronger, on that subject than I have done as soon as the probate question is disposed of. . . . I should rest very contented here was I not in constant anxiety about my family, whom I left in so peculiar a situation. If you should see them, please say that you have heard from me. Also please assure Esqr. Hoyt that every exertion which is in my power will be made for him, but I am sorry to say (and I say it in *confidence*) his case is a *hopeless* one, owing to his once having been a *Federalist.* Your very obedient servant in haste,

P. T. Barnum

## TO MR. BAKER

This letter obviously dates from much later than its location in the present collection would seem to indicate—possibly from December 1850, when Barnum was in Charleston with Jenny Lind; more likely from March 1853, when he was again in the city—but is included here on account of its connection with Joice Heth, the decrepit, hymn-singing Negro woman Barnum bought in 1835 and exhibited as the 161-year-old nurse of George Washington until her death in the following year. In his autobiography and elsewhere Barnum always insisted he himself had been duped by this imposition, and there is no reason to disbelieve him. In 1841 R. W. Lindsay sued Barnum in Pittsburgh for the value of a pipe of brandy, on which account the showman was briefly jailed. Twelve years after this event, Barnum writes in his autobiography, "he called upon me in Boston, with an apology. He was miserably poor, and I was highly prosperous. I hope I may be allowed to add that he did not afterwards lack a friend."

[no place or date, but probably c. March 1853]

Dear Sir,

Yours of the 3d inst. has been forwarded to me. Please read & then seal the enclosed to Lindsay. I send above $100, which I wish you to use in the best possible manner for *his benefit*. I really expect that if he had the money himself, he would lay it out foolishly, and that if a little pains [*sic*] was taken to get him into a hospital in Boston or elsewhere, that money or less would procure for him a *permanent cure* and then leave him in health to look out for himself. If he is allowed to *live out* this $100 in food and clothing, he will soon be begging again & the relief will be but *temporary*. I earnestly trust that you will *try* to have this prove a *real* benefit to him. On reflection, perhaps he had better not receive my letter nor know that you have got my check until you have got it cashed and looked about and determined how it is best to use it.

His assertions, that I understand he has made to others, that I am under obligations to him are *ridiculously false*. I never had anything to do with him except to buy from him, in *perfect good faith* & pay him the money for, an old *negress* which he falsely represented as the "nurse of Washington" and which he imposed on me as such by aid of a *forged bill of sale* purporting to have been made by the *father* of George Washington. I honestly *believed* all this & exhibited accordingly, as Lindsay had done for months previous. Finally she died & the imposition became manifest, and *I* have ever since borne the stigma of *originating* that imposture. I never denied it before— but I might have done so truly. This is all the "obligation" I am under to Lindsay, but he is a poor devil, and I hope to see him recover. Please take his receipt or some acknowledgement when he receives the benefit of this sum, if convenient. If not, no matter. I would be pleased to hear from you at Charleston, S.C.

Truly yours,

P. T. Barnum

[8]

{5}

## TO FRANCIS COURTNEY WEMYSS

John Diamond (1823–57), a celebrated blackface dancer who, Barnum claimed in his autobiography, was "the prototype of the numerous performers of the sort who have surprised and amused the public these many years," was first contracted to Barnum in 1839. "He could twist his feet and legs, while dancing, into more fantastic forms than I ever witnessed before or since in any human being," is how the manager Noah M. Ludlow later described him in his *Dramatic Life as I Found it*. Francis Courtney Wemyss (1797–1859), at this time active in theatrical management in Philadelphia, was later hired by Barnum to superintend the stage of the American Museum.

New York, 21 January 1840

Dear Sir,

I send enclosed in a newspaper a bill of Broadway Amphitheatre, in which will be seen the name of *Master Diamond*. He is beyond all doubt the best negro dancer in America; his singing is quite middling, but his dancing is absolutely beyond all calculation *astonishing*. At the National Theatre, Boston, he obtained the *largest benefit* 2 months ago of any performer this season, although he had been playing there over three weeks. Besides this kind of dancing, he is *good* in the *highland fling* and *sailor's hornpipe,* for both of which he has the proper *costumes.* Last night (his first appearance at the Broadway Amphitheatre) he was called out *five times* by an audience so crowded that no more could get in, and many having tickets were obliged to go away. So much for the *boy,* all of which is *warranted correct.*

Now, do you want him a week or two? His terms for a week would be $6 per night for five first nights and ⅓ gross receipts on the sixth night—second week $5 per night for five nights, ¼ gross on the sixth.

It is quite possible Mr. *Sweeny* may also be got with his *banjo,* which has never been before the public in Philadelphia but one night, but he is not yet *certain* that he can leave here before a month; but if he can, he & the boy would make a

[9]

*joint engagement* for $10 per night and on the sixth night ⅓ gross receipts.

There certainly is no mistake but with the *varieties* which can be given by Master Diamond and his *masterly* and *unequalled* dancing; he can draw crowded houses for a week or more, and if *Sweeny* can be with him of course the attraction will be all the greater. . . . This letter is written in haste and is not quite as *systematic* as might be wished, but you can doubtless understand it. You might certainly make a great *card* of Master Diamond for a week or two. Please write to me (whether you want him or not) by first mail . . . and much oblige

Your obedient servant,

P. T. Barnum

P.S. The boy's father is in the city, but being a foreigner & therefore not so competent to attend to engagements, he has given me power of attorney for the same.

## CIRCULAR LETTER
## TO VARIOUS FELLOW SHOWMEN

By the date of this letter Barnum had been on tour with Master Diamond for some six months, but with only indifferent success. Fogg and Stickney were managers of a traveling equestrian company that often appeared in theatres, and Ludlow and Smith, usually in partnership, were managers of several theatres in the South and West.

Mobile, 27 February 1841

To Messrs. Fogg & Stickney, Ludlow & Smith,
and all others whom this may concern
Gentlemen:

Whereas Master Diamond is lawfully, under an unfilfilled [*sic*] contract, bound to me by his guardian, Joseph W. Harrison of New York, legally appointed by the surrogate of said city, and whereas said Diamond has absconded from my employ, this is to caution you against employing or in any manner harboring him, on penalty of the law, as I am determined to pursue the legal course which is in my power against any person or persons who shall attempt to deprive me of my legal rights. Said Diamond has overdrawn the money due him to the amount of $95 and has during the last week expended a hundred dollars in brothels and other haunts of dissipation & vice.

P. T. Barnum

P.S. A full detail of his character and conduct will be published in the New Orleans papers of Wednesday next.

P. T. B.

## {7}

## TO SOL SMITH

After reclaiming his erring protégé, Barnum returned with him to New Orleans and offered his services to Sol Smith (1801–69) and Noah M. Ludlow (1795–1886), who had recently opened the New American Theatre in that city. The "divine Fanny" was the ballet dancer Fanny Elssler, then performing at the rival St. Charles Theatre. Despite the shaky start of their relationship, Smith and Barnum soon became fast friends.

New Orleans, 3 March [1841]

Mr. S. Smith:

Master Diamond has at last come to his senses and has *voluntarily* returned to me, to whom he is in every respect legally and honorably bound. As I have some business in this city to which I *ought* to devote five or six days, if you wish a little dancing as an offset to the "divine Fanny," I offer you Master Diamond's services 4, 5, or 6 nights on the following *unusually* low terms: I to receive 12½ percent on the gross receipts the three first nights; the *fourth* night being advertised for his benefit, I to have 30 percent; after which he can play one or two nights more (as you choose) for 12½ percent. On each night, if you wish, he will dance the "Black Bayadere" *à la Elssler,* also all his other dances, and play a little *burletta* which in Mobile took first-rate and was pronounced *the best thing he does.* . . . You cannot expect much *affection* on my part after telling Mr. Scott the very ridiculous story which you did about my taking another boat instead of the *Vicksburg* for the purpose of saving the paltry sum of *two dollars* (and by such false economy lose a night's performance), when in fact my only motive for not going up on the *Vicksburg* was to prevent a person in your company from tampering with Master D and attempting to seduce him from my employ. However, should we engage, nothing shall be spared on my part to ensure a successful engagement to the management, and should the *third* night instead of the fourth happen to be *Elssler's* night at the St. Charles, I have no objection to that being the *benefit* night.

Yours &c.,

P. T. Barnum

. . . .

## TO MOSES KIMBALL

Moses Kimball (1809–95), the indefatigable proprietor of the Boston Museum, was one of Barnum's closest friends. The two men were of nearly the same age and background and had even opened their museums in the same year. They frequently shared exhibits and performers and entered into joint speculations (the notorious Fejee Mermaid, a preposterous creation consisting of the dessicated head and torso of a monkey sewn to the body of a fish, which Barnum made so much of in 1842 and later years, was actually Kimball's property), and their extensive correspondence—in which they boasted of their weekly receipts, rejoiced or commiserated with each other over the success or failure of their respective enterprises, and crowed over their plans to humbug the public—contains some of the most uninhibited and revealing views we have of Barnum's early character. Unfortunately, the bulk of Barnum's earliest letters to Kimball, now in the Boston Athenaeum, was damaged some years ago in a fire. Hence the need for frequent editorial interpretation.

In late 1842, barely a year after he had become proprietor of the American

Museum, Barnum discovered and engaged the famous Bridgeport midget Charles S. Stratton, then only four years old. After carefully tutoring him in his role and re-christening him with the resounding name of "General Tom Thumb," Barnum exhibited him at the Museum and sent him on tour, originally in the care of "Parson" Fordyce Hitchcock, who was for many years in Barnum's employ. Both Mr. and Mrs. Stratton accompanied their son, the former acting as ticket seller. Yan Zoo was a Chinese juggler whose feats included balancing spinning plates on sticks; the fat boy was probably Master T. M. Reed, sometimes billed (after the famous English monstrosity) as "Daniel Lambert Jr." The reference to Peale's is to another New York museum, which Barnum bought in 1843 and ran for a few months as a "rival" establishment.

## American Museum [New York], 30 January 1843

Dear Moses,

. . . My business averaged but $70 per day last week. Sorry you[rs] is not better than that. As I have to raise $500 to pay a *private loss* before the 22 Feb., I send the General to Philadelphia on *Sunday next*. I shall run on & make arrangements next Thursday. He will probably be ready for you about 1st to 10th of March. In a few days I will send you some fine *lithographs* of him so that you can be giving him *notoriety*. . . .

*I must* have the fat boy or the other monster [or] something new *in the course of this week* so as t[o be] *sure* to put them in the General's place *next Monday,* [?*so*] *don't fail*! I don't want *Yan Zoo* unless he can perform on 8 feet [*sic*] stage & will come for $15 per week for two weeks with a privilege on my part, and he pay his own expences—indeed, I don't want him at all if you send the fat boy or something as good. Mrs. Smith will answer me *anytime* as well as Miss Mills, from whom I have heard nothing. I hope you will get the Mother Carys chickens for me. Now more about the *General.* I pay him and his father $7 per week and board & travelling expences for all three— father, mother, & son—and I have engaged my good frie[nd] Parson Hitchcock at $12 per week, board & travelling expen[ses, to go w]ith him and shew him off. . . . He will do the same at Philadelphia & Baltimore. When the Genl. goes to Boston the Parson may continue with him, or he may remain here and attend to Peale's Museum while the boy & parents go to Boston, and you pick up some genteel person in Boston to do it. Just as you please. I dare not trust my singer with him, lest he may tamper with the parents and try to hire them away. Indeed, I fear the same from any person you might employ. Hitchcock's wages may seem high, but he is genteel, industrious, and knowing the ways of the boy well; I think he will well earn all I pay him, and of course before returning from Phil. & Baltimore he will be *thoroughly rehearsed.* So do as you please about Hitchcock; only if *he* don't go to Boston, you must employ some person who won't *tamper* with the parents. Peale's took $60 last week. . . .

Don't fail to send me *some attraction* in time for next week.

Yours forever & a day,

Barnum

## TO MOSES KIMBALL

New York, 5 February 1843

My dear Moses,

I never was more *happily disappointed* [than when I rec.] your letter today about the giant booby. I had made up [my mind] that it would be a failure and that I should pay their expen[ses &] wages & send them back without exhibiting. A thousand thanks [for] saving me the trouble & expense. The fact is, a half & half giant [or] anything else is good for nothing. . . . Tom Thumb left for Philadelphia today; yesterday was his (adver[tised]) *farewell* benefit. I took $*280*! Did you ever hear the like? [The] day previous took $90 odd. I have the Rocky Mountain wild I[ndians] this week. Give them one half after deducting $*400* for the week's [expenses!] That is a *leetle* better than to give them *two thirds à la* Peale.

[14]

By the way, Peale wrote me the other day to ask if I c[ould] not send him a Tom Thumb or a two-headed man or [something] to create an *excitement*. . . . I replied that I could furnish [him with a] "beast with 7 heads & 10 horns" at short notice, or any other [?item] that he ordered; that Tom Thumb was made to my order six [?weeks] ago, and being now *nearly new* & without a rival, he was [very] *valuable;* that I thought he could take $1200 per week in Balti[more] Museum; and that he might engage him if he gave me [?half.] I shall let him chew upon that a few days. He certainly nev[er shall] have him for less than *half.*

I went to Philadelphia last [?Wednesday] night. . . . I engaged Masonic Hall *front room first floor* for only $12 per *week,* including *gas* & *fuel.* If I don't clear $1000 there I shall for the thousandth time in my life be mistaken. [I] hope to get through with Phil. & Baltimore & take him [south] myself, then let you have him by about the [middle] of March. But you must *drive* business when you get him, & to assist in that, I shall send you some *lithographs* to distribute about your whole city, especially in all public show windows—hotels, P. Office, &c. &c. . . . I have practiced [this] strong in Philadelphia, and I think with *great effect*. . . . I have sent to London for a [pony] there for sale, 30 inches high. Do you know of one not over 3 feet? [I] want it for Tom Thumb, to ride about the room on.

As ever [thine,]

Barnum

The Peale referred to in this letter was Rubens Peale—son of Charles Willson Peale, the famous painter, naturalist, and museum proprietor—who was then carrying on his family's business at the Baltimore museum that still bears their name.

# (10)

## TO MOSES KIMBALL

American Museum, 8 March 1843

Oh Temperance! *Oh Moses*!!!

What a big oat you must [have] swallowed crossways when you wrote me those [letters.] That of the 7th came *early* this morning—that of the *6th* [?three] hours afterwards. Well, you are in rather bad luck just [now] and you have *a right to be cross*: the armour was wrong, [the] Indian men were contrary, Harrington was wiffling, Barnum w[as] greedy and was keeping Tommy longer south than he promised, yo[ur] business was bad, you generously advanced that *"bitch"* $12 a[nd] got her the situation, and all that like a devilish clever fellow as [you ?are.]

*And you may get cross once in a while, and* [you] *may write me cross letters,* and I'll bear with [it like] a man; but you *must* permit me to *laugh* when I read your bitter effusions, for I know just how you feel, having felt exactly so a thousand times. But *don't* eat a fellow up now without giving him a chance for his life—pray don't! You may blow me up a little and swear at me if you are a mind to, and I'll g[ive] you full liberty to *lick* Miss Darling and ride her on a [rail] into the bargain if you want to, but don't—oh don't—tar [and] feather me and draw me in quarters on account of [your] *"cart loads* of gold and silver vases, ornaments,"* diamonds,* [&c. &c.]

I have not shown your letter to "Miss Darling" nor spoken of the contents, nor shall I—I'll wait for you to cool down. [I] told Frances that you did not like what I said about the appa[ratus.] She replied that Miss Darling told her yesterday that she hoped I [had] not written you anything about it that would give offence, for you had really been very kind to her and she would sooner work six months for nothing than to offend you, for she felt very grateful to you, and all that sort

[16]

of thing. . . . In keeping [*Tom*] *Thumb* longer south than I expected, I keep him out of my own museum as well as yours, and if he lives you shall have him, and at a time when you can make more money than he now could for you, and as for making *hay, excitement,* &c., it will be found an *easy* matter for you to raise an excitement on *Tommy* anytime, especially the *first* time. It hardly seems *sensible* to [go] to the expense of bringing him from the South where [he] is doing well, and then have to take him back there, perhaps in summer, when in fact *now* is the best season of the year to have him there. [?As to] the Big Boy, you may hold on to him as colla[teral] security for Tommy—or you may send him on whenever you please.

Do you want a pretty good-sized *bald eagle* skin? I bought two yesterday—shot on Long Island. . . .

As ever thine,

Barnum

The "bitch" and Miss Darling were one and the same—a female magician with a shady past. Barnum had advertised her as arriving from abroad, but the *Spirit of the Times* later disclosed her real name was Mills and that she had spent time in a Massachusetts insane asylum after robbing her father and running off with a lover who abandoned her. It was Kimball, apparently, who first gave her the chance to "rehabilitate" herself, ordering and overcharging her for some equipment for her act. When Barnum relayed her complaints about this, her benefactor exploded. Notwithstanding such ingratitude, Kimball joined Barnum in engaging her for a year at the rate of $6 per week and traveling expenses, which even Barnum conceded was "little enough." Both managers were also engaging various groups of American Indians around this time. Harrington was an exhibitor of dioramas who also made some props for Miss Darling.

## TO MOSES KIMBALL

American Museum, 20 March [1843]

Friend Moses,

. . . The *"bitch"* appears tonight for the first time. I reckon she'll make a hit. That brute of a Snelling *blowed* her yesterday. His informant is *Bennett,* who has returned and who pumped it out of Julius [?—*charred,*] Celeste's mother, or some other lea[king ?hulk.]

Some of our damned skunks have seen the Mermaid box stowed away on the top shelf of my office, and *that* has been tattled out, it seems.

Now how the hell to keep anything from the damned traitors except to do all the work and performing myself, I don't know. I have no time to say more.

As ever thine,

Barnum

When the *Spirit of the Times* printed its exposé of Barnum's new attraction, Barnum suspected Henry Bennett, who later in the year managed Peale's Museum for him, of leaking the story to the paper's correspondent. The Mermaid was the notorious one of "Fejee" extraction, which Barnum had exhibited at his museum the previous year. It was then sent on tour under the management of his uncle Alanson Taylor. But in Charleston, as Barnum wrote Kimball in a letter of 13 February 1843, the "bubble" burst, and Taylor was subjected to "everything that a mortal could stand" (*Boston Athenaeum*). In effect, the fraud had outraged the local scientific community, and the resulting ruckus was so great that Barnum himself, for once, seems to have been genuinely embarrassed. To spare its being made into "mince meat," the Mermaid was secretly shipped back to New York.

❮12❯

## TO MOSES KIMBALL

American Museum, 22 March 1843

Friend Moses,

Yours of yesterday is at hand. The *"Darling"* takes better and better every day—last night took $70 and all were delighted with the enchantress. She is bound to take pretty well. For fear the *Times* would be out on her again next Sunday, I concluded to advertise her *benefit* for Saturday next (day and evening), and I also advertised in her name that tickets might be got of her *personally* at the Museum office during the day, Friday & Saturday. I think that will help some, as I am not the only one who thinks her a "saint"—a vestal, in fact. [However, I] expect she will sell most of her tickets to those who *hope* she is *not quite* a saint. . . .

The *Times* men have just called to say they are *very sorry* they assailed me and Miss Darling, *will not do it again,* &c. I regret to say they were induced to this by a *large quid pro quo.* . . . If Bennett, as I believe, carried that information to the *Times,* I'll see [him] doubly damned before he shall come to my place. I'll sooner make enemies and let them pick the holes in my jacket than to succumb unnecessarily to d——d infernal knaves and traitors, *cunning* though they may be. His shrewdness, after all, is of the small-potatoe order, and I fear it not. . . .

The fat boy has been noticed this morning [in ?all] the papers and will be advertised Sunday. . . . Dr. Valentine commences with me Monday for $30 per week. I lose Miss Hood— *awful!*—and Mr. Jenkins. Express waits.

As ever thine,

Barnum

Dr. Valentine was a comic lecturer and impersonator of eccentric characters.

## TO MOSES KIMBALL

Despite their setback with the Mermaid in Charleston, Barnum had suggested to Kimball that, for the sake of the "excitement," they institute a suit against their chief antagonist in that city, the Rev. John Bachman. By the time of this letter Kimball was more enthusiastic over the idea than was Barnum, who in the meantime had consulted a Charleston journalist and lawyer, Richard Yeadon, on the subject. Celeste Williams was a juvenile dancer who was around thirteen years old at this time. Mary Gannon (1829–68), sometimes billed as "la petite Elssler" on account of her dancing, was also an actress who later attained some distinction in the American theatre.

New York, 27 March [1843]

Well Moses,

I have done as you directed—[read your] letter, *re*-read it, and *slept on it*—and all to no effect [as] far as changing my mind from the *first impression* made upon looking it over—viz., that although it would be wondrous funny and profitable withal to sue & *beat* Dr. Bachman, Yeadon does *not* [by] any manner of means feel *confident* that we could do so. First, he says *"provided* it be a *genuine* specimen" &c. Now my dear [Moses,] every devil among the scientifics would *swear* that its existe[nce] is a *natural impossibility,* and would they not raise suspicions too strong in the minds of the *cannaile* [*sic*] for us to use *them* to advantage? 2d, Yeadon says if the object is to get damages, "Dr. Bachman [may] have a *party,* and a *strong one,* & the chance of success would be *lessened"*—or in other words there *would be no chance at* [all,] for all lawyers are sure to put the smoothest possible [?side]. . . . However, it would be *Almighty Rich* if we *could* sue & *beat* Bachman, and I would join you in giving Yeadon $500 in case of *success.* . . .

Harrington is here. Williams (Celeste's father) is afraid that there will not be room enough for her to dance. Please measure & send me *depth* & *width* of what stage room you have. Then he talks about new clothes for her and many new fixins, as he says she has never been in "Bosting" & if she goes he wan[ts her] to *make a great hit.* Then he says he is not sure she can be ready *so soon,* as he wants her to take a *benefit* here before [leaving,] but is to tell me all in a day or two. I felt of him about *terms.* [He] said he thought it should be $15 per week. I told him I believed you [had] got Miss Gannon & two or three more for that. He stuck up his nose [at] the *comparison* between Miss G and Celeste &c. &c. *I* can spare her—glad of the chance. She would please *your people.* . . .

The Darling is *only* so-so. I have *not* "taken an *especial* fancy in that quarter" and *only as a matter of business* consider her or wis[h] you to consider her as anything particularly *extra.* Still, I believe she is *much better* than if she had *"turned out"* after her seduction, and I think it a *"charity"* and a good act to give her honest employm[ent] (*more especially* if we can do it *profitably*), *not* believing her to [be] "a d——d artful & hypocritical bitch." She *may* be, but *I* have seen nothing like it & *hope* I shall not. If I do, then are we [?well] stuck for a year! Remember the fat boy next Saturday & the *cut* on Wednesday or Thursday.

As ever thine,

Barnum

## TO MOSES KIMBALL

American Museum, 1 September 1843

Dear Moses,

I am grieved, vexed, and disappointed [to] hear of the sickness and *death* (for I know she will die) of the Ourang Outang. D——n the luck! I have puffed he[r] high & dry, got a large transparency and a flag 10 [by] 16 feet painted for her, besides newspaper cut engraved, [&c.]—and now, curse her, she must up foot and die. [This] is *peculiarly distressing* from the fact that Tom Thumb, Cole, his dog, & Great Western all leave this week to [make] room for *her*—& she can't come! But some p[ork] will boil that way & I must grin & bear it. The Par[k, Olym]pic, & Amphitheatre all open next Monday—and of course catch me with my breeches down. . . .

Barnum

---

"Great Western"—not to be confused with the steamship of the same name—was a comic actor who specialized in Yankee roles.

# (15)

## TO MOSES KIMBALL

American Museum, 26 September 1843

Dear Moses,

The Indians arrived and danced [?last] night. There are 5 Indians, 2 squaws, and a little [?papoose] five or six years old besides the interpreter. I have never *seen* them till last night—you may think that *stran[ge,]* but it is a *fact.* They dance very well, but do not [?look] so fine as those last winter. They rowed, or rather *paddled,* another [race] last Saturday at Camden. I hired them *out* for the oc[casion] for $100 and their board &c. Fitzhugh staid with them [and] brought me the money last night. You may as [well] get your puffs preliminary in the papers. I [?think] that I can let them leave here Saturday after[noon,] though I can tell better and *positively* on Thursday, [so] that you know Friday morning. . . .

Thine as ever,

P. T. Barnum

P.S. You must either get a [?building] near the museum for the Indians to sleep and cook their own victuals [in] or else let them sleep in the museum on their skins & have victuals sent them from some *Sweeny* shop. I boil up ham & potatoes, corn, beef, &c. *at home* & send them at each meal. The interpreter is a kind of half-breed and a decent chap; he must have common private board. The lazy devils want to be *lying down* nearly all the time, and as it looks so bad for them to be lying about the Museum, I have them stretched out in the workshop all day, some of them occasionally strolling about the Museum. D——n Indians *anyhow.* They are a lazy, shiftless set of brutes—though they will *draw.*

B

[22]

# (16)

## TO MOSES KIMBALL

American Museum, 12 October [1843]

Dear Moses,

. . . I have agreed to let John Sefton have t[he] General one night next week at Niblo's for his benefit. *I* am to take General on the stage & show him off, & have somebody in the boxes call out to ha[ve] him *passed round,* which I shall decline but express my *regret* at being obliged to do so, as he must return at once to the American Museum, but that they can see him, shake hands, & converse with him at the *Museum* any d[ay] during the week! Sefton gives me $50 and will not detain him 30 minutes. . . . Harnden's folks can't get *the* pony, but propose [to] get another. I *decline* & ask for my money, which they agree I shall have. Now my dear fellow, what must I give you for your *smallest?* Touch me like a *Christian* of some *fellow feeling* & write by return express.

As ever thine in haste,

Barnum

. . . .

John Sefton (1805–68) was a popular comic actor of the day. The pony Barnum was so eager to acquire was for the General's use. In a letter of 24 October to Kimball, Barnum writes that Tom Thumb "killed 'em dead" at Sefton's benefit (*Boston Athenaeum*).

# (17)

## TO MOSES KIMBALL

New York, 8 November 1843

Dear Moses,

. . . I send Hitchcock to Baltimore this afterno[on] to get those dirty, lazy, and *lousy* Gipseys. I expect they are too d——d low for me to do anything with them. However, I *must try*, f[or] if I don't do better than at present, I am sure to bust.

As ever thine,

Barnum

# (18)

## TO EDWARD EVERETT

From 1844 to 1847, with time out for flying visits to America, Barnum was in Europe with his sensational discovery Tom Thumb, leaving his museum and other interests in the hands of capable assistants, among them "Parson" Hitchcock. At the time of his arrival in London the distinguished scholar, orator, and statesman Edward Everett was U.S. Minister to Great Britain. It was Everett who helped Barnum attain a major goal of the tour: a "command" to appear before Victoria and her court at Buckingham Palace.

London, Saturday night, 23 March [1844]

Dear Sir,

Ten thousand thousand thanks for your kindness. General Tom Thumb and myself have just returned from a visit to Her Majesty the Queen, in compliance with the royal command delivered this afternoon by Mr. Murray. The Queen was delighted with the General, asked him many questions, presented him with her own hands confectionary &c., and was highly pleased with his answers, his songs, imitation of Napo-

[24]

leon, &c. &c. Prince Albert, the Duchess of Kent, and the Royal Household expressed themselves much pleased with the General, and on our departure the Queen desired the lord-in-waiting to request that I would be careful and never allow the General to be fatigued. I assured his lordship that I would strictly regard Her Majesty's injunction. I have now attained my *highest* desires and hasten to thank *you* to whom I am *entirely* indebted for this great gratification. Rest assured that your goodness will never be forgotten.

Had I anticipated this unexpected honor, I should not have written what I fear you will regard as a *presumptive* letter this morning. If so, I hope you will forgive it.

Hoping to have the pleasure of seeing yourself and friends whenever & *wherever* may suit your convenience, I have the honor to remain, dear sir,

Your obliged & humble servant,

P. T. Barnum

## TO MOSES KIMBALL

Norwich, England, 29 July 1844

Dear Moses,

I have hired the "Bell Ringers" at a roaring price—much too high to think of putting them in our museums at present. I have made them *"Swiss,"* procured *Swiss dresses,* got out a lithograph representing them in *Swiss costume,* & have sent the stone by this steamer *directed to you.* You must take it out of the custom house, pay duty if any (it cost only $12.50), & forward it to Hitchcock. Neither myself nor Hitchcock are to be *known* in the business, but the public are to suppose that the "Ringers" go to America *on their own hook;* and *you* must help us to prepare the public by means of lithographs & *extracts* for a grand *furore,* equal to the *Ole Bull* excitement; [and] when they arrive they must open at Tabernacle or Apollo in N.Y., take $300 to $500 per night *if possible,* then do the same thing for a week or two at Philadelphia, Baltimore, & Boston, and *then* take them in the museums. Now my dear fellow, I have made a *"strong venture"* in engaging these chaps. There are 7 ringers, besides one who goes along & keeps in continual practice so as to be ready in case one is sick. Then there is a violin player, making *nine* in all. I have advanced them over $300, paid their passages besides, & they sail in the *England* on the 1st of Aug. Now my boy, do help give them a lift in Boston, & I'll do as much for you. If you can give Hitchcock any advice, pray do so. Perhaps you know some driving fellow (musical or not) who could take charge of them & put them through those cities. *I* shall fix Wilbur & Smith's *Times* & the N.Y. papers. They *are* really the most extraordinary fellows in the world, & if the *fashion* will only stamp them, I don't see why they can't quite equal "Ole Bull" in attraction. If they *can't* go it *strong* alone, or by the aid of one or two good singers (which I *think* they *can*), why then they must go to the best theatres on shares, say *half* or thereabouts. If *I* was in America I would make a fortune on them. I hope you will advise H so that he can do it for me. They are *very funny* & *novel.*

I have also absolutely & truly obtained the *identical state robe* or dress worn by *Queen Victoria* at her levees & drawing rooms. It is positively *true, on my honor, so help me God!* If you knew the difficulty I had in obtaining it, you would excuse the earnestness of the above expression. It is *rayther* magnificent & ought to make $20,000 in America in three years. It is not *often* that queens' state dresses are exhibited to the public. I dare not tell *how* I got it—but I got it honestly & *paid for it*—& by & bye *you* must have a *shy* at it & thus help yourself & me too. I shall spend no more money for attractions for the present, I tell you, for I *have* spent after the big sort lately, you may depend. However, I must trust to luck & *hope* to get it back fiftyfold.

We are down in the very poorest part of England (*got*

*sucked*), take only $150 per day, but return to London next Monday, stay a week & then go into the very heart of England, & I *guess* will go it strong as ever. General is in capital health & spirits—improves every moment & don't grow a hair. Stratton's folks are first-rate; everything goes as smooth as oil. . . . I meant to have said that the Queen's dress *may* be sent to *you* by this steamer. If so, you must tell custom house officers it is second-hand wardrobe, & if they won't let it go duty free, you must call the second-hand cost price $*100* & pay duty on $100. But if nothing is said to them about its being the Queen's, I think you *may* get it through as *theatrical wardrobe—perhaps*. . . .

London, Aug. 1st

Since writing the foregoing I have come, as you see, to London. The Indians will be here tomorrow, and Catlin & self will make money on them I *think* to a large amount—but alas for the fallibility of all human expectations. We may *lose* a heap instead of make, but my *hopes* are *high* on the subject. . . . I have written Bennett of the *Herald* a letter which he must publish about the giant business. If he don't, I will cowhide him when I get to N.Y., no mistake about it. . . . Olmsted has written me & *hinted* that at the expiration of my lease he *may* convert the Museum into *offices*. Of course it is only done to frighten me & perhaps raise the rent, but I'll frighten him damnably, for I shall write *advising him to do so* and telling him that I have concluded to lease ground or buy & build a larger & more convenient museum in Broadway. I *know* it will scare him. . . .

Thine as ever,

Barnum

. . . .

The campanologists, who did indeed prove successful in America, were actually from Lancashire. Besides touring with Tom Thumb and sending back to America a steady stream of curiosities and performers, Barnum engaged in a number of other enterprises while abroad, among them an exhibition of American Indians in partnership with the famous artist George Catlin. James Gordon Bennett (1795–1872), the proprietor and editor of the *New York Herald,* was one of Barnum's most persistent ene-

[27]

mies, having been taken in by the showman's publicity practices as early as 1836 in connection with the Joice Heth affair. Francis W. Olmsted, who owned the American Museum building (by this date Barnum owned the collections), was happy to renew the lease.

## (20)

## TO MOSES KIMBALL

Bristol, England, 18 August 1844

My dear Moses,

I could not possibly get time to write you by the *Great Western* & have but a little chance to do so now. So I must go right into the merits of the case. I am sorry to hear that your "numerous & complicated businesses" are proving too *hard* for you and hope that your rusticating in the country will be of advantage to you. As for my own part, the more business I have the better I like it. I now have got the Indians under full blast, and what with them & Tom Thumb, my automaton writer exhibiting at the Adelaide Gallery, the Bell Ringers, Am. Museum & Peale's, giants, dwarf, &c., I guess I have about enough on hand to keep *one* busy. But for fear I might get out of business (notwithstanding I cautioned you about getting [*too*] *many* irons in the fire), I am thinking *very seriously* of buying out the Adelaide Gallery in London & carrying it on in company with the nephew of Catlin, a regular roarer. The chance for success is great—indeed, it is *sure*—and by that arrangement he could send me novelties to America & I could occasionally send him a fat nigger girl or something else. Besides, he is *at home* with the *press* & could *glorify in advance* anything sent to America, as we could also that sent to England. These inducements have great weight with me, and the whole investment required is only about $6000, with every prospect of clearing $20,000 per annum. I may not go into this arrangement, but it is perfectly feasible.

[28]

BARNUM and his FAMOUS MIDGET GENERAL TOM THUMB, dressed
in one of the costumes he wore in his skits.

DAGUERREOTYPE. COURTESY OF MRS. MORRIS S. BRITTO.

[29]

That "Yankee Dwarf" calling himself Tom Thumb will only help the real critter. There are at least 20 General Tom Thumbs now exhibiting in various parts of England, but that only paves the way for the approach of the *"conquering hero."* . . . We shall not get to Paris with the General before February, *if at all.* At present we are going through the best towns in England—average receipts $300 per day & I *guess* they will get over that before we reach Lei[cester]. . . . If the General keeps his health a few months longer (& he is as fine as ever), and if I keep my health, I *guess* I shall be able to take home enough to pay me for the trouble of coming over here! . . . The General's sales of books (lives) & pictures average him $30 per day, or $9000 per annum, more than half of which is profit & *their* perquisites. Not *werry* bad! His carriage, ponies, & servants in livery will be ready in a fortnight and will *kill the public dead.* They can't survive it! It will be the greatest hit in the universe, see if it ain't! . . .

As ever thine,

P. T. Barnum

## (21)

### TO MOSES KIMBALL

The parents of Tom Thumb, Sherwood and Cynthia Stratton, accompanied their son to Europe and, as this and other letters indicate, occasionally nettled the manager by challenging his authority. In his letters to the *New York Atlas* and later in his autobiography, Barnum ridiculed their pretensions and boorishness, sometimes disguising their identities. The "new administration" refers to the new contractual arrangements that took effect on 1 January 1845, whereby the General and his father, no longer on salary, now shared the profits equally with Barnum.

London, 30 January 1845

My dear Moses,

    . . . Since New Year's (the new Tom Thumb administration) *my* profits have averaged $800 per week, & I think if the General lives I may safely count on clearing $25,000 per annum. You may well say it is a "fairy business." The Strattons are crazy—absolutely deranged with such golden success. At first they were inclined to take airs, carry high heads, and talk about what *we* were doing; but when Mrs. Stratton began to be too inquisitive about the *business* & to say that *she* thought expences were too high & that I spent too much for printing &c., I told them both *very decidedly* that *I* was the *manager* & that unless the *whole* was left to my direction [I] would not stay a single day. Their horns were hauled in very suddenly, you may depend, & they are now down to their *old level,* where you may be sure I shall keep them. I can do business with blockheads & brutes when there is money enough to be made by it, but I can't be tempted by money to associate with them nor allow them to rule. . . . I want to get some beautiful dissolving views painted in London illustrating the *history of the American Revolution,* and in order to do that I must have correct prints, *colored* so as to give the correct colors of the *military costumes* &c., and as you know much more of those subjects than either Hitchcock or me, I must trouble *you* to collect them & send them to me *by the next steamer.*

First, I want the landing of our forefathers at Plymouth, then an Indian treaty or two (I already have *Penn's* treaty), then any pictures of their skirmishes with the Indians, then the picture of throwing over the *tea* in Boston harbor, then *all the different battles* both by *land* and *sea,* also a good view of *Bunker Hill as it now is,* &c. &c. &c.—affording a complete pictorial history of our country up to the close of the Revolution—& a group of Liberty, the American flags, shield, and the devil and all as a grand and glorious *finale* to the patriotic drama. A good view of Fannieul [*sic*] Hall, Washington's seat at Mount Vernon, &c. &c. would all help fill up the plot. Also correct portraits of all our Presidents, though on the whole I only care for those of Washington & Jefferson & [*pointing hand*] Jackson! Now my dear fellow, set your *wits* to work & give me the fruits thereof. . . .

I am glad the old Lowell museum is turning out so rich

[31]

& am also glad that you are so strong a National Republican. Put me down as one, for if ever I return I'll go that ticket. It's time to fight against *foreign* interference in our elections. . . .

I am truly yours,

P. T. Barnum

## {22}

## TO MOSES KIMBALL

Paris, 30 April [1845]

My dear Moses,

Yours of the 1st is before me [and I am] greatly rejoiced to hear of your continued & improved success. I trust that ere long the richest men in America will be *we museum* chaps. . . .

General is carrying all before him. He is as merry, happy, & successful as ever. Stratton is laying up $500 per week, & I guess Bridgeport will be quite too sm[all] to hold him on our return. And as for his wife, she will look upon N. York or Boston as dirty villages quite beneath her notice. Maybe there is not already a display of ringlets, earrings & other jewelry, $50 silk dresses with *low bosoms,* &c. &c!!! It's rich! Very!! . . .

Thine as ever,

Barnum

## 23

## TO MOSES KIMBALL

Bordeaux, 26 August 1845

My dear Moses,

Yours of Aug. 1st is recd. . . . I am indeed having "a glorious time" in France & elsewhere at the exp[ense] of the *public,* & in 15 days I am going with the General to see the Queen of Spain, who with her court will be within two days' jour[ney] from Bordeaux. I am managing the French *language* as well as French napoleons—beautifully.

Yes, the daddy & mammy of the Genl. are the greatest curiosities living, and [I] am now showing them up a little in the *Atlas.* I could not help it, for [there] were some jokes too good to be lost. For instance, when we were [in] Belgium, Stratton was surprized [*sic*] to hear *Dutch* spoken. He said [he "had] no idea the old Dutchmen ever travelled so far from *home."* I asked him where he supposed their "home" was. He said, *"In the western part of the state of New York"*! Wasn't that rich? . . .

The laws of France about exhibitions are very *funny.* They are made [to] protect theatres; & in all the towns of France except Paris, unless I can arrange with [the] manager of the theatre he can by law take 15 percent of my *gross* receipts & the hospital can take 25 percent of my *gross receipts*— in all, 40 percent! I have generally arranged with the managers to play in theatre nights & get half gross receipts, saving to myself the privilege of playing day times without giving manager anything. And generally [I] have paid the hospital from 5 to 20 francs per day. But in Bordeaux . . . the manager claimed 15 percent & the hospice would not [take le]ss than 20 percent—in all 35 percent on my *gross receipts.* So I have [give]n them a touch of *Yankee.*

In olden times Bordeaux was of course a little village,

and the little village of *Vincennes* joined it. Bordeaux now has 110,000 inhabitants & has extended so as quite to *surround Vincennes,* and yet singularly enough Vincennes has *preserved her rights* and stands, with *a mayor of its own,* almost in the middle of the city of Bordeaux! I have therefore arranged to exhibit the General in a magnificent saloon in *Vincennes,* where I pay the hospice 10 francs per day, and as there is no *theatre* in that commune, I [don't] pay a d——d sou for the theatre! Furthermore, they are all crazy [to see] the General & will do so at any price; so to be revenged I have [?put] the price of admission at *three francs each* (it usually out [of Paris] is 2 francs), and I'll raise hell here for 10 or 12 days & no mistake. There's plenty of money here & I'll get a good bit of it—& leave the hospital directors a lesson they will not soon forget.

This is a most *charming* country, & he who has not seen it has seen *nothing.* There is no ale here, but I guess there is a little *w[ine.]* Price for good wine, 6 sous per bottle! Wholesale pr[ice] of ditto, 3 sous or 2½ cents per quart! Of course, they have high[er] prices—6 francs per bottle—but the difference is much more in name than in quality. It makes a man's mouth water to walk through the vineyards here, often 50 & 100 acres each, all loaded with grapes. It's a great country, Moses, & you *ought* to be here a month with me—but there's no use talking, you won't come. . . .

Barnum

[34]

## 24

## TO MOSES KIMBALL

Brighton, England, 18 August 1846

My dear Moses,

I acknowledge and confess that I played all my friends, including yourself, rather a shabby trick in coming away so suddenly from America. But truth to say, I think if I had not come by the *G. Western,* I should not have come at all, for I should have been confined in an *insane retreat* before the next steamer sailed.

I *never* before experienced so much trouble, nay *misery,* in the same space of time as I was forced to endure during my stay in the States, and if I believed I should be obliged to go through the same vexations & annoyances when I returned, I would *never go back, by God*!

However, I hope yet to get a little peace of [*sic*] my life, though I shall not return to try it till next year.

I intended to have left New York on the 16th July, but my troubles only seemed daily to increase, and in a fit of very *desperation* I resolved to leave the 25th June by *G. Western.* So here I am, and although hard at work and not very happy, I have less *troubles* than when I was home. General is as usual *first-rate* and prospering. The speaking automaton has paid all the expences from Philadelphia to London and is now clearing $300 per week with prospect of a great increase next year in the *season*.

The *animal* that I spoke to you & Hale about comes out at Egyptian Hall, London, next Monday, and I half fear that it will not only be exposed, but that *I* shall be *found out* in the matter. However, I go it, live or die. The thing is not to be called *anything* by the exhibitor. We know not & therefore do not assert whether it is human or animal. We leave that all to the sagacious public to decide.

[35]

The bills & advertisements will be headed as follows:

"WHAT IS IT?
Now Exhibiting at Egyptian Hall &c. &c.
found in the forests of California &c. &c."

I hope you are succeeding in your *stupenduous* [*sic*] *enterprise* and that you will have a success exceeding your own most sanguine expectations, & *I believe you will.* If you do, then all the world will say, "Great is Moses, we always knew he was the cleverest, sharpest man in Boston &c. &c." But if you should prove unfortunate, then all the world will exclaim, "What a stupid fellow! We knew he would fail in his foolish enterprise and it serves him right!" Such is man—such is human nature—such is the world. The merest chance wind from Dame *Fortune* puffs an ass into a lord, a nabob, a philosopher—a very *god*—while an adverse breeze sinks the man of honor, genius, enterprise, and wisdom to a depth below the brutes!

Oh Moses, this is a d——d mean world, and fortunate is he who can succeed in extracting honey from such a flower—a flower whose root and every petal is bitterness.

And yet *we* belong to this same d——d mean world and are ourselves made of much the same material as all the rest—viz., *selfishness, selfishness, selfishness. I* plead guilty to this general crime & can only give as my poor excuse that it is a part of *human nature.*

But farewell & God bless you & let me hear from you, at the usual address: 25 Rupert Street, Haymarket, London.

Thine truly,

Barnum

Although Barnum had his family with him for a while in Europe, they remained in America for most of the time he was abroad with Tom Thumb. His daughter Frances died shortly after his departure in 1844, and when he returned home for a visit in the spring of 1846, he first saw his new daughter Pauline, who had been born on 1 March. The "troubles" he fled from so precipitately two months later are unexplained, although it is conceivable his wife was voicing a few complaints.

The "What Is It?" was a patent fraud that did, as Barnum feared, fail with the British public. In fact, the mysterious "nondescript" was the dwarf Harvey Leach, otherwise known as Hervio Nano, a famous man-monkey and human fly. The failure of the intended imposition and consequent "maltreatment" of Leach are sometimes said to have contributed to his death in the following year. The speaking automaton was purchased in America from its inventor, a German named Faber. Kimball himself was at this time expanding his activities and about to open a new museum in Boston. From later letters it is obvious he was hurt by Barnum's unannounced return to Europe, even going so far as to threaten to withdraw his friendship.

## {25}

## TO MOSES KIMBALL

Back in America, Barnum and Sherwood Stratton continued to tour with Tom Thumb, Barnum also resuming management of his American Museum and other enterprises. He was indeed overworked, since "Parson" Hitchcock, his faithful agent in his absence, had recently lost his wife and was unfit to attend to business.

Bridgeport, 30 March 1847

My dear Moses,

Stratton & self have been determined to get to Boston to see you, but upon my soul *we cannot manage* it, for I have ten men's works [*sic*] to do here and am obliged to go to Philadelphia early next week to prepare for our campaign which will commence in Phil. Monday of week after next. Stratton & self have talked up our Boston arrangements *pro* and *con* and looked at the matter in all its phases, and I give you below the result. As you justly remark, there is no necessity for any gammon or chaffing between us, and my only wish has been if possible so to arrange our affairs as to show the General in the museum, so that it should produce a good harvest for *you* without giving us less profits than if we opened in a hall alone. I fancy that the following proposal will effect that object, and if you agree with me, then we'll go ahead and pull as strong as possible together. If, however, you don't see it an object so to arrange with us, I beg you to consider it our *ultimatum*; and by placing yourself a moment in imagination in our shoes, I trust you can find sufficient philosophy to induce you to not be offended because we cannot see our mutual interests in joining teams.

The proposition is this:

The General to exhibit in the museum in Boston in his various costumes & performances from 11½ to 1 o'clock (or from 10½ to 12 o'clock), also in the afternoon 1½ hours, then to play once or *twice,* if necessary, in the evening in connection with your plays—he to appear in his costumes and *Bombastes,* or in *Hop O' My Thumb* or what you please, provided he finishes by 10 o'clock, on the following conditions:

1st. You to charge your usual price for daytime.
2d. [You to charge] 37½ cts. for evening.
3d. The General to exhibit Saturday evenings (if possible).

We to share the gross receipts for evening performances and to share the gross receipts in daytime whenever those receipts are less than $120—but whenever they are more than that, we to have all over $60. The General's *sales* of books &c. always to be his own affair.

Or if you prefer it, we make this proposal: To share gross receipts of the evening, and for the daytime you to have 20 percent of the gross receipts.

I need not tell you what my impressions are about the General's drawing in Boston or any other city of its size in whatever hall or building he may be put. You have a better facility for judging than I have. My receipts in New York were [ov]er $16,000—*so help me God!*—in four weeks. I believe they were $16,600. I believe he could have done about as well 2 or 3 weeks longer. At all events, thousands wished to see him who *dare*[d] *not* on account of the *crowds.* Our miniature equipage would be in Boston perambulating the streets daily. The little boys' liveries are all new and complete at present. . . .

Think of it & let me know in course of a few days, addressed to me at the Museum, New York. God bless you.

Truly yours,

P. T. Barnum

. . . .

[38]

## TO MOSES KIMBALL

Museum, 2 February [1848]

My dear Moses,

I plead a thousand times guilty for not writing oftener. Will try to do better in future. Yes, you guessed right politically. 2d, I am going the Teetotal & Sons of Temperance *strong* & believe it the most glorious cause on earth, and one that *shall not* be hampered by *priestcraft* without a fuss. . . .

H has left & I am at my old post continually from Tuesday morning till Saturday afternoon. Go home Saturday night, stop over Monday night on a/c of the Sons of Temperance, & then am off for N.Y. After a few weeks Greenwood will be able to do without me most of the time. Till then I work hard & like it as well as ever. We are running from $210 to $350 per day (according to weather) on the strength of our *giantess*. She is a *whopper*! . . .

Stratton is at Harrisburgh, Pa., exhibiting & grumbling as usual. You remember that neice [*sic*] whom we saw at Stratton's brother's house in Bridgeport, her in the *white* frock. She *eloped* the other Sunday with a young chap. The next day her father pursued them to Stamford, found them *after* they were married, blowed her sky high, and then said, "Now miss, I suppose you are ready to go home with me." *"No siree,"* replied the accomplished lady, "You don't get me home without my *husband* goes with me." So the old man at last took them both into his wagon & toted them home!

Would your piece of *The Drunkard* do here by changing localities a bit? How many characters are in it? . . . That spouting on the *Fejee Mermaid* is rich. *I* get all the curses for humbugging the public with that critter. How *bad* I feel about it! Call at Bridgeport when you come through. If I am not

[39]

there Charity will be, & be glad to see you. Respects to the family.

As ever thine,

P. T. Barnum

With Hitchcock no longer able to function, John Greenwood Jr. (1817–76) became Barnum's principal assistant and was for many years responsible for the day-to-day operation of the Museum. Born in England, he came to America at the age of twenty. After leaving Barnum's employ, he spent his final years serving as U.S. Consul in Brunswick, Germany. *The Drunkard,* a famous temperance drama by Kimball's stage manager William H. Smith, was eventually transplanted to New York and became one of the greatest hits on Barnum's stage.

## {27}

## TO MOSES KIMBALL

Museum, 10 April [1849]

My dear Moses,

Thank you for your two letters. . . . Your business is indeed *stunning*. It beats mine all hollow. I have only averaged $1850 per week. But *yesterday* we commenced picking up a little:

Receipts at the Museum                          $408
Receipts for *Col. Freemont's*! Wooly Horse  176.50!! first day!
                                             $584.50

All delighted & astonished at this *California Production*!! Glory enough for one day! . . .

Thine as ever,

Barnum

"Colonel Frémont's Woolly Horse" was another of Barnum's famous "nondescripts"— advertised as being "made up of the Elephant, Deer, Horse, Buffalo, Camel, and

Sheep"—and was exhibited separately from the Museum. The hoax was inspired by reports of Frémont's expedition to the Rockies and made possible by Barnum's acquisition of a small horse with curly hair the previous summer in Cincinnati.

## {28}

## TO JOHN HALL WILTON

New York, 6 November 1849

Sir:

In reply to your proposal to attempt a negotiation with Mlle. Jenny Lind to visit the United States professionally, I propose to enter into an arrangement with her to the following effect: I will engage to pay all her expenses from Europe; provide for and pay for one principal tenor and one pianist, their salaries not exceeding together one hundred and fifty dollars per night; to support for her a carriage, two servants, and a friend to accompany her and superintend her finances. I will furthermore pay all and every expense appertaining to her appearance before the public and give her half of the gross receipts arising from concerts or operas. I will engage to travel with her personally and attend to the arrangements, provided she will undertake to give not less than eighty nor more than one hundred and fifty concerts, or nights' performances.

Phineas T. Barnum

John Hall Wilton was Barnum's agent charged with negotiating the engagement with Jenny Lind, who eventually signed with Barnum on 9 January 1850. The specific terms of their contract called for payment to Jenny Lind of $1000 per concert for 150 performances, $25,000 to her musical director, Julius Benedict, and $12,500 to Giovanni Belletti, the baritone who accompanied her to America—besides expenses for servants, a secretary, and companion for Lind, and travel expenses for the entire party. An extraordinary feature of this agreement was Barnum's pledge to deposit, in advance, the entire salaries of all three artists with Baring Brothers of London. The present letter and contract were translated into Swedish for Jenny Lind's approval.

[41]

## (29)

## TO JAMES GORDON BENNETT

Having made what many considered a ruinous agreement with Jenny Lind, Barnum launched a massive publicity campaign in advance of her arrival in America, even enlisting the aid of his old enemy Bennett.

Museum [16 April 1850]

Dear Sir,

I engaged apartments at the Irving [House] today for Jenny Lind & suite and the above is a copy of the letter sent to Mr. Howard by myself. I have also today put up the large amount of money required by Jenny Lind to be lodged in the hands of Baring Brothers and send it by tomorrow's steamer. If any of the above is found of *public* interest sufficient to get in tomorrow's *Herald,* I shall feel much obliged, as I wish to send it in print across the Atlantic tomorrow.

Truly yours,

P. T. Barnum

## (30)

## PRINTED CIRCULAR LETTER

After opening another museum in Philadelphia, Barnum closed his New York establishment for extensive renovations, especially of the "lecture room" or theatre. This announcement preceded the reopening on 17 June.

American Museum [c. June 1850]

Sir:

This establishment is undergoing extensive improvements and additions and will soon be reopened and conducted on the same plan as that adopted at my museum in Philadelphia, which receives the approbation and countenance of the great body of clergymen, the religious community at large, and all of the first families in that city, as well as strangers who visit Philadelphia and do not approve of theatres and theatrical exhibitions as at present conducted.

My plan is to introduce into the lecture room highly moral and instructive domestic dramas, written expressly for my establishments and so constructed as to please and edify, while they possess a powerful *reformatory* tendency. The moral domestic drama of *The Drunkard, or The Fallen Reclaimed* has been represented over *eighty* times at my Philadelphia museum, and it is universally conceded to be one of the most powerful auxiliaries that the temperance cause has ever received in this country. Incorrigible inebriates have been brought by their friends a distance of forty miles to witness this drama, and never, to my knowledge, has this been done without resulting in their signing the temperance pledge; and I am personally cognizant of the fact that *thousands* have been induced by this drama to renounce intoxicating drinks *in toto*.

*The Gambler,* a companion piece to *The Drunkard,* written expressly for my Philadelphia museum, has also been produced there with great moral effect. Goldsmith's *Vicar of Wakefield* has just been dramatized by a clergyman of celebrity and will soon be produced there.

My whole aim and effort is to make my museums totally unobjectionable to the religious and moral community, and at the same time combine sufficient *amusement* with instruction to please all proper tastes and to train the mind of youth to reject as repugnant anything inconsistent with moral and refined tastes.

Every vulgar or profane allusion and gesture is scrupulously avoided, and nearly every person in my employment, both in Philadelphia and New York, is a *teetotaller*.

No intoxicating beverages are allowed on my premises, and all improper characters, male or female, are excluded.

At the reopening of this museum, I expect to produce the drama of *The Drunkard* and shall feel obliged if you will

[43]

accept the enclosed ticket of admission and witness its representation at such time as shall suit your convenience.

I am, truly, your obedient servant,

P. T. Barnum

(31)

## TO O. C. GARDINER

Bridgeport, 16 August [1850]

Dear Sir,

I have but a moment to write. Jenny Lind leaves in *Atlantic* 21st inst. & will probably arrive in N.Y. 2 weeks from next sabbath. She brings with her a female companion who has travelled with her for years; a private secretary; Mr. Jules Benedict, the eminent composer and pianist; Signor Giovanni Belletti, the famous baritone (& an old friend of Jenny Lind's) from Her Majesty's Theatre in London; and *probably* a Miss Andrews (sister-in-law to Hoffman, the pianist); & also *probably* a violinist whose name has been announced, but which I have forgotten. Benedict & Belletti bring their own servants, & I have provided servants here for Jenny Lind.

The length of time which they remain in N.Y. will depend entirely upon the patronage. In fact, the same may be said of any other city in the Union, *inasmuch as Jenny Lind gives me the privilege of going to England & there using any portion of the 150 nights or concerts for which she is engaged. I may be induced under this offer to have her go there (to London) in time for the World's Fair in 1851. All will depend on the patronage here.*

The hall in New York being *much larger* than in any other city, our intention is to have most of the concerts given there—that is, *more* than in any other city. In Philadelphia the Musical Fund Hall only holds about 1000 to 1200 persons, &

[44]

the price of tickets must therefore in that city be *very high* to warrant her in singing there. Philadelphians had better come to New York.

The expense of building & decorating the hall in *Broad-way* (not *Mercer* St., as the entrance is in B-Way) opposite Bond St. will exceed $100,000, besides the *land*. The hall proper is 130 feet long by 100 feet wide & 50 feet high. It has a gallery on three sides. It will seat over 5000—I think 5600, but cannot tell till the plan of seats is finished next Tuesday. Most of the audience will be on the ground floor.

I have in my possession the programme for the first concert as dictated by Jenny Lind herself & sent me by Mr. Benedict. I cannot divulge it now, but will say that it is all that Mr. Benedict states in his published letter, and in addition to that programme will be the new song for which I have offered $200. The committee, which I think is a *good* one, was selected before your letter was recd., although the gentlemen you name certainly stand *very high*. . . . I requested Mr. Bryant to be one of the committee, but he declined.

I will add that I *think* the first concert will be given on 18th Sept. No price whatever will be at *first* fixed to tickets—but all will be sold at public auction about one week previous to the 1st concert. Every seat & ticket will be *numbered* so there will be no *crowding* & *no standing*.

The orchestra in New York will consist of 60 of the best musicians, every one a *picked man* & capable of playing a solo. *Hoffman* the pianist is engaged to travel with Jenny Lind.

Truly yours,

P. T. Barnum

P.S. A capital story ("London Correspondence") is told of Jenny Lind in today's *Herald.*

B

---

Gardiner was editor of the *American Musical Review.* The new music hall (Tripler Hall) that Jenny Lind was to inaugurate was not finished in time for her first New York concerts, which consequently took place at Castle Garden at the foot of Manhattan. To further stir up "excitement" in advance of her debut, Barnum had offered a prize of $200 for an "ode" to be sung by her. The judges of the contest eventually selected Bayard Taylor's "Greeting to America," which was set to music by Benedict (one of the judges) and thereafter sung by Lind at many of her concerts. The first concert was actually held on 11 September.

(32)

## TO J. S. REDFIELD

J. S. Redfield was one of the judges charged with selecting the winning ode. He was also the publisher of the first edition of Barnum's autobiography.

Irving House [2 September 1850]

My dear Redfield,

Jenny Lind has determined to give her first concert *early* next week, or surely by the *middle* of the week. It is *indespensible* [*sic*] therefore that the committee *meet this day or evening & decide at the earliest possible moment on the fortunate song,* inasmuch as *it must be set to music* and *learned* in time to be sang [*sic*] at the first concert. Now my dear R, I am to have a confab of 2 hours this morning with Jenny and therefore beg of you to take this scrawl in your hand, call on each of the committee this morning, & *fix* the thing definitely. All I can say is that the said committee shall hear that song sang at the first concert.

Truly yours,

P. T. Barnum

Mr. Benedict says go ahead & make your selection—then let him read some 10 or 20 of the *best* & he will join you in deciding. He is busy every moment.

JENNY LIND'S INAUGURAL CONCERT at Castle Garden, New York, on 11 September 1850.

COLOR LITHOGRAPH BY N. CURRIER. COURTESY OF THE BARNUM MUSEUM, BRIDGEPORT.

## (33)

## PRINTED CIRCULAR LETTER
## TO MEMBERS OF THE PRESS

American Museum, 6 September 1850

My dear Sir,

I regret to inform you that the tickets for Mlle. Jenny Lind's first concert are not yet printed, but you may depend that I shall at the earliest possible moment (certainly by Monday, 9th inst.) cause to be delivered to the conductors of the public press as many cards of admission for Wednesday evening as under the circumstances can reasonably be expected.

Notwithstanding I am fully convinced that all persons, after hearing and knowing Jenny Lind, will concur in acknowledging that her talents and musical ability are only equalled by her estimable character, and that neither have been overrated by the public press, yet I confess myself under many obligations and impressed with deep and unfeigned gratitude for the kind spirit in which that noble engine of human thought and progress has sustained me in the gigantic undertaking, whose result is now to be witnessed in listening on these shores to the Queen of Song in the very zenith of her vocal powers and popularity.

Looking hopefully for the continuance of your favor, which I assure you is properly appreciated and in my person will never be abused, I subscribe myself

Most faithfully yours,

P. T. Barnum [*signed*]

## TO MOSES S. BEACH?

[New York, c. 24 September 1850]

My dear Fellow,

No man ever fought harder for his *bread* than I did to get Jenny to your office yesterday. I got her consent once (she declaring from the beginning she could only visit *two*), but when she found your office was *so near* the *Herald,* she backed out through *fear* of the immense crowd waiting in front of *Herald* office.

She never sees any person the day she sings. She has to be busy all day tomorrow before leaving for Boston; & I assure you that although I would gladly do *anything* to accommodate you, I should risk her displeasure & *could not* get her consent by asking it at present.

I sent you 6 tickets. If not enough, let me know immediately.

Yours truly,

P. T. Barnum

As this letter indicates, Jenny Lind was mobbed throughout her American tour. The recipient appears to have been Moses Sperry Beach, one of the proprietors of the *New York Sun.* Lind left New York for Boston on 26 September.

## TO JOSHUA BATES

Almost from the moment of Lind's arrival in America, Barnum had to contend with a group of self-interested "advisers," led by her attorney John Jay, who traduced the showman on every occasion and contributed to the rupture between the singer and her manager the following spring. Barnum himself, at least in his public pronouncements, was always careful to profess the greatest admiration for the "angelic" Jenny—he could not, after all, very well betray the legend of his own making—but in private he was somewhat less laudatory. The present letter, eventually published by Barnum himself, was omitted from the 1855 edition of the autobiography. Bates was with Baring Brothers, the London banking house with which Barnum had deposited Lind's earnings in advance.

New York, 23 October 1850

Dear Sir,

I take the liberty to write you a few lines, merely to say that we are getting along as well as could reasonably be expected. In this country you are aware that the rapid accumulation of wealth always creates much envy, and envy soon augments to malice. Such are the elements at work to a limited degree against myself, and although Miss Lind, Benedict, and myself have never, as yet, had the slightest feelings between us, to my knowledge, except those of friendship, yet I cannot well see how this can long continue in face of the fact that, nearly every day, they allow persons (some moving in the first classes of society) to approach them and spend hours in traducing me. Even her attorney, Mr. John Jay, has been so blind to her interests as to aid in poisoning her mind against me by pouring into her ears the most silly twaddle, all of which amounts to nothing and less than nothing—such as the regret that I was a "showman," exhibitor of Tom Thumb, etc. etc.

Without the elements which I possess for business, as well as my knowledge of human nature acquired in catering for the public, the result of her concerts here would not have been pecuniarily one half as much as at present—and such men as the Hon. Edward Everett, G. G. Howland, and others will tell you that there is no charlatanism or lack of dignity in my management of these concerts. I know as well as any person that the merits of Jenny Lind are the best capital to depend upon to secure public favor, and I have thus far acted on this knowledge. Everything which money and attention can procure for their comfort they have, and I am glad to know that they are satisfied on this score. All I fear is that these continual backbitings, if listened to by her, will by and by produce a feeling of distrust or regret which will lead to unpleasant results.

The fact is, her mind ought to be as free as air, and she herself as free as a bird, and, being satisfied of my probity and ability, she should turn a deaf ear to all envious and malevolent attacks on me. I have hoped that by thus briefly stating to you the facts in the case, you might be induced for her interests as well as mine to drop a line of advice to Mr. Benedict and another to Mr. Jay on this subject. If I am asking or expecting too much, I pray you to not give it a thought, for I feel myself fully able to carry through my rights alone, although I should deplore nothing so much as to be obliged to do so in a feeling of unfriendliness. I have risked much money on the issue of this speculation—it has proved successful. I am full of perplexity and anxiety, and labor continually for success, and I cannot allow ignorance or envy to rob me of the fruits of my enterprise.

Sincerely and gratefully yours,

P. T. Barnum

## TO JENNY LIND

After visiting several other cities, the Jenny Lind troupe returned to New York, where Tripler Hall was finally ready to receive them. The present letter was in response to a request from Lind that Barnum reduce the price of tickets to this immense hall and prevent speculators from profiting from her concerts. Both letters are in the New-York Historical Society and bear the notation at their tops "items leaded agate, 12 slips immediately." The exchange was probably engineered by Barnum for its publicity value.

Irving House, 24 October 1850

My dear Miss Lind,

I hasten with much pleasure to say in reply to your letter of this morning that the great capacity of Tripler Hall will enable me to comply with your suggestions, and that accordingly I shall fix the prices to the entire first floor and second circle at $3.00 each, the front row in the first circle at $5.00, and all other seats in the same circle at $4.00 each. I shall give immediate directions that these prices apply to the concert of tomorrow (Friday) evening and all future concerts during your brief stay in New York. I have the honor to remain

Truly your obedient servant,

P. T. Barnum

## {37}

### TO THOMAS RITCHIE

Barnum's Hotel, Baltimore, 14 December 1850

Dear Sir,

In reply to your letter of yesterday inquiring whether there is any truth in the report that Mlle. Jenny Lind has given a donation to an association of abolitionists, I beg to state most emphatically that *there is not the slightest foundation for such a statement.* I feel no hesitation in saying that this lady never gave a farthing for any such purpose, and that her oft expressed admiration for our noble system of government convinces me that she prizes too dearly the glorious institutions of our country to lend the slightest sanction to any attack upon the union of these states.

I have the honor to remain

Your very obedient servant,

P. T. Barnum

Thomas Ritchie was editor of the *Washington Union.* This letter was written while the troupe was on its southern tour, which included both Baltimore and Washington.

# {38}

## TO SOL SMITH AND NOAH LUDLOW

Charleston, 26 December 1850

My old Friends,

Yours of the 20th is recd. . . . I trust there will be no trouble between us & have no fear of it. I do most heartily detest seeing a set of ragged dirty chaps located right under the eyes & noses of respectable ladies & gents, as is generally the case where there is a *pit*; but as none but decent people generally attend the Lind concerts, it may be best perhaps to still keep the *pit*. Of that, however, my agent will decide before we arrive. . . .

Now as regards music. I enclose a line from Benedict, telling what we have & what we want. He thinks that in order to conciliate the *French* population (you know Jenny never sang in Paris) that the French orchestra, being as he is informed *very good,* had better by all means be engaged for the 3 nights, & yours on the 4th together with such others as are needed & can be got. If yours can be used *with* the French & ours, & the number still not exceed about 40, why let us have *all* & I will then take yours at $50 per night if they are all good & acceptable to Benedict. Or if French company ask too much or will not come, then we must do without them. But if the French orchestra can be had 3 nights per week for $5 each person per night, please engage them sure for first 3 concerts with privilege on my part for the balance (3 per week). And so in respect to the *other* musicians necessary to be had according to Benedict's list. I will pay $5 each per night, but we can use none but *first-rate.* I am glad to accept your offer to procure me the musicians & wish you would be so kind as to set about it *at once* & write me the result to Havana. I expect that 8 of my musicians will go from here to N.O. to wait for us, as we have no use for them in Havana. I think we can give 15 concerts in New Orleans—possibly more.

Yours,

P. T. Barnum

P.S. I am sorry that the Mobile theatre is so small & the price so large. Both are, I think, insuperable objections. Can you learn for me the capacity of the largest hall or church (if it can be got) in Montgomery? Could not a large church be got in Mobile?

What about your St. Louis theatre? Can you give me its exact capacity & your terms? You are pretty fellows to talk about wanting to make money out of Jenny Lind excitement. Why, she fills every theatre, hotel, store, & shop with money wherever she goes, & sheds blessings on cab drivers, shoemakers, milliners, tailors, and every calling under heaven. But you should be satisfied with your share in the general scramble & not try to make money out of *me*!

I propose shedding immortality on some good, sober, temperate, & steady steamboat captain who will take us from N. Orleans to Vicksburg, Natchez, Memphis, & such other towns on the Missi. as we can give one concert in, wait for us to give the concert, then take us on board & go ahead the same night. His boat would *fill* with passengers independent of our company, which would number 30 or more, & the delays would not be long. If you think of a *good* captain & a good boat, please name this to him.

Barnum

Barnum had been negotiating with his "old friends" Sol Smith and Noah M. Ludlow for Jenny Lind's appearance at their New Orleans theatre since the previous October. The party arrived there in early February after an unsatisfactory engagement in Havana.

## (39)

## TO SOL SMITH

Charleston, 31 December 1850

My dear Uncle Sol,

I suppose you have business *enough* of your own. Still, I *must* trouble you a little & trust that you will be recompensed therefor in this world or the world to come.

I enclose some documents which I really have not read a word of, for lack of time, but which I leave to your kindness & *discretion* to distribute in such quarters as they will *immediately* see the light—not all in *one* place—and perhaps you will then be so good as to write me at Havana whether such things are *acceptable* in N. Orleans, and if so, enough more can be furnished *"of the same sort."* I need not tell you that even *Our Saviour* needed John the Baptist as an *avant courier.* Why then, may not an "angel" require the heavenly rays of *"Old Sol"* to light her pathway to the Crescent City? The angel Gabriel uses a *"trumpet,"* and *you* know that *we must* do likewise! But *Mum* if *you please.*

Yours truly,

P. T. Barnum

Off in the morning in *Isabel* for Havana. Charge postage &c. to me.

B

# {40}

## TO MOSES S. AND ALFRED ELY BEACH

*Confidential*

New Orleans, 10 February 1851

Messrs. Beach Brothers:

Undoubtedly your Havana correspondents have told you of the banquet given . . . at the country house of Count Santavenia on Sunday night, 2d Feby. I was there the next day, saw the tables, crockery, empty champaigne [*sic*] bottles, &c. *Bennett* of the *Herald* was one of the guests. This you may rest *assured* of (though probably you already know it). The old Castillians have *bought* him body and soul, boots and breeches. They have made a most ruinous bargain, *whatever* the price may be that they have given, for his influence is much less than nothing. But you may now depend upon seeing the colum[n]s of the *Herald* devoted to puffing the new Captain-General & the old Spanish government, until the liberal and liberty party outbid the Spaniards—which they will never do, as they totally refused to trust him with the minutest portion of their secrets.

Mrs. Bennett has cut up some strange antics in Havana, which has [*sic*] caused much amusement to the Americans. She openly boasts that *she edits* the *Herald,* and none doubt it who know much on the subject. She was a steady and almost nightly visitor to the Dominica, a drinking shop frequented mostly by Americans (men), and there with a gang of rollicking men gathered about her, she would keep up a loud conversation until an hour arrived at which she declared she must go home, for her husband scolded her strong and had forbid her going to the Dominica. They left Havana by the *Falcon* for New Orleans. Bennett, not satisfied with the accommodations offered Mrs. Bennett, threatened to publish the *Falcon,* but the purser told him to do so and be d——d, for no one on board the

[56]

*Falcon* cared a curse for him, his wife, or his paper. This sharp rebuke gave great pleasure to the passengers.

*Jenny Lind* and Barnum were passengers by the same steamer, but neither would speak to Bennett or his wife. In fact, no person scarcely spoke with them, and during the passage they appeared the most lonely and disconsolate outcasts that can well be imagined. Mrs. Bennett had several animals with her, including a dog and a very noisy screaming monkey; and such time as Bennett was not wrapped up in his cloak and a brown study in some dark corner of the ship, he was occupied in attending to the wants of Mrs. Bennett's monkey and other members of her menagerie.

Mrs. Bennett had intended to have given a ball in Havana, but finding too great a prospect of a *sparse* assemblage, she gave it up and must now try and think of some other way of gaining her darling object—viz., admission to the fashionable circles of New York. This is the great desire of both Mr. & Mrs. Bennett, and their chances are about as good as they would be of entering straight into paradise—boots, monkies [*sic*], petticoats, and all.

Truly yours,

P. T. Barnum

P.S. Please make what use you can of these facts & keep my name *secret,* though I hold myself responsible for all that I write.

P. T. Barnum

At the time of this letter Alfred Ely Beach, and possibly Henry D. Beach, were joint owners of the *New York Sun* with their brother Moses Sperry Beach. Mrs. Bennett's eccentric behavior was a frequent cause for comment by many people.

# (41)

## TO EDITOR OF THE *SUNDAY COURIER*

Barnum's Great Asiatic Caravan, Museum, and Menagerie began touring in the spring of 1851. This letter, in a hand other than Barnum's, is typical of those sent to various editors to "prepare" the way.

300 Broadway, 31 May 1851

Editor of the *Sunday Courier:*

You will perceive by the advertisement of my collossal [*sic*] travelling exhibition that the grand procession which passes through this city on Monday next will really exceed in *splendour* and *novelty* anything ever before seen in this country. It is worth going a hundred miles to see, and people from the country will come in large numbers to witness it. The grand state carriage of the late Queen Dowager of England, with the original gold-decorated harness, liveries, &c. &c., will appear in the procession and really make such a display as republican eyes have never beheld in a republican country.

May I beg you to add to the many obligations I already owe you by giving an elaborate article on this procession. The whole exhibition has cost me *$136,000* & has been got up as matter of pride as well as profit.

Truly your obedient servant,

P. T. Barnum

## {42}

**TO EDITOR OF THE *COURIER***

In 1851 Barnum became the American agent for a newly invented fire extinguisher—a venture that quickly ended after the "annihilator" failed a public demonstration.

Bridgeport, 1 November 1851

Mr. M'Makin:

The article in your last *Courier* in relation to *Phillips' Fire Annihilator* is an *error*. Neither "Dr. William A. Graham" nor any other person in America has ever pretended to have invented what Mr. Phillips has produced—viz., an atmosphere in which flame or fire cannot exist, but which can be inhaled with perfect ease and safety. This apparrent [*sic*] miracle *has* been accomplished by Mr. Phillips, and the public will soon be witnesses and recipients of his beneficent discovery.

Truly yours,

P. T. Barnum

## {43}

**TO UNIDENTIFIED CORRESPONDENT**

Bridgeport, 29 November 1851

My dear Sir,

Yours is recd. I am sorry you could not hear the strange lady, for she is *one of them*. However, I have not the slightest interest in her and do not even know where her address is. Nor do I ever expect to speak with her again.

I hope you will not fail to secure me a ticket for the editorial Kossuth dinner, and I would much like also to have

[59]

one for Rev. E. H. Chapin, who writes much for the press. I am quite willing to pay for his ticket, & he would give probably the *best speech* on the occasion.

If it is preferable to have him one of the invited guests, be it so. I don't care which.

Truly yours,

P. T. Barnum

Coming so soon after the breakup with Jenny Lind, who was now touring America on her own and at the time of Barnum's writing singing in Boston, this letter is indeed intriguing. The Universalist minister Edwin H. Chapin was a good friend of Barnum and the same who converted him to teetotalism.

## TO NATHANIEL P. BEERS

Nate Beers was a cousin of Barnum's wife Charity. He often performed errands for Barnum in New York City and, together with his wife Emma, was a frequent guest in Bridgeport.

Bridgeport, 6 February 1852

Friend Beers,

Please send me 500 segars by Adams' Express Saturday (get them there by 2 o'clock P.M.) and inform me for what price I can sell some for you for cash. I may not be able to sell any, but Francis the barber says he would like several thousand *good segars* for $22. But he must see mine as a *sample*.

I will also try Wells & others, but as I leave home Monday morning, I *ought* to get the segars Saturday night.

Respects to your lady.

Truly yours,

P. T. Barnum

## (45)

## TO WILLIAM MAKEPEACE THACKERAY

Iranistan [Bridgeport], 29 November 1852

My dear Sir,

Since seeing you the other day, it has struck me that you can do me a *great favor* which I shall highly appreciate and reciprocate to the extent of my ability. I am associated with others in the publication of a new pictorial weekly journal similar to the *London Illustrated News* [*sic*], the first number of which will appear some ten days hence. We shall publish an edition of 100,000 to commence with, and expect to have 50,000 *bona fide* subscribers before the 1st of Feby., as the price will be only *half* that of the *London News.*

Now I wish to get you to write us an article for the *first* number, on any subject you please, of from half a column to one, two, or three columns, and if you can continue to do so for subsequent numbers, I shall be very glad. We shall of course expect to meet your pecuniary demands for the same and will do all in our power to serve you otherwise. I hope that this may lead also to future arrangements for supplying us with the first sheets of works which you may write hereafter, for which I am sure we can make everything satisfactory to you.

Your name will be a tower of strength to us, and we have naturally a very great desire to show the public an original article from your pen in our first number.

Our journal will be one of the first class and the highest respectability, as you will be assured by Genl. Morris or Mr. Wyllis [*Willis*] of the *Home Journal,* L. Gaylord Clarke of the *Knickerbocker,* or any other of our literary men.

I most sincerely hope you will gratify us at least as far

[61]

as the first number is concerned, and rest assured *you shall never regret it.*

Truly yours,

P. T. Barnum

. . . .

On 1 January 1853 Barnum and Alfred Ely and Henry D. Beach launched their weekly paper the *Illustrated News*. William Makepeace Thackeray, then in America, declined the invitation to contribute.

(46)

## TO BAYARD TAYLOR

Bayard Taylor (1825–78), whose ode had won the prize in the Jenny Lind contest, was a good friend of Barnum, who sought his advice on many occasions. A prolific writer and journalist, he was best known for his travel narratives, based on personal observations made in nearly every corner of the globe. The "Japan Expedition" mentioned in this letter was that led by Commodore Perry which succeeded in opening Japan to the West.

American Museum, 16 December 1852

My dear old Friend,

I have a great favor to ask of you. I have just invested $20,000 with two others of $20,000 each in getting up an illustrated weekly paper here similar to the *London Illustrated News*. We intend that it shall soon equal that paper. Of course, we want drawings & sketches of everything interesting in all parts of the world, and by advice of Messrs. Greeley & Dana I write you & forward the letter through them, asking you to use all influence you can in getting us drawings &c. of all important & interesting *things* and *events*, & especially when connected with the *Japan Expedition*. We will agree to pay liberally for all sketches sent us which *we use*, & we shall try to use everything important. I wish to trouble you to name these facts

[62]

to all the artists in the expedition with whom you become acquainted, and *especially* does Mr. Dana recommend *Mr. Heine* who writes for the *Tribune.* One of our editors is Dr. Rufus W. Griswold, who sends you his best respects & good wishes and joins me in hoping you will not fail to exert yourself for us. If you yourself have any sketches to spare, I hope you will send them on. By the way, do you ever see any curiosities alive or dead, animate or inanimate, which remind you of the *Museum?* If you see anything particularly stunning in that line, for heaven's sake nail them for me, or fix it so that I can do it, and inform me. Your letters are doing much towards keeping the *Tribune* in its present proud position of the best & most influential paper in the country. May Allah protect & bless thee now & evermore. Pray let us hear from you often. Let the artists direct either to me or the *Illustrated News,* New York.

Truly yours,

P. T. Barnum

## TO EDWARD EVERETT

Bridgeport, 7 February 1853

My dear Friend,

I assure you I felt quite ashamed of your likeness as it appeared in our "Illustrated." We shall pretty soon make a good one & apologize for the other. You can have no adequate conception of the embarrassments attending the advent of such an enterprise; but we have patience, faith, & determination.

We have parted with Dr. Griswold because he insisted on *absolute* control of the columns of the paper, & that is what of course we who *pay* will give to no man. We want much to get a *good* writer & compiler for about $1000 to $1500 per year. Not more than ⅓ to ½ his time would be required. We have several pretty good assistant editors now.

We shall be delighted to print the autograph letter of the Duke of Wellington & feel deeply obliged to you for the same.

I beg to congratulate you (*& the country much more*) on your recent election to the U.S. Senate.

Truly yours,

P. T. Barnum

## TO EDWARD EVERETT

Bridgeport, 19 February 1853

My dear Mr. Everett,

Your favor of the 17th is most thankfully recd. The *fac-simile* of the Duke of Wellington's letter is indeed a valuable & *highly interesting* document.

I shall take it to New York on Monday next & Mr. Beach will either remit you $15 by mail or I will hand it to you on the 2d or 3d March, as my intention is to be in Washington at that time.

I have been confined to my house for some ten days by sore throat caused by temperance lecturing, and hardly know how our "Illustrated" is progressing in regard to *editors*. At the last accounts Dr. Griswold had receded from the stand he took at first, claiming undisputed *control* of the editorial columns, and was willing to come back as leading *editor*, submitting his proofs for approval or rejection by the proprietors. But the Dr. is so strong in his literary prejudices that Mr. Beach had nearly concluded to dispense with him altogether.

The copying of the Duke's letter is *admirably* done & is well worth the $15. And if it were not, we should gladly send it, the copyist being poor.

Again thanking you for your kind consideration, I am most sincerely

Your friend,

P. T. Barnum

## TO FRANKLIN PIERCE

Iranistan, Bridgeport, 23 March 1853

Mr. President:

I have claimed to be the *greatest curiosity* in the Democratic party, for thank God, *I want no office*! But I beg the liberty of saying a single word. *Edward Taylor*, Esq., of Danbury, Conn., at present judge of the county court, is a most excellent judge of law & has practiced at the bar for about 30 years. He desires the office of U.S. judge (just vacated by the death of Hon. A. T. Judson). Others will doubtless apply, probably some who have been in office many years. I believe no man in our state is more deserving or better qualified for the office than Judge Taylor. He *needs* the office (pecuniarily), and I sincerely hope he may obtain it. He is a faithful Democrat and commands the respects of all classes. Senator Toucey knows him—also, I think, Hon. Lorin P. Waldo.

Most respectfully yours,

P. T. Barnum

Barnum may have wanted no office for himself, but he did for a relative. Edward Taylor was his uncle.

IRANISTAN, AN ORIENTAL VILLA.

P. T. BARNUM TO FRANKLIN PIERCE, 23 March 1853. The engraving depicts Iranistan, Barnum's first mansion, which was modeled on the Brighton Pavilion. The same impressive stationery proved a major factor in Jenny Lind's decision to sign with Barnum for her American tour.

# {50}

## TO THEODORE SEDGWICK

Theodore Sedgwick was president of the company of stockholders that financed the ill-fated New York Crystal Palace. Located near the site of the present-day 42d Street library, this great edifice—like its earlier counterpart in London, devoted to the exhibition of the arts and industries of both the "new" and "old" worlds—opened its doors in July 1853 and burned to the ground in 1858.

*Confidential*

American Museum, 15 April 1853

Dear Sir,

I have just learned for the first time that one or more articles have appeared in the *Sun* against the World's Fair, and that *Mr. L. C. Stuart* has insinuated that I was the author or instigator of them. Knowing Stuart to be a great talker, as well as an inveterate *storyteller,* it struck me that very likely he might have poisoned your ears with such falsehoods. I write therefore to say that I have never before seen nor heard of any such articles, that I have never for a moment felt anything but the warmest friendship for the whole enterprise in which you are engaged, that the same feeling is entertained by all connected with the *Illustrated News,* and that anything which I or the publishers of that print can do to forward the interests of the "Exhibition of the Industry of All Nations" will be most cheerfully and gladly done, so long as it maintains its present character of being a national work and calculated to redound to the honor of the American nation. Indeed, the publishers of the *Illustrated News* intend at an early period to devote a great portion of their space to the illustration of all articles of interest connected with the Exhibition, and are anxious at all times to receive and publish interesting intelligence regarding the same, as well as drawings of such articles as are now or may be accessible at an early day.

The fact is, L. C. Stuart is such an abominable *Munchausen* that it is hard to tolerate him after he is once found

[67]

out, and owing to his dreadful propensity of "drawing on his fancy for his facts," he is not permitted to enter the Museum free as heretofore, and it is hoped he will never attempt to enter by paying, for he is not such a man as we ever wish to see. I once before hinted to you his propensities that way, but had then no idea to what an extent his egotism and love of romance, as well as ingratitude, would carry him. I shall never intentionally lay a straw in his way, but I feel it my duty to take the proper steps for preventing his doing me an injury by *falsehood.*

Hoping that the nature of this subject, although disagreeable, will be considered by you a sufficient apology for this letter,

I am very truly yours,

P. T. Barnum

## (51)

## TO DR. RUSSELL T. TRALL

American Museum, 27 April [1853]

Dr. Trall:

I was much pleased with Miss Stone's speech last night and concur with nearly all her views. I have written her to Boston to send me her daguerreotype for publication in the *Illustrated News,* and if you choose to write a report (say of a column or less) giving a little biography of her and a definite statement of her arguments, I will see that it is spread before over 100,000 subscribers and possibly 500,000 readers. Please address it to me here, marked "Private" on the envelope. Any time within a week will be in time. I know it will help her cause.

Truly yours,

P. T. Barnum

Lucy Stone (1818–93) was a popular lecturer on woman's rights and abolitionism. Barnum appears to have been frequently among her audiences. The New York physician Dr. Russell T. Trall (1812–77), a writer on hygiene and a temperance advocate, had recently established a medical school for both male and female students. His wife later served as a judge at Barnum's baby shows. From a transcription in the National Woman Suffrage Association Papers in the Library of Congress. The location of the original letter is unknown.

(52)

## TO SOL SMITH

During much of 1853 Barnum busied himself on behalf of "Uncle" Sol Smith, recently retired from theatrical management to his home in St. Louis, who was trying to place an autobiographical work with the New York publishers. When *The Theatrical Journey-Work and Anecdotal Recollections of Sol Smith* finally appeared in Philadelphia in the following year, it included a flattering dedication to Barnum. Possibly inspired by Smith's example, Barnum now set out to write his own autobiography. Despite persistent rumors to the contrary, it was entirely of his own composition.

Bridgeport, 19 December 1853

My dear Uncle,

Yours of the 9th is recd. . . . Appleton says he sent your *MSS* as requested. As soon as it comes I'll try Stringer & Townsend, & I hope & think successfully. At all events, I'll do the best I can. Had you not better have a portrait engraved for the work?

I think of writing my life this winter. What do you think about its taking? . . .

Truly yours,

P. T. Barnum

[69]

## (53)

## TO MOSES KIMBALL

[Bridgeport, 1853?]

My dear Moses,

. . . Look here, old fellow, don't talk in such a foolish manner about my finding better friends &c. You *know* better than that. The fact is, I have foolishly got so many thousand irons in the fire that I don't have time to write *anybody*. But I'll dig out if I live & find leisure to write & visit my old friends, among whom I am always proud to number *Moses Kimball* as the *first*. So no gammon, *if* you please. . . .

Truly yours,

P. T. Barnum

## TO DR. RUSSELL T. TRALL?

Bridgeport, 11 February 1854

My dear Sir,

The Methodists are building a church here and need help very much. They want our friend Lucy Stone to lecture for them one night. If she will do so, I will guarantee that they shall pay her any sum she asks not exceeding $50, and if she should want more than that, please let me know and I'll see what can be done.

I wish her to make my house her home, and that of any friends who may accompany her. They would be glad to have her lecture on Friday night, the 3d of March, if she can do so—if not, some subsequent evening would probably answer, though not quite so well. I write to you thinking you will have her address. . . . I think the lecture on Woman's Rights would suit them here—at all events, they ought to hear it. But she can select her own subject.

I really hope she won't fail to come.

Truly yours,

P. T. Barnum

The recipient of this letter was very likely Dr. Russell T. Trall, to whom Barnum had written about Lucy Stone the previous year. From a transcription in the National Woman Suffrage Association Papers in the Library of Congress. Location of original letter unknown.

## (55)

## TO SOL SMITH

Museum, 14 February 1854

My dear Uncle Sol,
. . . I am now in the midst of our poultry show—8000 chickens in the Museum. Gods! What a crowing!

Truly yours,

P. T. Barnum

## (56)

## TO HORACE GREELEY

Horace Greeley (1811–72), the distinguished proprietor and editor of the *New York Tribune,* became one of Barnum's closest friends, Barnum even naming one of the bedrooms in his mansion Waldemere after him. Shortly after writing this letter, Barnum was elected president of the Crystal Palace Company, an honor he soon decided he could easily have done without.

Friend Greeley,

Having heard of some remarks which you have dropped to a mutual friend that prove to me you are laboring under *misapprehension* in regard to my position with the Crystal Palace, I hasten to give you the *simple facts,* which I shall be glad to verify and prove by reliable evidence if you think you have any information that justifies you in doubting my statement. I beg farther to say that this letter is *not* intended as a confidential communication, but although written in haste and without revision, I give you full authority to show it to any and every person who has led you astray in regard to me—or to make any other use of it you please.

Some three weeks ago (Friday, 17th Feb.) a Mr. Hooper called at the Museum and requested me to allow my name to be run as one of the directors of the Crystal Palace. I replied with the most perfect frankness and sincerity that *I could not consent to it,* that I did not own a dollar's worth of the stock nor never did, and that no inducement could be offered me to devote the time & labor necessary to infuse new life into the institution. Besides, it was so deeply in debt that I had great fears & doubts of its stock ever being worth much.

He insisted on using my name, *I resolutely opposed it,* and he finally withdrew, leaving me to understand that he would not mention my name again in connection with the management of the Cyrstal Palace.

The following Sunday I saw that my name with that of Mr. Genin was published in this connection, and noting that the stock was running up and believing this false impression to be the cause, I felt it an act of duty & justice to state the fact that I was not a candidate. And so help me God, at the time of publishing the "card" with Genin I neither owned a dollar's worth of stock *nor had the remotest idea of doing so,* nor of becoming a candidate. Nor do I believe Genin had.

But after the card appeared, nearly half the friends I met winked & looked wise and said they perfectly understood my dodge—that it was to depress the stock with a view of purchasing &c.

Seeing that the public *would not* believe what I stated in the card, but would continue to run up the stock, I merely as a business operation authorized my broker to buy 100 shares of the stock at 30, not expecting to retain it more than a few days. Nor did I.

He bought the hundred shares, and I authorized him to sell them again in five days afterwards, and he did so—at an advance.

Mr. Hooper, it seems, heard from my broker that I had bought. But I had sold out again & was *not* "the owner of 100 shares of stock" as Hooper stated at the Metropolitan meeting (no doubt in good faith) that I was.

In the meantime many persons were writing & calling on me, begging me to permit my name to be placed on the list of directors.

I never fairly & explicitly agreed to do so, but finally & reluctantly remained *passive* in the matter, though I confess the remarks made against me at the Metropolitan meeting aroused the "old man" a trifle (& only a trifle) within me, & I concluded to throw no obstacle in the way of my election. . . .

I am now elected, & although I do not covet the labor attending the position, I shall not perhaps feel justified in refraining from *working* if there is any chance for the resuscitation of the Exhibition. *That* I can better judge of after examining the details of its affairs. At all events, rest assured that if I work at all, it shall be for what I conceive to be the best interests of the Exhibition and of the City of New York & our common country.

I would like exceedingly to see the Palace crammed with visitors for at least another season, and if such a thing is feasible I shall be glad to do all in my power to bring it about.

As for the presidency, I care not a millionth part of a hair about it, & shall neither say nor do anything towards securing it. I only hope the directors will take such action as shall best serve to make the enterprise successful and to continue it in its present character of an "Exhibition of the Industry of All Nations."

Truly yours,

P. T. Barnum

This letter is too long—but I hope you will read it.

P. T. Barnum

## (57)

### TO REV. THEODORE L. CUYLER

The Rev. Theodore Ledyard Cuyler (1822–1909), although Presbyterian, was another prominent man of the cloth who counted among Barnum's closest friends. A prolific author of devotional and travel works, and a popular speaker in the evangelical mode, he was also one of the leading lights in the temperance movement. Bridgeport was often in need of his services.

American Museum, 21 March 1854

Dear Sir,

I want to beg of you to go to Bridgeport with your lady next week, Wednesday the 29th inst., with me—stop at my house & make a temperance speech there in the evening of Wednesday 29th inst. I will see that you are fairly compensated therefor. Please say *yes* at once so that I can give the proper notice. We need you there *exceedingly,* for our election takes place 1st Monday in April.

Truly yours,

P. T. Barnum

[74]

# (58)

## TO JAMES GORDON BENNETT

In public, Barnum liked to claim he did not care what people wrote or said about him, so long as they said something. In private, it was often a different matter. This "flag of truce" was evidently written during a fit of respectability, while its author was struggling as president of the faltering Crystal Palace Company, and is on stationery bearing the letterhead "Office of the Association for the Exhibition of the Industry of All Nations."

New York, 28 April 1854

Dear Sir,

I send you this letter as a *Flag of Truce* and *not* for publication.

I doubt whether you really entertain any enmity against me, from the fact that you have frequently told Mr. Cromwell that you did not. But having been in the *habit* of making me a kind of target for the last 18 years, this habit has become a kind of "second nature" to you, and thus do we find "Mermaid," "Joice Heth," "Woolly Horse," &c. stereotyped, as it were, and it has sometimes struck me that your readers would think you were dosing them *ad nauseum* [*sic*].

Well, I think your experience in this instance has convinced you that I am not to be killed by newspaper bulletts [*sic*]. So far from it, I rather liked your attacks or squibs when you did not attempt to impeach my integrity.

But now comes the question: Don't you think it is time to let me drop? I mean as a *target* for ridicule. I decidedly think *it is,* and respectfully request you to do so. For myself personally, I don't care two straws for all the newspaper squibs that could be written in a century. But I am now engaged in managing a public enterprise which I hope & believe will be made highly conducive to the interests and reputation of this city and the country at large.

Second, I have a family growing up around me, am myself not quite as young as I once was, and all things considered, I have to request that you will hereafter *not* speak of myself or my actions in a spirit of ridicule or abuse, except I, or they, *really deserve* it.

If, in addition to desisting from such a course, you should (for a wonder) begin to speak of me and my efforts with some little degree of respect and encouragement (selecting some *other* butt for your sarcasm for the *next* 18 years), I really think you will consult your own interests as well as oblige

Truly yours,

P. T. Barnum

## TO MOSES KIMBALL

Bridgeport, 14 July 1854

My dear Moses,

Weary, fagged, tired, and almost sick, I have quit New York for the season and I trust *forever* as a resting place. Thank God I have got enough to live comfortably on here in the country & then have enough left to ruin & spoil my children.

I was an ass for having anything to do with the Crystal Palace. Its distance from the centre of the city would itself have killed it, without the awful management which it was cursed with.

The question now occurs, what will be done with the Crystal Palace? Here are some statistics for you to ponder. The Palace & iron fences cost over $700,000. If economically built now, they would cost over $500,000. They would all probably be sold by the present directors for $250,000.

All can be taken down, transported to Boston, & put up again for $50,000 to $75,000—but say $100,000.

The interest on $350,000 at 6 pr. ct. would be $21,000.

Now if the Crystal Palace could be put on Boston Common and managed by Boston men—*businessmen*—would it not clear as an exhibition $50,000 & probably nearer $100,000 per annum? The daily expense need not exceed $80 to $100, except when kept open evenings & gas was used. The daily expences now are not over $100 in New York, for the snuff boxes, Jew's harps, eyeglasses, & other little things which people might *steal* have been put under *glass,* and the number of police reduced to *ten. Five* policemen would suffice—for people won't steal grindstones, furniture, pianos, statues, paintings, &c.

If *properly* conducted, exhibitors would pay *rent* for the space they occupy. In Sydenham Palace they have taken $500,000 for *space* to exhibitors. The refreshment saloons would pay the proprietors of the Crystal Palace 20 pr. ct. of their gross receipts, which percentage will amount in Boston to $40 per day, or $12,520.00 per annum, for the refreshment receipts will average $200 per day. But call it half that or ¼— it will be a good item.

If used as *bazaars* are used in London, Paris, & elsewhere (besides being for the exhibition of industry & arts), the counters would really rent for many thousand dollars per annum.

Mr. Sherman of the firm of Duncan & Sherman, Bankers, told me yesterday that if Bostonians would take that matter in hand, he would take $25,000 worth of stock—for, said he, none of us would live long enough to ever see it closed again if they should open it. I would myself take $15,000 to $25,000 worth of stock in it.

It is universally acknowledged that the N.Y. Crystal Palace is a magnificent building—far more so than that of London.

A lecture room capable of seating 5000 persons could easily be spared in one portion of the Palace, & thus it could monopolize all the great *lectures* of the season, & such men as Thomas H. Benton and all our greatest statesmen would each deliver at least *one* lecture there, on human government or some other subject, which would draw large sums of money &

*cost nothing.* The same room could also be used for musical purposes, and as one side of the room would be formed of canvass, the canvass could be removed when required so that 10,000 to 20,000 persons could hear. The Palace will contain 50,000 persons even when as full of goods as at present.

I need not say to you *how much* the Palace would help Boston if located so centrally as the Common. Nor need I say how much it would help your museum. My museum last year cleared $50,000, about double what it would have done had it not been for the Crystal Palace. New Yorkers who now think the Palace *too far off* to visit would positively go to Boston to see it, and if Boston men should really take hold of it in earnest, they would put New York to shame. Now Moses, if this happens to strike you aright, you can probably bring about the biggest thing you ever thought of touching & gain both gold & glory. How does it strike you?

Truly yours,

Barnum

P.S. I hope, unless you are *opposed* to this idea, you will set it a going in your papers. I don't *know* that less than $300,000 would buy the C. Palace—*that* would be dog-cheap for it. The American Institute wants to retain it in N.Y. Philadelphia is talking of getting it.

Sunday night concerts would do in the C. Palace in Boston.

Think of this subject & write me.

## (60)

## TO BAYARD TAYLOR

*Private*

Bridgeport, 4 August 1854

Friend Taylor,

I am about acting on your hint to write a lecture on the science of humbug.

I shall esteem it as a special favor which I will be glad always to reciprocate if you will take 15 minutes to think & tell me in what way you think I should handle it.

I have a plan of my own, but before commencing I would feel infinitely obliged for some hints from you on the subject.

Truly yours,

P. T. Barnum

Barnum's lecture and articles on "humbug" eventually led to his 1865 book *The Humbugs of the World.*

## (61)

## TO BAYARD TAYLOR

Bridgeport, 24 August 1854

My dear Sir,

Yours is recd. with *many thanks.* My lecture is about ⅔ds completed, but having promised Redfield to give him all the

*MSS* for the autobiography by November, I have laid aside the lecture for the present.

Truly yours,

P. T. Barnum

## (62)

### TO MOSES KIMBALL

Mermaids—the "Fejee" one and those of other extraction—recurred regularly in Barnum's career. They and other equally absurd fabrications (frogs with human hands, the fabulous phoenix itself) were a Japanese specialty, and on at least one occasion the showman imported a large quantity of such curiosities direct from that country. Part of Kimball's museum collections eventually went to Harvard, where two mermaids may be seen to this day in the Peabody Museum of Archaeology and Ethnology. One of them is said to be the Fejee lady herself.

Bridgeport, 4 September 1854

My dear Kimball,

I want you to hire me the old Mermaid for a year or two, or sell it outright for my museum.

I have been so much Mermaided late years that I fancy the thing would attract some notice if placed in the Museum. At all events, I would like to try it.

I am hard at work on my autobiography, the publication of which I *hope* will help make up my losses by Crystal Palace.

Please write me *here* the terms of Mermaid & oblige

Truly yours,

P. T. Barnum

## (63)

## TO MOSES KIMBALL

Bridgeport, 6 September 1854

My dear Kimball,

Have you any objection to my publishing in my book your and my contract in regard to the Mermaid? If you earnestly desire it, I'll not have your name at all connected with it, but I guess you had better let it rush [*sic*] just as it was.

Pray tell me if the story of the old sailor getting it in China was really true, and also give me all particulars of its origin that you can. If it *was* insured in Boston before you got it, *do* try & learn in what office it was done. These *antecedents* of the Mermaid are highly essential to me. Nevertheless, I'll keep your name out if you desire it. But I'll not hurt you—*nohow*.

If you have one of the pamphlets containing cuts & history of mermaids, pray send one & oblige &c.

Barnum

P.S. Redfield publishes my book with illustrations—retail $1.25. He *starts* with an edition of 50,000. Will have all the *MSS* in his hands 15th Oct.

## (64)

## TO MOSES KIMBALL

Bridgeport, 28 September 1854

My dear Moses,

Business is business. From the notoriety which I *can* give the Mermaid, I had ought to have it a year at my museum without charge, for if I am to have it there, I will give it such a lift as will make it worth more to you after the first year than it ever would be *without* my book. Now I will tell you what I will do. I will announce in my book, which will be out early in December, that the Mermaid belongs to *your museum* and will be seen there until the *1st day of April* next, on which very appropriate day it will make its appearance at my museum and remain there for one year, after which it will go to your museum to rest forever as a fixture. Thus you will get it for the first four months (nearly), and my book, with its *illustrations* of the Mermaid & its anecdotes concerning it and fixing it eternally as belonging to your museum, will establish it *permanently* in the public mind as a Boston Museum *fixture,* & this you know will make it better for you than if I did not publish my book at all. Besides, I will give you $200 for the use of the baby that period, & advertise in my bills that after 1st April 1856 it goes to you forever.

I think you should say "yes" to this without hesitation, & then I'll dress it up in a way that will make it an object for both of us.

Please answer at once & oblige

Truly yours,

Barnum

. . . .

Barnum and Kimball did arrive at an agreement, and the "baby" was again exhibited at the American Museum in conjunction with the publication of Barnum's autobiography.

## TO VARIOUS EDITORS

Nearly identical copies of this and the following letter—sometimes in Barnum's hand, sometimes not—were sent to editors throughout the country to publicize the forthcoming autobiography. The lucky publisher, determined upon well before the letter was written (see the 6 September letter to Kimball), was J. S. Redfield of New York, who had served on the Jenny Lind prize ode committee; although the contract itself, which called for the delivery of the manuscript on the following day and publication on or before 20 December of the same year, was not signed until 27 October 1854. The retail price of the book was set at $1.25, on which Barnum was to receive a royalty of 30 percent.

*Private*

Bridgeport, 6 October 1854

Friend Gray,

Will you have the kindness to announce that I am writing my life & that fifty-seven different publishers have applied for the chance of publishing it.

Such is the *fact*—and if it wasn't, why still it ain't a bad announcement.

Let me reciprocate when I can.

Truly yours,

P. T. Barnum

## TO VARIOUS EDITORS

Office American Museum, 15 October 1854

Gents:

I am now engaged upon my life—with no intention of taking it off, however, otherwise than with the pen. I am on the closing chapters, and I take the liberty, as a whilom brother of the Order Editorial, to write you that my autobiography will make its appearance before the public and in your sanctum sometime in December. Any assistance you can lend me in making known the fact of its approaching publication will be gratefully remembered by

Yours truly,

P. T. Barnum

P.S. The Boston, New York, and Philadelphia publishers are after the book in a swarm. I will advise you the moment I shall have made my selection which of them will issue it.

This letter is in a hand other than Barnum's, although signed by him. At least three copies, with minor variations, are extant.

{67}

## TO MOSES S. BEACH

New York, 30 November 1854

My dear Moses,

Not finding you in, I enclose the book for you to review & cut up—but pray *don't cut me up.*

As the book is not to be published till 14th, please not let your *review* appear before the 11th.

Your father's name is mentioned at pages 217 & 220.

Truly yours,

P. T. Barnum

P.S. Of course you will have a perfect copy soon as it is *bound.*

B

Moses Sperry Beach continued as proprietor of the *New York Sun* until 1868. His father Moses Yale Beach, the newspaper's former proprietor, had befriended Barnum at the start of his career.

# (68)

## TO J. R. TRUMBULL

Further publicity for the autobiography was generated by a series of lectures during the winter of 1854–55.

New York, 11 December 1854

Dear Sir,
Yours of the 9th is recd. I will therefore deliver my lecture for your society on Thursday, Dec. 21st.
*Subject: "The Philosophy of Humbug."*

Truly yours,

P. T. Barnum

. . . .

# (69)

## TO DAVID K. HITCHCOCK

Bridgeport, 28 February 1855

My dear Doctor,
Yours is recd. O.K. I see that Burns the fugitive slave is bought & is on his way to Boston. I'll give him $500 to go into my museum 5 weeks & there tell his tale to our visitors, provided he don't first appear elsewhere in New York & also pro-

[85]

vided he will commence in N.Y. by the 15th March & as much sooner as may be.

Please name this to his friends & let me know.

As ever truly yours,

P. T. Barnum

Anthony Burns was a fugitive slave who became a *cause célèbre* when he was liberated by abolitionists in Boston during the spring of 1854. David K. Hitchcock was a member of the Massachusetts senate from Newton.

## TO REV. THOMAS WENTWORTH HIGGINSON

The Unitarian minister Thomas Wentworth Higginson (1823–1911), an ardent abolitionist and social reformer, was one of the ringleaders of the raid that had freed Burns in Boston. The first sheet of this letter has not been located. Its extant envelope, however, permits identification of the recipient and an approximate date.

[Bridgeport, c. April 1855]

P.S. I had no room in the other sheet to thank you for your three pamphlets. I read them all last night with *great* satisfaction, both to myself & wife. My wife attends the Unitarian church, but her hatred of slavery is so strong that they are *too tame* for her. I have travelled much in the southern states & have got to abhor the curse from witnessing its fruits. I have spent months on the cotton plantations of Mississippi, where I have seen more than one "Legree." I am quite your disciple as to woman's rights, & as to the idolatry of the Bible, your remarks on that subject have served to help me much, for I have long felt that there should be some hurricane which should drive out the chaff from the wheat. Much in the Bible we should burn if it was printed in an almanac or any other book.

I once stepped into Tripler Hall for the purpose of seeing Lucy Stone. I had never then seen her. She was speaking on woman's rights & I became enchained to the seat & remained there till she had finished, which was 1½ hours, or nearly so. I have several times tried to get her to Bridgeport to lecture. I would still like to do it. Can it be done? If so, can you give me her address? . . .

This is a hurried hodgepodge letter, but I have written just as I feel & have no "ulterior motive" except what appears upon the surface. The fact is, I am not, nor never was, half so cute nor cunning nor *deep* as many persons suppose. I generally speak right out, just as I think, & have neither time nor inclination to engage in duplicity. My pecuniary success is owing (more than to anything else) to doing with all my might whatever I undertake & not be content in *half-doing* a thing.

If you can come & stop with me over Sunday—coming on a Friday or Saturday & preach for us Sunday (if you bring your family with you, all the better)—we should all be delighted, & I will see that you are satisfied pecuniarily. If you could come *next* Sunday, I think we have no preacher engaged, in which event we should be *glad* to have you come. Please answer & oblige

Truly yours,

P. T. Barnum

I don't often get betrayed into so *long* a letter—which is lucky for my correspondents.

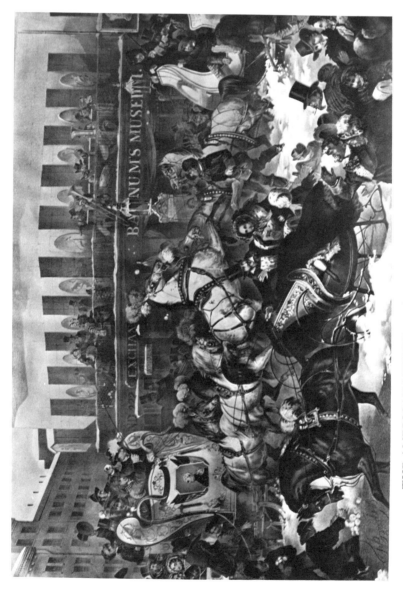

THE AMERICAN MUSEUM and NEW YORK TRAFFIC congestion around 1855. The musicians on the balcony were always the worst Barnum could find, so they would drive people into the Museum.

# (71)

## TO SOL SMITH

New York, 2 April 1855

Dear Uncle,

Will you see if there is a chance for the "four babies" to visit my Baby Show? They would almost surely get the $250, & I'll *guarantee* them $150.

Truly yours,

Barnum

Among the various contests got up at the American Museum was Barnum's "Grand National Baby Show," first held in June 1855, with prizes awarded for the "finest baby," "second finest," "third finest," "fattest child," etc. A premium of $250 was offered for the "finest quatern," or set of quadruplets. Smith's reply from St. Louis, written at the bottom of this letter, was "No babies of the kind—not even a pair of *twins* to be found."

# (72)

## TO THOMAS BRETTELL

Thomas Brettell was a London printer who resided at St. James's Palace by virtue of his wife's position as custodian there. He and Barnum became good friends during the latter's first visit to London in 1844, when Brettell printed the first of several pamphlets on Tom Thumb. Mrs. Tom Thumb writes about his wife and her living quarters at the palace in her autobiography. Sherwood Stratton died at the age of forty-four on 29 December 1855—of a "heart ailment," according to one of his son's biographers.

Iranistan [Bridgeport], 8 May 1855

My dear Brettell,

About a year since (or 8 months) I sent over to you a coat of arms & some documents of a man named Chauncey, I

[89]

think, who expected to get a fortune which is left there by one of his ancestors. The ignorant jackass now begins to think that I have got the money on his papers & will not hand it over! So if there is no chance for him, do, for God's sake, send me back his papers with a letter saying he *cannot* get anything, or else I shall be in a sad pickle. . . .

Stratton is still in the insane retreat—not much chance of his getting better. It is caused by his return to strong drink. The little General is travelling as usual. Our folks are all well & send best regards to you & yours. I hope (& so do all Americans) that the Allies will soon scratch out the eyes of the Russian Bear—but we don't like the squinting of Austria & Prussia. You must set free the Poles, Italians, & Hungarians, & then the Allies & *Liberty* will triumph.

Truly yours,

P. T. Barnum

{73}

## TO SOL SMITH

*Private & Confidential*

New York, 2 November 1855

My dear Uncle,

H. L. Bateman, who is about opening a theatre in St. Louis, owed me some $4000 by his notes of hand. I got judgement against him in California, & by garnisheeing Page, Bacon & Co. where Bateman deposited, I secured $1800 odd. I have now a certified & sealed copy of the judgement for the balance, some $2400. I want some *cute* lawyer or other individual to watch his chance & secure this balance. I suppose that on some benefit night the receipts might perhaps be attached to the amount of the claim, or perhaps he may deposite [*sic*] in his name with some banker who might be factorized or garnisheed. Bateman, however, will be very *wary,* as he is suspicious that I'll try to catch him napping. He tried three weeks ago through Le Grand Smith to buy the claim for about *half. . . .*

Business is pretty good, health first-rate, & the world wags merrily with me. I hope it is the same with you. With compliments to your family, I am as ever

Truly thy nephew,

P. T. Barnum

Henry L. Bateman was father of the famous "Bateman Children," Ellen and Kate, who made some stir as juvenile actors in the 1850s. Barnum at one time engaged them for his museum and afterwards sent them to London under the management of Le Grand Smith, who had previously served as advance agent during the Jenny Lind tour.

{74}

## TO UNIDENTIFIED CORRESPONDENT

By early 1856 Barnum was bankrupt through his dealings with the Jerome Clock Company of New Haven and his plans to bring the company to East Bridgeport, which he was then developing. Prior to his failure he had sold the Museum's collections to John Greenwood Jr., his former manager, and H. D. Butler. Circassian girls, on account of their reputed beauty, were highly desirable articles at the time, and Barnum and his agents were frequently at pains to secure one. A famous example was Zalumma Agra, "Star of the East," whom Greenwood, as was reported in a pamphlet describing her, discovered in Constantinople.

New York, 2 February 1856

My dear Doctor,

The clock folks have *wound me up.* Never mind. My wife owns the Museum lease, which will give her an annual income for the next 23 years that will support us.

Greenwood in getting up the "Congress of Nations" wants two beautiful Circassian slaves. I have written Mr. Brown, our consul in Constantinople, about it, but it struck me that you could perhaps manage it through your young dental Turk. Will you try?

He wants to *hire* 2 beautiful Circassian girls & their mother or father or some other protector for 1 to 2 years. I suppose they would have to be bought, then give them their freedom and hire them, making contract through U.S. consul. Will you tell me whether it is feasible to get them & do what you can to aid Greenwood in the matter?

For my own part, I have renounced business & care forever.

Truly yours,

P. T. Barnum

## TO W. C. CURRY

Barnum's many friends rallied around him once his bankruptcy became known, but he steadfastly refused most offers of assistance.

New York, 14 April 1856

Friend Curry,

Yours of the 11th is recd. You can't imagine how your words of sympathy thrill my heart. Adversity at least is a blessing so far as it tries one's friends. I am glad to say that I have warm personal friends of long standing & *relatives* of substance whose kindness renders it unnecessary for me to accept your kind offer of pecuniary aid. Your goodness of heart, however, you may depend, is deeply appreciated & will never be forgotten. The health of my wife is very poor. She joins me in best wishes for you & yours.

Truly yours,

P. T. Barnum

# {76}

## TO WILLIAM H. NOBLE

In April 1856 a large body of Bridgeport citizens met to publicly "sympathize" with their bankrupt fellow townsman—an event that received considerable attention in the national papers. Barnum himself, who had removed with his family to Long Island, was not present, but sent this "characteristic" letter, which was read at the meeting. William H. Noble was Barnum's partner in his plans to develop East Bridgeport.

New York, 24 April 1856

Dear Sir,

I have just received a slip containing a call for a public meeting of the citizens of Bridgeport to sympathize with me in my troubles. It is headed by His Honor the Mayor and is signed by most of your prominent citizens, as well as by many men who by hard labor earn their daily bread and who appreciate a calamity which at a single blow strips a man of his fortune, his dear home, and all the worldly comforts which years of diligent labor had acquired. It is due to truth to say that I knew nothing of this movement until your letter informed me of it.

In misfortune the true sympathy of neighbors is more consoling and precious than anything which money can purchase. This voluntary offering of my fellow citizens, though it thrills me with painful emotions and causes tears of gratitude, yet imparts to me renewed strength and fills my heart with thankfulness to Providence for raising up to my sight, above all this wreck, kind hearts which soar above the sordid atmosphere of "dirty dollars." I can never forget this unexpected kindness from my old friends and neighbors.

I trust I am not blind to my many faults and shortcomings. I, however, do feel great consolation in believing that I never used money or position to oppress the poor or wrong my fellow men, and that I never turned empty away those whom I had the power to assist.

My poor sick wife, who needs the bracing air which our

[93]

own dear home (made beautiful by her willing hands) would now have afforded her, is driven by the orders of her physician to a secluded spot on Long Island where the sea wind lends its healthful influence, and where I have also retired for the double purpose of consoling her and of recruiting my own constitution, which, through the excitements of the last few months, has most seriously failed me.

In our quiet and humble retreat, that which I most sincerely pray for is tranquillity and contentment. I am sure that the remembrance of the kindness of my Bridgeport neighbors will aid me in securing these cherished blessings. No man who has not passed through similar scenes can fully comprehend the misery which has been crowded into the last few months of my life; but I have endeavored to preserve my integrity, and I humbly hope and believe that I am being taught humility and reliance upon Providence, which will yet afford a thousand times more peace and true happiness than can be acquired in the din, strife and turmoil, excitements and struggles of this money-worshipping age. The man who coins his brain and blood into gold, who wastes all of his time and thought upon the almighty dollar, who looks no higher than blocks of houses and tracts of land, and whose iron chest is crammed with stocks and mortgages tied up with his own heartstrings, may console himself with the idea of safe investments, but he misses a pleasure which I firmly believe this lesson was intended to secure to me, and which it will secure if I can fully bring my mind to realize its wisdom. I think I hear you say

> When the devil was sick,
> The devil a saint would be.
> But when the devil got well,
> The devil a saint was he.

Granted, but, after all, the man who looks upon the loss of money as anything compared to the loss of honor, or health, or self-respect, or friends—a man who can find no source of happiness except in riches—is to be pitied for his blindness. I certainly feel that the loss of money, of home and my home

[94]

comforts, is dreadful; that to be driven again to find a resting place away from those I love and from where I had fondly supposed I was to end my days, and where I had lavished time, money, everything to make my descent to the grave placid and pleasant—is, indeed, a severe lesson; but, after all, I firmly believe it is for the best, and though my heart may break, I will not repine. . . .

P. T. Barnum

{77}

## TO BENJAMIN WEBSTER

By the end of 1856 Barnum was in England again, where he eventually succeeded in retrieving his fortune through his tours with Tom Thumb and a lecture he got up entitled "The Art of Money-Getting" (which he candidly acknowledged might more appropriately have been called "The Art of Money-Losing"). Among the other attractions he managed during this period was the Howard family, famous for their interpretation of *Uncle Tom's Cabin*. Benjamin Webster was manager of London's Adelphi Theatre at the time.

London, 20 December 1856

Dear Sir,

I have with me an exceedingly talented *trio,* Mr. & Mrs. Howard & their little daughter Cordelia, an exquisite actress of eight years.

They have made their mark in America, and I am *certain* that they would draw large & delighted audiences to your theatre if you should decide upon giving them a trial. We are in no particular *hurry* about their first appearance in London, as we knew before leaving New York that the pantomime season would absorb public attention the first month in the year, and we came prepared to *wait*. If, however, you should think it advisable to entertain the idea of engaging them after your holiday entertainments commence falling off, I should feel honored in an interview at such hour & place as will suit your convenience.

[95]

I scarcely need assure you that, situated as I am, I should never have crossed the Atlantic with an attraction which I did not *know* possessed every element of immense success.

Very truly yours,

P. T. Barnum

## {78}

## TO REV. ABEL C. THOMAS

The Rev. Abel C. Thomas (1807–80), authór, editor, historian of Universalism and compiler of its first hymnal, served most of his pastoral career at the First Universalist Church of Philadelphia. Barnum frequently corresponded with him and members of his family.

London, 9 March 1857

My dear Abel,

The Lord reigns—let the earth *rejoice*. Time rolls on, troubles come and go, we have darkness at one hour & sunlight at another—but away up, *high* up above all, is calmness and everlasting quietude. With us, all is excitement, strife, turmoil; but we are but ants, struggling & striving, ever busy, ever anxious about our little anthills, while true wisdom should say to us, "Fret not thy gizzard." We cannot *control* fate or destiny, but out of all our chaos & troubles, our excitements & disappointments, we gather lessons of experience & wisdom; and truly wise is he who sees the hand of the good Father in everything.

How mole-eyed are those who cannot see that very often "apparent evils are blessings in disguise." In one sense there is *no* evil or trouble to those whose heart is in the right place. Last summer, in my poverty & seclusion at the seaside with my family, I found more peace & contentment than Iranistan ever afforded me—& even on the Atlantic & this side of it, hope & happiness have been and are my handmaidens. All

[96]

praise to Him for permitting me always to look upon the bright side of things. My health & spirits are much better than I would like to have many suppose. My hopes of a prosperous future even in the present sphere are by no means extinguished. On the contrary, they brighten daily. But this is *mum*. Elements are continually at work which will evolve the right sort of thing, but time & patience are requisite.

Your claim—principal & interest—has never been jeopardized. I only regret that "the ready" was not available & forthcoming when you wanted it. But it will all come to the uttermost farthing & to your entire satisfaction, & with it my everlasting gratitude. If you will write me at once telling me about the works of that watch & anything else I can do for you, it shall be faithfully attended to. I can command the money here sufficient to cover any of your orders, and the goods will reach you duty-free. So speak out at once.

I believe my wife is in better health, and the rest of my family are well. Here I have no news further than that all things seem to work & move and bring about results exactly such as I most desire. I have learned to be patient & submissive, & that was a great and most important lesson for me to acquire. It was just the lesson which I needed—in fact, my whole troubles have been and are just what I most stood in need of. *Of course* so, for they are sent to me by Divine & Parental wisdom, and I receive them with earnest thankfulness. The eye of faith sees the object & the *end* of such things. . . . Accept the most fervent & honest assurances of my everlasting gratitude to you & of my never dying esteem for yours, & believe me to be as ever yours to serve,

P. T. Barnum

. . . .

## (79)

### TO ALFRED ELY BEACH?

Barnum returned to America in the summer of 1857. As this letter concerning advertising in the *New York Sun* indicates, he still had his say in the management of the American Museum, despite his public assertions to the contrary. The recipient was apparently Alfred Ely Beach, although he is generally said to have sold out his interest in the paper, to his brother Moses S. Beach, by this date.

New York, 9 July 1857

Mr dear Alfred,

Just as I am on the eve of leaving town, Greenwood tells me you want to put the screws to us by charging $360 for what has always heretofore been $100. Now my dear fellow, I am sure the old quarter-dollar museum can't afford this, and I hope you will not bite off your nose & ours too by charging it. The $100 per annum is but a *small* portion of what we pay you for extras, and you know we have always hitched horses so well together that no favors are with[h]eld by me *ever* when they can be given for the *Sun's* benefit.

Pray reconsider a minute & let the $100 charge stand. It will be all right & pay you well on the long run.

Truly yours,

P. T. Barnum

## (80)

### TO MOSES S. BEACH

New York, 11 January 1858

My dear Moses,

Your young man has just taken the $400 C[rystal] P[alace] bonds. I had meant to have seen you today & will do

[98]

so next Saturday if I can manage to be in town. In the meantime I hope you will look sharply about you & see what chance there is to do one of 3 things—viz.:

1st Extend the lease of C.P. 25 years free of rent & free of taxes, or

2d Have the state purchase it for the perpetual exhibition of machinery, inventions, &c. &c., or

3d Have the city buy it & rent it to the American Institute, who will pay $10,000 per annum for it.

When I see you I will endeavor to show you that besides being a great public loss & disgrace to destroy such a beautiful building, there are *other* considerations which would seem to justify your looking closely into this subject.

Truly yours,

P. T. Barnum

## (81)

## TO WILLIAM W. BRAGG JR.

New York, 22 April 1858

My dear Sir,

Yours of yesterday is recd. I am sorry to say that my *autograph* is already too common in Boston & elsewhere. You could find it attached to many thousand-dollar notes which I had been lured to give under *false pretences*. They are scarcely worth the paper they are written on & no doubt could be purchased cheap from Mr. W. K. Batchelder, firm of Ladd & Co., Music Warehouse, Washington St.; Mr. Hovey, firm of I. C. Howe & Co.; Benjn. French; Jesse T. Alderman; Mr. Atwood, hotel keeper, *Brighton;* and *Bradley* (& his friends), late agt. for the Jerome Clock Co.; & many others. *Such* an autograph can hardly be worth possessing, but at your request I send it.

Truly yours,

P. T. Barnum

{82}

## TO UNIDENTIFIED EDITOR

Back in England, Barnum toured the provinces lecturing on "The Art of Money-Getting" during much of 1859. The speech was not the only attraction on the program, and even the Fejee Mermaid was again pressed into service. This letter is in a hand other than Barnum's, although signed by him.

St. James's Hall [London], 25 January 1859

Sir:

At my lecture on Friday night, the 28th inst., I shall introduce a *Bavarian* minstrel whose *instrument,* though smaller than Picco's, produces more peculiar & startling orchestral effects.

The presence of your reporter is respectfully solicited.

Your obedient servant,

P. T. Barnum

{83}

## TO W. GUERNSEY

The following was written in connection with a prospective engagement in Dublin.

Newcastle upon Tyne, 5 April 1859

Dear Sir,

Yours of the 4th is recd. The musical performances of Herr Knope add materially to the interest of my entertainments. He is a very superior artist. I should prefer to keep him with me. I also am compelled to take a man with me to put up & take down the paintings, exhibit the Mermaid at the close of the entertainment, &c.

Now I am willing to furnish these two men, the Mermaid, and myself for 12 consecutive week nights on the following terms: £325 and railway expenses for myself & 2 men. . . . I am willing to receive in London three days before starting a London sight-draft for £100. But before commencing my entertainment I must be secured for the next £125 by having it lodged in the hands of a respectable banker in Dublin who shall hand it to my order on the night of the 6th entertainment; and before giving the seventh entertainment the remaining £100 must be deposited with a responsible banker (satisfactory to me) who shall pay it to my order on the night of the 10th entertainment. . . .

The fact is, some speculators have made money by engaging me & paying me—but ano[ther (in B]radford) made money by *not* paying according to agreement, and I prefer doing my own business & taking my own risks to letting other parties do it if I am still to incur risks. Hence I must be fixed & firm on this point. . . .

When I engaged Jenny Lind, I deposited £37,500 three months *in advance,* & I have frequently done the same thing (on a smaller scale) when speculating in minor things like "Barnum on Money-Making," & I think *it is right.* For success or failure often depends upon *management,* & the party having nothing to do with management & no direct interest in receipts should at least be *sure* of the sum agreed upon for him to receive. I am in Durham 7th, Darlington 8th, & London early on the 9th. I start from London for Plymouth Sunday 10th. Hoping to hear from you as soon as Saturday, I am

Truly yours,

P. T. Barnum

P.S. The Oxford affair was misrepresented. The students crammed the house to suffocation & tried to enjoy themselves by lampooning. But I was quite delighted with it & so were they. No person threw anything at me. But they begged me to remain a week, promising full houses every night. . . .

## (84)

### TO MOSES KIMBALL

Bridgeport, 25 June 1859

My dear Moses,

I have returned bringing the Mermaid in good order, & for which I give you many thanks & owe you heaps of gratitude. Greenwood will send the "crittur" by express. . . .

My poor Charity still continues very ill, & I am not quite well as the *clock wheels* are running in my head yet & make me dizzy sometimes. I hope to see you ere long & in the meantime am

As ever thine,

P. T. Barnum

## (85)

### TO MESSRS. R. GRIFFIN & CO.

This letter was written to an English publisher who was about to issue a brief biographical sketch of Barnum, in which he was characterized as "a celebrated American charlatan," a failed "strolling player," and as "duping the world" with such notorious frauds as Joice Heth. In the newly written sketch by the "highly respectable clergyman" that Barnum now sent the publisher, the word "charlatan" was diplomatically emended to "showman," the imposture regarding Joice Heth was said to have originated with her former proprietors, Barnum's civic qualities were extolled, and mention was now made of Barnum's management of Jenny Lind and celebrity as "Prince of Humbugs."

*Private*

Barnum's American Museum, 27 January 1860

Gentlemen:

Your lithographed letter of Dec. was duly recd. The sketch you sent me would, if published, do me an *injustice.* As I desire *nothing* but what is fair and right, I sent your letter to a highly respectable clergyman who knows me about as well as I know myself, and asked him to send me a fair & candid sketch for your book. He has enclosed me the sheet which I now send to you with a single alteration by myself, after having cut off his address.

It is a *fact,* as you will see in my autobiography, that the story of Washington's nurse did not originate with me, but that *I really believed it myself* when I entered the speculation. It is also a fact that my nett [*sic*] profits by the Jenny Lind enterprise exceeded £70,000, while hers were about £40,000. The exact figures as taken from my account books are published in my autobiography.

As a general thing I have not "*duped* the world," nor attempted to do so; but while I do not attempt to justify all I have done, I know that I have generally given the people the *worth of their money twice told.* The Mermaid, Woolly Horse, Ploughing Elephants, &c. were merely used by me as skyrockets, or advertisements, to attract attention and give notoriety to the *Museum* & such other really valuable attractions as I provided for the public. I believe hugely in advertising and blowing my own trumpet, beating the gongs, drums, &c. to attract attention to a *show;* but I never believed that any amount of advertising or energy would make a *spurious* article permanently successful. No man really believes less in *shows* than myself. I should dislike to be thought so poor a student of human nature as to believe that money can be made from the public without giving a full *equivalent* therefor. I don't believe in "duping the public," but I believe in first *attracting* & then pleasing them.

Very truly yours,

P. T. Barnum

## (86)

## TO SOL SMITH

Out of bankruptcy, Barnum quickly resumed the proprietorship of the American Museum, with his trusted assistant Greenwood continuing as manager. The new "What Is It?" was the deformed Negro William Henry Johnson, otherwise known as "Zip," who continued on exhibition—first at the Museum, then in circuses and variety theatres—until well into the present century.

Museum, 4 April 1860

My dear Uncle Sol,

A certain museum proprietor in St. Louis—I don't know his name—saw a queer little crittur exhibiting in Phila. a few months since. I have since secured it, and we call it "What Is It?" I think the sd. museum proprietor offered to buy it. It would take a big figure to buy it, but I would like to learn what he will be willing to pay per week to exhibit it 6 to 10 weeks, & I am also open for an offer to buy it. If he is a proper & responsible person I would like to open correspondence with him in regard to novelties which I might occasionally furnish him, & perhaps he could also sometimes supply me with something attractive alive. If he is not the right sort of a chap, don't speak to him. I guess you are not sorry I have dug out again. I can make $90,000 per annum in this museum.

Truly yours,

P. T. Barnum

## (87)

## TO UNIDENTIFIED CORRESPONDENT

Museum, 23 April 1860

My dear Sir,

Yours is recd. We have had a specimen of the Mohawk Monster in our aquaria before & would like yours as well as one or two more of the same sort if they turn up. Please send the "crittur" at my expense & allow me the pleasure of seeing you when you come to town and thanking you in person, as I do now most sincerely by pen.

Truly yours,

P. T. Barnum

## (88)

## TO SAMUEL FRANCIS DU PONT

Museum, 23 May 1860

Dear Sir,

I do not propose to *bore* you, as I fear you have too much of that sort of thing. I am confident, however, that we have many curiosities here which the Japanese Embassy have never seen & that they would be interested in, especially our *grand aquaria* & several singular *living curiosities*. We have prepared numerous flags, banners, &c. for the occasion of their visit to the city, & I hope you will kindly gratify *them* & me by having them visit the Museum. If you will give me a day's notice I will *exclude visitors* while they are here, if you require it. I also hope they will visit *Adams' California Menagerie*.

Truly yours,

P. T. Barnum

Samuel Francis Du Pont (1803–65) had been detailed by the Secretary of State to escort the first Japanese embassy that visited America during the spring of 1860. Adams' California Menagerie, presided over by the fabled Grizzly Adams, was then being run by Barnum as a separate establishment.

{89}

## TO UNIDENTIFIED CORRESPONDENT

Museum, 29 May 1860

My dear Sir,

Do come and see our improved aquaria & especially the "angel" fish from the Gulf of Mexico, if it is yet alive when you inquire for it. It is immeasu[r]ably the most elegant fish I ever saw—& no fish story!

Truly yours,

P. T. Barnum

## TO JOHN NIMMO

John Nimmo was connected with the English-language newspaper *Galignani's Messenger,* published in Paris, and often performed errands in that city for Barnum.

Museum, 20 September 1860

My dear Nimmo,

I believe I justly owe you about two pounds or $10 for something, & I really forget what. If it is more, pray let me know. I enclose that amount. And now for another commission. We are playing *religious dramas* here and have already got *Joseph and His Brethren* and *The Prodigal Son.* I hear that several religious or Bible subjects have been dramatized in Paris and played. If these plays have been published, they can be bought for a franc or two each, in which event I want you to buy & send me a copy of each one published. You may perhaps pick up the dramatized story of Samson, Saul, Queen Esther, &c. At all events, send me all that are published.

My wife is better, & I am driving business, trying partially to make up my losses. Greenwood sends his compliments though he never saw you. My family all join in kindest remembrances to you and yours. Hitchcock (whom you remember) is again in my employ & sends his kind regards.

Truly yours,

P. T. Barnum

# (91)

## TO J. B. TOHEY

Although Barnum declared his solvency from the stage of the Museum early in 1860, not all of his notes outstanding at the time of his bankruptcy had yet been taken up. It is interesting to compare the contents and tone of this letter to those of other letters written around the same time—that of 4 April 1860 to Sol Smith, for instance.

Museum, 4 December 1860

Sir:

I more sincerely regret than you can that any calamity should ever have placed me in the position which I shall frankly confess to you I am in; but all regrets are in vain, and *a struggle of five years* has inured me to accept with some degree of resignation a visitation which *cannot be helped.*

I was aware of the existence of the note described in your letter of the 5th inst., as well as some $67,000 more that was not presented to my estate—viz., $48,000 in this city and $19,000 in Boston. It is quite possible that there are thousands more of which I have never heard & of which I have no means of knowing.

I tell you candidly & honestly that *I do not possess a dollar's worth of property in the world,* & the prospect of ever doing so grows darker as I grow older. Although ostensibly proprietor of this museum, I have only hired out my name & services to the real owners for a monthly salary, quite inadequate to support my family, except aided by a small income which my wife holds in her own right. The real proprietors of the Museum (Messrs. Greenwood & Butler) bought & paid for it in /55, & most of their purchase money was seized by clock creditors. Messrs. G & B mortgaged the collection to the owner of the Museum building to secure rent. The Museum has lost money for several years, but since using my name & services it has done better. But now the cold weather & dull times are again operating against it to such a degree that my services will possibly be dispensed with, a fact which I shall not much regret, as I now work 15 hours in nearly every 24.

The New York holders of similar paper to yours have asked 25 per ct. for it, counting no interest. But $12,000 is more than my friends would advance for a trifle over two thirds of the clock notes known to be out, so the affair has remained in *statu quo* until today. But today the agt. of N.Y. creditors offers to take 15 per ct., which will be $7200 for the $48,000.

The party in Boston who holds $19,000 for himself & others asks 30 cts. on the face of the paper. My friends have offered him 15 cts. provided the N.Y. paper could be got for the same, which offer he refuses. Now as the N.Y. creditors will accept the 15 per ct., the Boston party shall be paid 25 *per ct.* upon the face of his paper, yours included, if you & he think proper to accept it. But it of course is no object to attempt to buy one piece or ten pieces of the paper unless *all* is bought.

I confess that at my time of life it is of very little consequence whether or not obstructions are removed which would prevent my again engaging in the turmoils & risks of business on my own account. I have lost nearly all of my ambition—and all I care for is to have my family live *comfortably.*

One thing, however, is certain. My estate has all been sold by receivers & assignees, & the proceeds paid to holders of clock paper for which I never received one dollar's benefit. Very likely I pronounced your note "right & correct" when I was in Boston with the Baby Show. I then considered that *all* such paper was right & correct, not dreaming of the insolvency of the clock co. nor of there existing uncancelled a tenth part of the paper which did so exist (I had been told that the acceptances I was continually signing were used to pay others which were maturing—but *this was false*). Nor did I know when in Boston that this clock paper was being sold at usurious rates of interest—a fact which would of itself have opened my eyes if I had been cognizant of it.

But why dwell on this unpleasant theme? I have been

[109]

and still am overwhelmed with financial embarrassments. I see but little encouragement in trying to get out any farther than I am. Still, I have never ceased to offer all that I could command to be able to say, "The clock notes are all cancelled." I own no property, & if I should die (which I *must* sometime), no note or debt against me will be worth the paper it is written on. *These are all candid facts.*

The party in Boston who holds the $19,000 is Mr. W. K. Batchelder, Piano Warehouse, 296 Washington St. If you or your agt. think proper to call & show him this letter, and if he thinks proper to abate 5 per ct. from his demands so as to accept 25 per ct. on the face, and yours is put in with the rest, you will receive by 10th January next for your note $375. But I repeat that unless Mr. Batchelder sells my friends his paper, yours is not worth to me or to my friends anything whatever. I have until 1st Jany. next to accept or decline the offer of N.Y. creditors to take 15 per ct. & therefore this proposition is open to you & Mr. Batchelder until 28th Dec.

I sincerely hope that your position in life is such that the loss by this misfortune is not seriously felt by you. I have lost many, many thousands besides & before the clock misfortune.

Truly yours,

P. T. Barnum

## TO JOSEPH GREEN COGSWELL

Cogswell had been librarian of the Astor Library since its founding in 1842.

New York, 20 January 1861

Dear Sir,

The South African savages now here express a great desire to see the *Astor Library,* as it is hard for them to conceive how *books* or *writing* can be made to communicate *ideas*. If not incompatible, with your arrangements, will you kindly permit me to bring them at such hour as you may name on *Thursday* next & oblige

> Truly yours,
>
> P. T. Barnum

## TO UNIDENTIFIED EDITOR

New York, 19 February 1861, 8½ P.M.

Dear Sir,

President Lincoln has just assured me that he will positively visit the Museum tomorrow, Wednesday. Will you please notice this fact & oblige

> Truly yours,
>
> P. T. Barnum

## TO HENRI DRAYTON

New York, 4 March 1861

Sir:

You having refused to perform with such accompaniaments [*sic*] as you had in Europe, & such *only* as I ever heard you sing to in Great Britain, I see no way except to let you take the consequences of that refusal.

I have already (as you are aware) notified you that the

performances (owing to your neglect in furnishing music & selecting a pianist, or agreeing to rehearse with one) are suspended till March 11th under my right to suspend as per *agreement,* and you have refused to perform on and after the 11th accompanied by such music as I can prove was agreed upon by you at the making of your contract with me.

Four thousand dollars ($4000) have been lost by your parlor operas in consequence of my temporarily listening against my better judgement to your plan of making an *orchestra* the *feature* instead of *yourselves.*

I have finally *insisted* upon adopting the original and only feasible plan for securing *success* and giving a performance which should reflect credit upon you & Mrs. Drayton, instead of a band of instrumental music. You will therefore accede to my request contained in my former letters to you. You will also please bear in mind that a few days' notice is necessary before giving your operas, and the longer you delay the notice of acceding to my request, the more time & damages will you have to account for.

Truly yours,

P. T. Barnum

## TO DR. OSCAR KOHN

New York, 8 March 1861

Sir:

As my engagement with you expires in 2 weeks for the Albino Family, I now propose to you if you will transfer them to me under your written agreement with them, I will pay you fifty dollars ($50) bonus. They are acting very disagreeable [*sic*] with you, but if I have your agreement transferred to me, I will put them in jail if they don't behave. I will still employ you in the Museum. Give me your answer Monday.

Yours &c.,

P. T. Barnum

Dr. Oscar Kohn remained in Barnum's employ for many years and seems to have been primarily responsible for looking after the animals at the Museum and later in Barnum's circus. The Albino Family—consisting of Rudolph Lucasie, his wife, and son—had first been seen and engaged by Barnum while he was traveling in Holland.

( 96 )

## TO ABRAHAM LINCOLN

Lindencroft, Bridgeport, 30 August 1861

Honored Sir:
The late events which have occurred in this vicinity, concluding with the arrest of *Schnabel,* have rendered Secessionists *so scarce,* I cannot find one for exhibition in my museum.

Those who one week ago were blatant Secessionists are today publicly announcing themselves as "in for the country to the end of the war." The *"strong arm"* has a mighty influence here.

Truly yours,

P. T. Barnum

Ellis B. Schnable, described elsewhere by Barnum as a "broken-down politician from Pennsylvania," had been speaking against government policies at various "peace meetings" in Connecticut. He had just been arrested by the deputy sheriff of Litchfield County on orders from Secretary of State William H. Seward. A few days before this event, on 24 August, he had been scheduled to speak at a meeting Barnum and a gang of Bridgeport loyalists broke up in a neighboring town, and had remained to heckle (and was kicked for it) Barnum when he made a speech of his own. Schnable spent the duration of the war in confinement.

# (97)

## TO GIDEON WELLES

By the date of this letter Barnum's old friend Gideon Welles had become Secretary of the Navy. Barnum's super-patriotism during the Civil War is well documented. On one occasion the offices of the *Bridgeport Farmer*—the "Copperhead" newspaper referred to in this letter—were sacked by a mob that had been stirred up by one of his speeches.

Bridgeport, 14 September 1861

My dear Sir,

The Prudential Committee and the Union Committee of this city, composed of our first citizens without regard to party, have written the Hon. Secy. of the Treasury in regard to the *disloyalty* of Philo C. Calhoun, sub[scriptio]n agt. for the National Loan.

The appointment of Mr. Calhoun gives *great offence* to all Union men here, & not one of them will subscribe a dollar at his hands. Indeed, they demand his removal & the substitution of Clapp Spooner, Esq., pres[iden]t of the Pequonnock Bank and one of the principal owners of the *Adams Express Co.—a loyal man.*

Calhoun is a rabid political Democrat of the *Bridgeport Farmer* school. He has $100,000 invested in a saddle & harness shop in Charleston, S.C.; his daughter lives in Virginia, having married a Secessionist; & his wife and daughters are outspoken Secessionists. At the defeat at Bull's [*sic*] Run, they drove to the *Bridgeport Farmer* office, called out the editors, and gloated & laughed with them in the public streets over our defeat.

Calhoun has always been an active, noisy man in relation to everything connected with our union, state, county, city, & even with school districts, but he has never opened his mouth in favor of our government. He has not given *a dollar* towards helping our volunteers, though all loyal men have done so, & he *refused* to sign the call (signed by thousands of our citizens)

[114]

for a meeting to *sustain the government* & to listen to the speeches of Hon. D. S. Dickinson & Col. Thos. Francis Meagher, here today. The Prudential Committee telegraphed Mr. Chase this morning to suspend Calhoun's appointment until he gets their letter, which they send by this mail. I implore you, notwithstanding the many calls upon your time, to send this letter to Mr. Chase & *add your word* in favor of dropping Calhoun & appointing Mr. Spooner.

*I* ask no favors of the government for *myself,* but I join my loyal fellow citizens in respectfully *protesting* against the putting forward of *rebels* to the neglect of men who are ready to give all their money and their blood to sustain our government.

*Great indignation* exists over this appointment.

Calhoun is now making $30,000 to $50,000 by his harness & saddle jobs here for the U.S. government, and is probably doing as much in *Charleston,* S.C., working for the *rebels.* For heaven's sake, have an *example* made of this traitorous Calhoun. It will do *a world of good* to the cause of the Union.

Respectfully yours,

P. T. Barnum

## TO CAPTAIN TREAT

Bridgeport, 28 November 1861

Captain Treat:

This being *Thanksgiving Day,* I thought I would give a *treat* to Captain *Treat.* You said the other day that you had not elbow room on the west.

Now since you have built such a nice house, which is an ornament to that part of East Bridgeport & a benefit to my property, you are welcome to 15 feet on the west. You may fence it in if you like and have it.

Truly yours,

P. T. Barnum

## TO ROBERT BONNER

Robert Bonner was proprietor of the *New York Ledger*.

Bridgeport, 5 February 1862

My dear Mr. Bonner,

I am laid up for a few days here at home with a bruised leg caused by a fall. I wrote Mr. Greenwood the other day to send you a family season ticket to my museum.

We sell no rum nor segars there; we long since excluded improper characters; we keep it nice & genteel & are patronized by the *best class* of society.

The aquaria is by far the most neat & complete of any in the world; the great hippopotamus from the Upper Nile is the *only* animal of the kind ever seen here; the living whale is a rare novelty to place on public exhibition; and Commodore Nutt is the crowning triumph of the establishment. If you will venture into the lecture room, you will hear nothing vulgar nor profane & on the contrary will see by far the most *gorgeous* & *interesting* spectacular exhibition ever seen in N.Y.

The expenses of the Museum are now double what they ever were before, and I sadly want & need in your columns a statement of *the facts* concerning the manner in which I am now catering for public *improvement* as well as public amusement.

I am already under numerous obligations to you, & I know I am asking for something unusual for you to do. Still,

I hope that you will see that I am doing *good* to the community in which we live, and as you are doing the same, I have presumed upon your kindness once more.

If it is utterly inconsistent with your feelings to do as I desire, I shall still feel as ever

Your grateful friend,

P. T. Barnum

## {100}

## TO W. C. CURRY

Bridgeport, 21 March 1862

Dear Sir,

During the last eight days I have been an anxious watcher at the bedside of my poor wife, who we have often thought could not live an hour. Three days since, as if by a miracle, she began to revive, & we now almost feel that she is out of immediate danger.

This explains my not answering your letter sooner. I shall be *very* glad to see "Mrs. Curry & Lizzie" with you when you come to N.Y., & for fear they might stick you for the "quarters" at the door, I enclose the needful. I cannot use the old Bible. It is not a thing that can be exhibited & *examined* in the Museum.

As ever truly yours,

P. T. Barnum

. . . .

## (101)

### TO PHILO H. SKIDMORE

The nineteenth century was a great age for punsters, and Barnum could hold his own with the worst of them. The present letter was written to one of his Bridgeport neighbors, who once had occasion to complain—evidently in no uncertain terms—about some bear wagons Barnum had left parked on Elm Street after they had been repaired and repainted at Hall's Carriage Shop. In 1862, the year of this exchange, Barnum had not yet embarked upon his career with the "Greatest Show on Earth." But he did have a menagerie in his American Museum, and around this time he was also managing the separately run "California Menagerie" of the famed Grizzly Adams, whose troupe of bears included an immense grizzly that went by the name of "Old Sampson." Notwithstanding the fact that Adams was suffering from a mortal head wound—inflicted by one of his bears—that left his brain exposed, Barnum sent him and his charges on a tour of Connecticut and Massachusetts, the two men having first made a wager as to whether Adams would live long enough to finish the engagement. It was this exhibition, presumably, that now made an unscheduled stopover on Elm Street near the residence of Philo H. Skidmore. No doubt the latter had plenty to complain of, since the cages do not appear to have been empty.

Bridgeport, 17 May 1862

Dear Sir,

On returning home last night I found your kind letter of the 15th inst. Profoundly lamenting the palpable absence of taste for the "fine arts" which prevails in Elm Street, and seeing that like "casting pearls &c." the artistic display from Hall's Conservatory of Art is more than you are willing to *bear,* I shall not *pause* nor hesitate, especially after reading the finishing *clause* of your eloquent epistle, but shall at once order the bears to "dig out" lest there might be mischief a *brewin'* in your vicinity.

I am rejoiced at the evident tendency to "spiritual things" which is manifest in Elm St. from your desire to cast off the "Old Adam." The proprietors of the "Conservatory" will today *haul* the palaces of "Old Sampson" & his courtiers to "Gaza," in order that more appreciative eyes may *gaze-a* while upon the "wreck of matter" ere it falls (perchance) into the hands of the ruthless "Philistines." I hope that in descending the hills the horses will be relieved by placing a "skid" upon

[118]

the wheels, but if they require further relief, I shall be obliged to call on you for one *Skid-more.*

I hardly know where I shall place the "palaces," but if I cannot find a more suitable locality for them, I will *Barnum.*

## {102}

### TO OLIVER WENDELL HOLMES

In 1857, through arrangements Barnum had made the previous year, the first public aquaria in America opened at the American Museum. Barnum's Aquarial Gardens in Boston, which he managed around the time of his writing to Holmes, were an extension of this initial venture.

Barnum's Aquarial Gardens, Boston, 29 July 1862

My dear Sir,

I shall feel obliged in your acceptance of the enclosed season ticket to our Gardens & shall be *very* glad to know that you call often.

I am extremely anxious that the Boston public should know how much I am trying to do for them at the low figure of a "quarter."

Truly yours,

P. T. Barnum

## {103}

### TO THOMAS BRETTELL

New York, 10 October 1862

My dear old friend Brettell,

It does me good to see your charming "phiz" looking so natural as it does in that picture sent by friend John P.

Howard. I would give all my old boots and shoes for the pleasure of taking you again by the hand. God grant it may be so, but I see no immediate prospect of going over the Atlantic. The truth is, I don't feel like leaving my own country while she is in peril, nor do I relish visiting another country when I have none of my own to hail from. But I trust in God and Liberty that ere long this rebellion will be crushed and the Union, stronger than ever, be restored. I believe it will be so, but I don't want to argue the point with you or anybody else. I know this thing from beginning to end, and I know it is the d——dest barbarous, mean, and causeless rebellion ever known—not excepting that of the Sepoys—but I have been shocked and disappointed to see the English nation taking sides with the political slaveholders. But never mind. History will set this matter right, and I am doing all in my power to assist in *making history* about these times. But let this drop. . . .

Of course you have heard of my wonderful little Commodore Nutt, just what Thumb was 16 years ago—looks like him, talks like him, and acts like him, but is sharper and more clever. Nutt and Thumb are engaged to travel together for several years and will probably be in Liverpool before Xmas or soon after. They may perhaps run to London for a few weeks, but that is not certain. I have a small finger in the pie, *sub rosa*.

My health never was better, and I delight in working as much as I ever did. I take it easy at home in summer—fishing, sailing, bathing, riding, &c.—but from Oct. to May I work as hard as ever and love it. My business thus far has been good all through the war, but if needs be I am willing to be reduced to the last shirt and the last dollar—yes, and the *very last* drop of blood—in case that will help to preserve this nation as one and inseparable. . . .

I send pictures of Nutt and Thumb. I fancy you could get *Illustrated News* to publish likenesses with statement that they are coming to London soon. Pray try it. You need not use my name. Show them enclosed extracts.

May God bless and preserve thee and thine is the earnest prayer of

Your old friend,

P. T. Barnum

This letter was originally published (with the name of the recipient misspelled) in an article by Charles Hamilton, "P. T. Barnum, Genius of Humbug," in the March 1953 issue of *Hobbies* magazine. The location of the original is unknown. Commodore Nutt (George Washington Morrison Nutt) was another midget Barnum had recently engaged.

## (104)

## TO MR. MORSE

One of the great social events of 1863 was the wedding of Tom Thumb to Lavinia Warren on 10 February in New York's Grace Church. Witnesses were admitted to the church by ticket, and Barnum and his agents were besieged by requests for these precious items.

New York, 7 February 1863

Dear Sir,

Mr. Hitchcock *could not* (as he says he did not) *promise* tickets to the wedding. He promised to *try his best,* & he did. *We* have *no power* in the premises. Miss Warren & Genl. have been beset until *every place* in the church is taken, & the rector declares that not one person shall *stand* in the church. I can get you 6 cards to the *reception* which takes place same day at Metropolitan Hotel between the hours of 2 & 3 o'clock. They remain in their bridal costumes, & their wedding presents will be seen there. Mr. Hitchcock tried his best for you, but more than 6000 applicants have failed even to get reception cards.

Truly yours,

P. T. Barnum

[121]

# (105)

## TO SYDNEY HOWARD GAY

Sydney Howard Gay (1814–88) was managing editor of the *New York Tribune* during the Civil War.

New York, 16 April 1863

My dear Mr. Gay,

Mr. Eastman has just called & wants to take our drummer boy Robt. Hendershot to his school in Pokeepsie [*sic*].

But I have been keeping and paying him for several weeks in anticipation of your establishment presenting him the drum and publishing a notice of the same.

I hope you will kindly publish the notice as soon as convenient, and that I can have the use of the little hero for one week after the article appears.

Truly yours,

P. T. Barnum

# (106)

## TO GIDEON WELLES

New York, 4 February 1864

My dear Mr. Welles,

A most reliable friend of mine, just arrived here from the south, tells me that when in Nassau the four following blockade runners all arrived from Wilmington on one morning (viz., the 1st or 2d Dec., 1863): the *Alice*, the *Pet*, the *Beauregard*, and the *Dee*. The last named steamer is said to be owned by the Confederate government.

He says Nassau is overrunning with money and with successful blockade runners—that they say one successful run pays for the ship & cargo &c. Perhaps you already know all this & perhaps it can't be helped, but it is awful aggravating to us loyal workers and taxpayers, & I could do no less than write you this. I *know* my information is correct.

Truly yours,

P. T. Barnum

## ⟨107⟩

### TO MOSES S. BEACH

This letter was written to Beach in his capacity as treasurer of the Working Women's Protective Union.

American Museum, 22 March 1864

Sir:

I take pleasure in sending you fifty dollars for what I regard as the most sensible and effective organization that has yet been formed for ameliorating the condition of women who desire to gain their livelihood by their own honest efforts. It is high time that this class was not only effectually "protected," but also that other avenues were opened for their maintenance. They should learn bookkeeping, telegraphing, money-changing, &c. In France females not only act as accountants, clerks in stores, offices, &c., but they also sell the tickets at public places of amusement and engage in hundreds of other branches of light labor that are here filled by men. I could give permanent employ to several females of good character who are judges of money and competent to sell tickets. In fact, I think they have but to fit themselves for many light and pleasant avocations in order to find plenty of chances for employment at such salaries as will enable them to live comfortably and respectably.

Truly yours,

P. T. Barnum

## (108)

### TO C. F. WADSWORTH

The present letter shows how Barnum often went about acquiring exhibits for his museum—and the following letter indicates how one astonished recipient reacted to such a proposition. Ward's Natural Science Establishment, with which Wadsworth apparently was connected, had been founded by the eminent naturalist Henry A. Ward in 1862.

American Museum, 5 April 1864

My dear Sir,

Please send me a list of your restored extinct animals & the price you will charge for a set as specimens in this museum—also list of models of anything else which is *curious* that you may make.

If you mark a *low figure,* I will place a set here and place your name on them for a while as the maker. Or I will do it *perpetually* if you like to present a set to the Museum. It would be a great advertisement for you.

Truly yours,

P. T. Barnum

# (109)

## TO MESSRS. FOWLER & WELLS

American Museum, 20 April 1864

Gentlemen:

I confess I am surprised at your view of my proposition.

I supposed (and still do) that whatever was done here in that line would on the whole lead to *inquiry* on the subject & be the means of sending parties to you for "further particulars." I would not for a moment desire you to do anything contrary to your own feelings or interests.

Truly yours,

P. T. Barnum

# (110)

## TO JOHN GREENWOOD JR.

Museum, 14 May 1864

My dear G,

I still have faith in a beautiful Circassian girl if you can get one very beautiful. But if they ask $4000 each, probably one would be better than two, for $8000 in gold is worth about $14,500 in U.S. currency. So one of the most beautiful would do, but be sure & get a decent-looking chap of 16 years old or more. If you can also buy a beautiful Circassian woman for $200 [?$2000], do so if you think best; or if you can hire one or two at reasonable prices, do so if you think they are pretty and will pass for Circassian slaves. But in any event have one

ZALUMMA AGRA, "STAR OF THE EAST," Barnum and Greenwood's
beautiful Circassian girl.

SMALL CARTE DE VISITE. COURTESY OF THE BARNUM MUSEUM, BRIDGEPORT.

or two of the most beautiful girls you can find, even if they cost $4000 or $5000 in gold. Don't fail to have rich-appearing costumes for her and the eunuch, & bring one girl alone with eunuch if you think they will be attractive enough to pay. But of course one or two additional girls will help it if they can be hired right & are pretty, especially if one can pass for a Grecian. But after looking the thing over, if you don't find one that is beautiful & possesses a striking kind of beauty, why of course she won't draw and you must give it up as a bad job & not get them, for there is nothing in her to attract & fascinate, and the papers would cry her down & it would prove a loss. But if she is beautiful, then she may take in Paris or in London or probably both. But look out that in Paris they don't try the law and set her free. It must be understood she is free. . . .

Yours truly,

P. T. Barnum

If you get the woman with horns, let American newspapers & correspondents understand that you had a big race for her with European showmen & that the price paid for her was immense. Remember to find every avenue for publicity of the fact that an agent of Barnum's Museum is in the East seeking curiosities. Also, when you get to Paris you had better advertise that an agent for Barnum's Museum, now in Paris, is anxious to secure novelties for America. You had better write all the French which would be likely to give you any new ideas. Write here to the editors giving items of intelligence, among which name the agency. Also describe any curiosities that you may secure, then give the editors here your address (privately). They will publish your letter because it comes from so far.

The "G" of this letter was John Greenwood Jr., whose managerial duties at the Museum had temporarily been taken over by Barnum's sons-in-law David W. Thompson and Samuel H. Hurd. In the spring of 1864 Barnum sent Greenwood to Cyprus in quest of a woman who was reported to have horns growing out of her head—a futile trip, as it turned out, since the horns were merely "fleshy excrescences." On his way home Greenwood stopped over in Constantinople and disguised himself as a Turk in order to visit the slave markets. It was there, presumably, that he obtained the beautiful slave girl Zalumma Agra who, after tutoring by Greenwood, was exhibited by him in Europe and America. From a badly typed, inaccurate transcription in the University of Texas at Austin, Hoblitzelle Theatre Arts Library. The location of the original letter is unknown.

{{111}}

## TO REV. THEODORE L. CUYLER

Bridgeport, 3 August 1864

My dear Cuyler,

I was glad to see by the *Independent* that you are so near to us. I think after this blessed rain your family & self will luxuriate on that beautiful Greenfield Hill. It is difficult to find in this country (to my mind) any place more fresh and charming than the borders of Long Island Sound from New Rochelle to New Haven, and among all the localities none reach up to a more delightfully pure atmosphere than the place where you are rusticating.

I am *loafing* to a most extraordinary degree (for me) this summer, though thus far I have not been farther from home than to a clambake on Long Beach or a picnic at Samp Mortar Rock. My youngest daughter, Pauline, has just completed her education, & I have promised to go with her a week to Niagara and another week to Quogue, Long Island, in the course of the summer. But I dislike *crowds* (unless they pay me a *quarter* each), & I prefer to be at home where I am not stuck in a garret with bedbugs (*hum*bugs are quite enough) nor squeezed down to a ¼ mile table to eat cold victuals and be elbowed out of my propriety. Then again, I have plenty of horses & carriages & can take a ten-mile gallop on horseback or roll over the ground behind a spanking trotter—which, though I don't exactly care to be considered "one of the b'hoys," is nicer than to be jammed into watering-place omnibusses or city R.R. cars.

My wife's health, although feeble, is much better than it has been. My eldest daughter, her husband Mr. Thompson & child 10 yrs. old live next door to me; & my other daughter, Mrs. Hurd, is boarding with her children in this neighborhood.

Now when you find that you can't do better, I want you to fix a day that you will come with your wife & babies & join us in a regular family gathering. . . . I hear you are to preach here Sunday night, 14th inst., in the Methodist church. If this is so, I shall be sure to be there if in town, for I love your fresh, earnest, unctuous, & zealous efforts—though when I see your writings & your efforts so full of *generous love for your fellow men,* I often wonder & regret that you cannot see the final *triumph* of our good Father & Saviour over *all* sin & wickedness, so that all things shall finally be *reconciled* to Him, & He—the Almighty, the *Infinite* in power, knowledge, & mercy—shall indeed be All, and in all. Thus would all your prayers & the prayers of all good men be answered, and the angels would rejoice forevermore. But never mind. I love and admire you and your works. We cannot all see alike, but *we can all do good.* My family join in love.

Truly yours,

P. T. Barnum

Greenfield Hill, which is only a few miles from Bridgeport, is still one of the most attractive spots in Connecticut. Samp Mortar Rock is nearby. The remarks on religion toward the end of this letter are in reference to Barnum's Universalist beliefs, with which Cuyler—a Presbyterian—did not agree.

## TO REV. THEODORE L. CUYLER

Bridgeport, 11 August 1864

My dear Cuyler,

I have not before answered your welcome letter of the 5th because I intended to do it in person next Sunday if you did not call before. But now I have got *melted out,* & Pauline & I start for Quogue, Long Island, tomorrow to remain till 22d or 23d. . . . I am glad that the *twins* are to be in the family party. Make sure that with recollections of former baby shows, I shall regard them with the eyes of a *showman.* . . .

Your sincere admirer & friend,

P. T. Barnum

P.S. Do you know when I first saw & loved you? It was at Tripler Hall when you told of the deer-hunting neophyte who, when he saw the old buck, declared it was "the devil with an armchair on his head!"

B

# BARNUM'S AMERICAN MUSEUM.

## Christmas and New Year Holiday Bill.

The Manager has been determined to make these Holidays the most attractive and bewitching of any of their predecessors, and trusts that the following combination of Novelties, Curiosities, and Dramatic Entertainments, will prove this determination successful.

### THE GREAT
# LIVING WHALE

From the Coast of Labrador is alone a wonder worthy the attention of every educated and scientific person, as well as the merely curious. He is seen at all hours swimming about his large tank in all his native grace and grandeur.

### THE LIVING
# HIPPOPOTAMUS

From the River Nile in Egypt, the great Behemoth of the Scriptures, see Job, chap. 40, is the first and only one of these colossal animals ever brought to America, and the greatest wonder of the world.

### SIGNOR PIETRO D'OLIVERA'S
## 200 EDUCATED WHITE RATS

Perform a great variety of amusing and interesting tricks ; Children especially find this exhibition replete with interest.

## The Aquarial Garden,

Occupying one of the large Halls of the Museum, is of itself an Exhibition worth more than the cost of Admission to the entire Museum. Its numerous crystal ponds of River and Ocean water, abounding with Living Fish from nearly every River and Sea, are alive with interest to all classes. One tank has 8 LARGE SPECKLED BROOK TROUT, the largest and finest ever seen together ; another has 12 BEAUTIFUL SEA HORSES, the most interesting tiny inhabitants of the great deep, the heads and necks of which resemble, in their graceful curves, those of the horse. No visitor should fail seeing them. Indeed, every tank in the entire collection is replete with interest.

### THE LIVING HAPPY FAMILY
In the upper Saloon, is always surrounded with a crowd of smiling faces.

**THE LIVING MONSTER SNAKES** are more wonderful than pleasing, yet always surrounded by crowds of interested spectators.

**THE LIVING LEARNED SEAL** is regarded universally, as a *"Beautiful Creature !"* and his sparkling eyes are the admiration, if not the envy, of many of his fair admirers. These, and many more curiosities, are all to be seen at all hours, while EVERY AFTERNOON AND EVENING during the entire Holiday Season there will be

### SUPERB DRAMATIC PERFORMANCES,
and on CHRISTMAS AND NEW YEAR DAYS these Performances will be given nearly EVERY HOUR, Day and Evening, that every visitor shall be enabled to see one such performance, as well as all the Curiosities.

☞ To add still further to the interest of THIS GREAT FESTIVE SEASON, the Manager has expended over Seven Thousand Dollars in the preparation of a New Holiday Piece, never before seen in America, entitled,

### THE BOWER OF BEAUTY,
OR, THE
### HOME OF THE FAIRIES
In the Enchanted Forest, in which occurs a
### GORGEOUS MECHANICAL SCENE
By Randall, of London, in which appear
### 40 BEAUTIFUL YOUNG LADIES,
*NYMPHS OF THE AIR.*

This scene will be one of dazzling splendor, the most magnificent thing of its kind ever gotten up in this country, and will alone repay fourfold the cost of admission to the entire Museum. It will be produced every Afternoon and Evening during the entire Holiday season, and at each performance on Christmas and New Year days.

## Admission to all only 25 cts.  Children under 10 years, 15 cts.

Wynkoop, Hallenbeck & Thomas, Book and Job Printers, 113 Fulton St., N. Y.

AN 1864 BILL for the AMERICAN MUSEUM, listing the great variety of attractions offered to visitors.

## (113)

### TO SYDNEY HOWARD GAY

New York, 3 April 1865

My dear Mr. Gay,

I have just recd. a telegram that I am elected on the Union ticket to the Connecticut legislature from the Town of Fairfield by a majority of 187.

I will feel obliged if you will kindly publish the fact.

Truly yours,

P. T. Barnum

## (114)

### TELEGRAM TO EDWIN M. STANTON

Bridgeport, 15 May [1865]

I will give five hundred dollars to Sanitary Commission or Freedman's Association for the petticoats in which Jeff Davis was caught.

P. T. Barnum

This is an original autograph telegram, signed by Barnum, to the then Secretary of War. An undated note in the Fred D. Pfening III Collection, to an unidentified correspondent who wished to sell one of Davis's carriages, is possibly related to the same escape attempt: "A shell without the oyster is useless. Send Jeff Davis with the carriage and I can utilize the two." Davis had been captured by Union forces on 10 May 1865.

# (115)

## TO THEODORE TILTON

Theodore Tilton (1835–1907), orator, ardent abolitionist, and eventual victim of the woman's rights movement, was editor of the Congregationalist journal the *Independent*. This and the following letters are in reference to a speech Barnum made in the Connecticut legislature on 26 May 1865 on the subject of the enfranchisement of Negroes. The speech, which was widely reported and praised in the press, is given in the autobiography. Although the present letter is headed "P.S.," it seems to be complete.

Bridgeport, 29 May [1865]

*P.S.*

My dear T,

. . . I expect to go to Europe early in July with my daughter, 19 years old, and shall go into Russia in August. I would *like dearly* to have your foreign readers (as well as domestic) see an extract or a digest of my speech in your columns. I think I put one or two points there which they can't get over. The Conn. senate adjourned and came in a body to hear me. Old Governor Ellsworth & many other dignitaries were present, including Lieut. Gov. Averill. The latter gentleman as well as the 1st representatives of Hartford & New Haven & many others complimented me on it. Some ladies were present, & it went off finely. I only intended to speak 25 minutes, but the opposition interrupted me and put me on my mettle, & I gave them an hour & a half without tiring anybody. Those who undertook to interrupt me hauled off for repairs sometime before I finished, but they sat & heard it all.

Rogers of Milford brought in *your* name, & I used it in reply. The Copperhead [*Hartford*] *Times* is the only paper which happened to include that fact in their report. Rogers said that when freedmen asked anything of Congress, they immediately had such men as Charles Sumner & Theodore Tilton to back them up. I replied that it was astonishing, when the first statesmen and the first scholars and the first newspapers in the

country were striving to do justice to the Negro, the poor pur-
blind Copperheads could not see "the signs of the times," turn
from their miserable delusions, and bow to the logic of events.
I will enclose you a *Times* report, which although not so *full* as
the other which I enclose, still has several passages (which I
mark) omitted in *Courant's* report. I *hope* the *Independent* will
help put me *right* before its readers. For 30 years I have *striven*
to *do good,* but (foolishly) stuck my worst side outside, until
half the Christian com[mu]nity got to believe that I wore horns
& hoofs. And now as I have got old, I begin to feel a desire
that the present & future generations shall "nothing extenuate
or set down aught in malice." Let them show me *as I am*—&
God knows that is bad enough!

Truly yours,

P. T. Barnum

## ⦅116⦆

## TO THEODORE TILTON

Hartford, 29 May 1865

My dear Tilton,
        Pray don't get alarmed, but after mailing you my letter
this A.M. from Bridgeport, I recd. the enclosed from the mayor
of Biddeford, Maine. He (C. A. Shaw, Esq.) sent me a speech
which he recently made in the Maine legislature, & as it was
*secesh* in its tendencies, I wrote him a letter, an extract from
which it seems he allowed to be published, for the printed slip
enclosed is that extract, & I kept no copy of my letter to him.
Thinking that possibly you might make some use of it, I send
it & ask you to do me the favor to *mail* it to me at Bridgeport,
Conn., if you don't use it. I know this is asking an unusual
favor, but as you are an unusually good fellow, & I a sort of

lawless individual, I don't mind trespassing a little on your good nature.

Truly yours,

P. T. Barnum

(117)

## TO DANIEL STEVENS DICKINSON

Daniel Stevens Dickinson was a lawyer and prominent New York politician.

Hartford, 7 June 1865

My dear Sir,

Your kind letter of yesterday affords me great pleasure, for a compliment of such a nature from such a source I regard as *no small thing*.

I had only intended to speak some twenty minutes, but the interruptions from the other side of the house put me upon my mettle, and feeling as I did and do from my heart of hearts that my position is the *only* just and truly democratic one, I easily consumed an hour and three quarters in discussing the subject. The Copperheads hauled off for repairs.

But oh, my dear sir, is not the present prospect of our country's future position most glorious? Was there ever a struggle wherein the hand of a Beneficent and Almighty God was more plainly visible?

Could there ever have been a more pusillanimous termination to the rebellion than Jeff Davis gave it in his petticoats?

Truly yours,

P. T. Barnum

[135]

## (118)

### TO MR. MURPHY

On 13 July 1865 the American Museum burned while Barnum was speaking before the Connecticut legislature. Almost immediately he commenced plans for a new museum. The Mr. Murphy addressed in this letter is not included in the Library of Congress's list of diplomatic agents in 1865, but was obviously in a position to express a "German" opinion.

New York, 15 July 1865

My dear Mr. Murphy,

My museum is all destroyed. I am cast down but not dismayed. I think of building a new museum. If you can consistently [*sic*] send me a short letter (of condolence) stating that probably many persons in Germany will gladly contribute curiosities for my new museum, it would help me much with our public, and at the same time I should expect nothing further from your letter. If you cannot do *something* like this without touching upon your own ideas of good taste, please burn this & let its contents pass to *oblivion*. In any event, please consider this *strictly confidential* & oblige

Truly yours,

P. T. Barnum

## (119)

### TO BAYARD TAYLOR

Bridgeport, 16 July 1865

My dear Taylor,

You know that my entire museum collection is destroyed. I have sufficient property (all told) to erect and stock another museum & purchase also the land, which last item costs $300,000. I *must* erect such an establishment (in Broadway above Houston St.) because there's no disputing the fact that the destruction of the Museum is a *national loss* and no living man can command the facilities which I possess to get up a new one. But the next one must be of a much *higher grade* than the other was, although the price must remain 30 cts. for the accommodation of the million. It will be a vast building with every accommodation: immense lecture room on ground floor (rear) where I can trot in circus horses 12 weeks every winter, a picture gallery, a hall for statuary, full collection of specimens of natural history in all its departments, and on *the roof* a *zoological garden* reached by the *screw elevator ride* [*as in the*] Fifth Av. & Continental Hotels. Over the animals will of course be placed a well ventilated roof enclosed at the sides &c. This building & collection will cost about $300,000 more, perhaps $250,000. I think I can see my way through it all.

But I have a *great plan* touching things abroad wherein I want your advice and perhaps also your personal assistance; but I shall not expect the latter unless I can afford to satisfactorily remunerate you. I wish I could talk with you an hour, for that would throw more light than a ream of written paper. *First* then, everybody (almost) sympathizes with me & feels that the public are losers as well as myself. Hence by timely & proper notices in newspapers & by proper circulars thousands of persons in this country may be induced to send me relics & specimens of conchology & other branches which would be properly labelled with their names as donors and also serve to make up a *valuable* assortment of museum curiosities. *The same process* might awaken the attention of all sea captains & Americans abroad, & *their* contributions would be immensely valuable.

But the *great idea* which I am fostering and which if successfully carried out is worth all the rest ten times over is this: to get presents for my new museum from all the public governmental museums in Europe. Thus a specimen or two or more from the Louvre & Versailles, labelled "Presented by

[137]

Louis Napoleon, Emperor of France"; ditto museum at Kensington, presented by Queen Victoria; ditto Emperor of Russia; mummies &c. from Viceroy of Egypt; ditto public museums in Holland, Berlin, Dresden, Vienna, British Museum, East India Museum, London, and a score of other public & private institutions. Also from dukes &c. in Florence & Rome; also from the Pope of Rome; a present from Jenny Lind; d[itt]o John Bright & as many public characters as possible. No matter scarcely how little the intrinsic value of these contributions, the *names* of the donors would render them *very attractive.*

Now as a starting point to accomplish all this, I can procure, I think, a document signed by Pres[iden]t Johnson & his entire cabinet & as many other dignitaries as need be stating whatever is requisite—perhaps stating that the destruction of my museum is a national loss and that the American people will duly appreciate the kindness shown by parties abroad in contributing interesting objects to the new museum, &c. &c. &c. &c.

Now my dear sir, is this not feasible? And if it is, pray tell me *who* is the best person to start off at once (by 1st to 10th August) and visit the courts & principal cities in Europe on this business? Should *I* accompany such a person or not? I have thought of Horace Greeley, Harriet Beecher Stowe, &c. Greeley probably cannot go if he would, as he is still writing his book of the war, and Mrs. Stowe possibly would not go if she could. Yet many things are possible. Of course, I should expect nobody to go unless I paid them what their time was worth. If the step should become properly dignified through the public press & the influence of our *highest* govt. officials, need the mission be anything but a pleasant one? It could be accomplished by November.

Is not *Bayard Taylor Esq.* the best man living for such a mission, and could he not be induced to make the trip? You can scarcely imagine how intense and general the sympathy & regret are for the loss of the Museum. Offers of shells, minerals, and preserved specimens of birds, beasts, &c. are already being made in considerable quantities, & if the fever is once cleverly started, I think the collection can be half made up gratuitously in this country. Please consider this letter *strictly confidential*, & do please give me your ideas frankly about it, addressed in enclosed envelope.

You can defer lecturing till Nov. & have a pleasant summer trip, and I will pay you to your full satisfaction if you will go either with me or without. The new museum is to be next door below Laura Keene's theatre and extend down to Houston & back to Crosly St. I own all that property & it is all paid for. In haste,

Truly yours,

P. T. Barnum

## {120}

## TO BAYARD TAYLOR

Bridgeport, 22 July 1865

My dear Taylor,

Your letter has done me a world of good, for its encouraging tenor strengthens my confidence in myself. I have [*sic*] once (after talking with Mr. Greeley) *resolved* to *retire* & live in comparative quiet & ease, but the morning's sun lighted up my hopes, gilded my enthusiastic imaginings, warmed my old blood, and set it to boiling for a new conquest. So you will see I have already began [*sic*] to lay & pull my strings, and among my *influences* which are to set the ball a rolling are Governor Buckingham, Prof. Norton of Yale College, Hartford, Conn., Historical Society, all the newspapers with James Gordon Bennett *in person* more enthusiastic than all the rest. The *N.Y. Observer* advises the missionaries to help with their contributions from all heathen lands; the *Independent* (Tilton) promises a big article, but I fear that *Bowen*, on a/c of some

[139]

old mercantile or Jenny Lind pique, will cut it out. Clergy without number, including Rev. Bidwell of the *Eclectic*, and the public generally are with me. Prosper M. Wetmore has prepared a letter to Prest. Johnson which is signed & to be signed by Moses Grinnell, Shepard Knapp, Sim Draper, Surveyor Abram Wakeman, Moses Taylor, Greeley, Bennett, Raymond, Thurlow Weed, &c.

But now something has occurred which opens my eyes, longings, & intentions to an entirely *New Chapter—New Visions & New Arrangements*! I have sold my 12-year lease of the old museum. The price which I get for it in cash is fabulous, incredible—indeed, for the present I dare not speak it loud, for it must not go into the papers until the millionaire purchaser consents. So I tell you *in confidence,* as I have already told Mr. Gay, the sum I get in cash is Two Hundred Thousand Dollars! $200,000! The same purchaser has paid $450,000 for the *fee*— in all, $650,000 for 56 feet by 100! Restrain thyself! Abner L. Ely & Homer Morgan told me I could clear $30,000 to $40,000 per annum if I would erect a building on the old site, but I prefer a $200M certainty to any uncertainty. Besides, all trouble of building there is off my hands.

Now I find myself worth a million of dollars more or less—more likely more than less. Astor gave the public a *library;* Cooper gave them an institute. A. T. Stewart, who owes his wealth to *ladies,* is erecting that large marble building in 5th Av., at an expense of $700,000, for the interior of which he has already purchased $200,000 worth of *paintings* & will purchase many more; then instead of his *living* there, this building & contents are to be open *free* to *ladies,* so when they drive or walk out in the morning they can call & regale themselves from the munificence of him whom they have made rich.

Barnum has been made rich by catering for *the children.* The youth of America regard the loss of Barnum's Museum as a loss irreparable. Fathers & mothers mourn its destruction on account of their children. Why should not Barnum (who in fact was always more of a philanthropist than a humbug) establish a *free museum* for the instruction and edification of the *Youth of America*! In fact, erect a fireproof building and open in it a well stocked collection of the works of nature & art, relics, &c. open free to the public—the same as is the British Museum, the Louvre, Versailles, Japanese Museum of Holland, &c. One is *governmental* & the other an individual enterprise. I want to do this & I *will* if it is feasible. Listen:

1st. A million of dollars would not *begin* to give, or would only *"begin"* to give us a British Museum in extent, value, &c.

2d. A part of the million would be needed to pay annual expenses, repairs, additions, &c.

3d. A part of the million I need for my family to live on.

So I go on the principle that half a loaf is better than no bread, & therefore I propose to erect a *National Free Museum* which shall contain collections of natural history and shall also contain all specimens of *everything* presented by our govt. in any of its departments & everything presented by *anybody* in this or any other country. Thus potentates, rulers, & mighty men—authors, poets, statesmen, celebrities, *everybody*—may contribute their presents, relics, antiquities, &c. All public institutions at home or abroad may send their duplicates; the Patent Office, War Office, Navy Department may send their models &c. &c.—all being assured that they shall be placed in Barnum's National Conservatory or Institute (or some better name—pray *name it*) which P. T. Barnum presents to the Youth of America in particular and to the public in general, Barnum regulating & controlling the same and pledging himself that the public *shall* have access to it *free,* in the same manner that the public have free access to the British Museum and other governmental collections in Europe, I pledging myself *never* to claim or hold this property as my own & that my heirs shall keep it (the collection) perpetually & forever so open to the public free, & whenever they fail to do so *all* of said collection shall become the property of the general government.

Now for the nigger in the fence. And after all, it is no contraband, for if I undertake this thing I will do *all* I promise & thus make this a solid and everlasting public benefit. But here is my plan:

The British Museum is open 3 or 4 days in the week

from 9 or 10 to 4. Every year there are also a few weeks when it is closed altogether. The same is true with all other governmental museums which I am acquainted with.

Now alongside of Barnum's *Free National* (something) I propose to erect Barnum's American Museum with its giants, dwarfs, fat women, bearded ladies, baby shows, dog shows, wax figures, theatrical & occasionally *equestrian* "Lecture Room," polytechnic hall with working models of machinery, aquaria, zoological garden, living wild beasts top of Museum, curiosities of all sorts in natural history which *I purchase,* picture gallery, &c. &c. To this museum I charge an admission fee of 25 or 30 cts., children half price. Museum open from sunrise till 10 P.M. All Museum visitors admitted to *National* (concern) free at all hours from sunrise till 10 P.M. The *public* admitted to National concern *free* at *fixed hours—same* as in Europe—& *fixed days*—same as in Europe. At the division entrance between the free *National* & the paying *Museum* is a ticket seller who sells Museum tickets to such free visitors *only* as happen to wish to visit the Museum. I *suppose* that ⁹/₁₀ths of the National visitors will conclude to visit the Museum, but if they don't, there's no harm done. The National Institution shall be superb, & my pride will be to add to its attractions & conveniences every year & every day and have it perfectly *free* for all well behaved persons & thus be an entirely *distinct* thing from the Museum. Now to this Noble Free National Institution can the government object to contribute from its stores, or can it with[h]old its influence abroad for this great object?

Of course I have herein shown you the interior—the skeleton, the internal machinery, &c.—but to the public it will *look* a little different, for it will simply be announced that for such & such reasons Mr. P. T. B. will do so & so (Free National &c. &c.) in which *everything* will be placed that is contributed by any person or institution in the world &c. &c. Aside from this, Mr. B also intends to rebuild & reestablish his American Museum wherein he will introduce his lecture room and all living curiosities & sensational attractions which made his late museum so famous.

[142]

Now my dear Taylor, what do you say to this? Pray give me your suggestions.

In the meantime I hope you will write me a letter of 3 to 10 lines *for publication,* showing your sympathy and offering relics (whether you ever give them or not), and all the better if you make the letter one declining the position I have offered you to go to Europe, & saying that next year when you go abroad you will undertake to execute commissions for me. (Depend on it, I will gladly pay you *for* executing these commissions, & there shall not be a smell of *humbug* left to my name 2 months hence, so it will be quite respectable for you to execute those commissions.) Pray excuse this *long* letter & do give me your ideas.

As ever thine,

P. T. Barnum

The "millionaire purchaser" of Barnum's lease on the old Museum property was none other than James Gordon Bennett, who later demanded, but did not get, his money back when he realized he had paid far too much for the property in question. After reading this letter, the mind boggles at the prospect of what Barnum might have accomplished had he ever been offered the secretaryship of the Smithsonian.

## {121}

## TO BAYARD TAYLOR

Bridgeport, 28 July 1865

My dear Taylor,

Before I recd. your last I had got my $200,000 from J. G. Bennett for my lease, invested all in greenbacks, & had become so *conservative* that I had really about concluded to abandon all my projects & take Greeley's advice—"go a fishing."

Your letters inspired me again, so now I am going to

## HEADQUARTERS OF
# BARNUM'S AMERICAN MUSEUM,
## No. 539 and 541 Broadway, N. Y.

P. T. BARNUM, Proprietor and Manager.
S. H. HURD, Assistant Manager.

*Bridgeport Aug 11 1865.*

*My dear Taylor — The "Nation" slashed my old Museum 2 weeks ago & I wrote a private letter to Richards the publisher asking him to have his writer set me right & in that letter I gave (for the eye of that writer) my ideas & intentions about my new Museum. Richards published my letter verbatim a thing I did not dream of. If I had I should not have said that I was "worth 2 millions of dollars" nor that I had sent to hire Bayard Taylor to go to Europe". I should have used a different style of language if I had supposed that Richards would have presumed to print my private letter. I wrote it in great haste & I much regret that the Nation published it, in the*

P. T. BARNUM TO BAYARD TAYLOR, 11 August 1865. The engraving depicts the first American Museum, which had been destroyed by fire by the date of this letter.

publish one of them & be guided somewhat by the other. The *armory* hall is excellent, though *historical* armors will be expensive. Still, *something* that way can be done. Most of your other ideas are *excellent,* & I shall want more of them. I guess I shall go to Europe last of August & hope to take proper documents from government officials. I want dreadfully to approach all the big-bugs & big institutions abroad that can help with their names & contributions to enrich the Free National Museum. Can you think of any other word to use instead of "museum" that will be so expressive?

I cannot tell you how much I am obliged for your kind efforts in my behalf.

Very truly yours,

P. T. Barnum

## (122)

## TO GEN. WINFIELD SCOTT

New York, 22 September 1865

My dear Sir,

In common with millions of others I have ever been an ardent admirer of you and your career.

Anything connected with you must always possess *great historic interest* to the patrons of any public institution. I learned the address of your hat manufacturer from your attendant Louis, and I have taken the liberty to send you a hat by express which I hope you will do me the honor to accept. I have determined on getting together a collection of hats worn by 100 of the most celebrated men of the present day. I hope it will include that of Prests. Lincoln & Johnson and the most noted generals and statesmen of our own country, besides foreign potentates and such men abroad as John Bright, the late

[145]

Mr. Cobden, Humboldt, Livingston, Bulwer, Tennyson, Dickens, Dumas, &c. &c. &c. &c.

May I ask that you will kindly contribute your hat to the illustrious collection and add to my profound gratitude by placing your autograph on a card to accompany it.

Trusting that you will not regard this as an impertinence on my part, I have the honor to be

Your very humble servant,

P. T. Barnum

## {123}

## TO GIDEON WELLES

New York, 26 October 1865

My dear Sir,

I intend visiting Washington next week prior to my immediate departure for Europe in quest of curiosities for the new American Museum. As I wish to avoid trespassing upon your time for more than a few minutes, I enclose several documents which I hope you will do me the honor to read & consider.

As our various squadrons have more or less opportunity to make collections in natural history, I presume they do so for the Smithsonian Institute.

The American Museum, when properly restored, will have thousands of visitors where the Smithsonian has tens. Hence our facilities for instruction are so immense, I trust you will see no impropriety in giving me a letter which will empower and encourage all persons connected with the U.S. Navy to do whatever they choose towards obtaining specimens for the American Museum, provided that the interests of the government shall in no way be damaged thereby. Such a letter

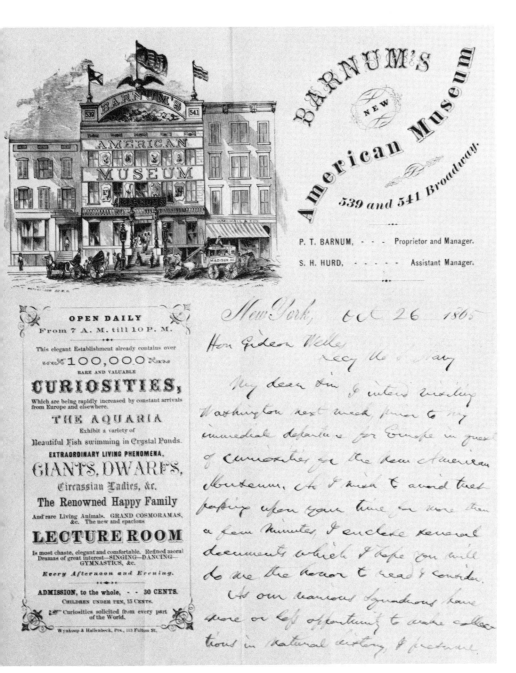

P. T. BARNUM TO GIDEON WELLES, 26 October 1865. The engraving depicts Barnum's "new" American Museum, which occupied the premises of the old Chinese Museum.

from you will be of great public benefit & will very deeply oblige

Your friend & servant,

P. T. Barnum

# {124}

## TO MR. WILSON

Bridgeport, 30 December 1865

My dear Wilson,

Now that the weather has become cold, I wish you would get a good man to clean out my mother's privy and put the contents on the lot back of her house and send the bill for the expense thereof to me. Of course, you will get it done reasonable as you would for yourself, and let the man at the same time put up the stones properly which have tumbled from the top of the privy wall. If you can find a man who will do the job for the privilege of taking the contents of the vault, let him do it if you think that will be *better* for my mother than to pay him & use the contents on her own lot. Horace Ferry once offered to do it on these terms. Whoever does it must leave everything *clean* and in *good order*.

I would like also to give my mother a pleasant surprise next spring by having you get a small neat water closet built on the rear of her house at the back of the woodshed or woodhouse, so that she could walk into it through the room where the water runs and then through the woodshed without going out of doors. Perhaps it should stand a foot or so off from the woodshed, but be closed in tight. Yet I don't know but it would be best to bring it close to the woodshed, for there is no *cellar* under the woodhouse. Of course, no door would lead to it from outside, as the present privy would be for the use of those who live in the house, but mother is too decrepid [*sic*] to get out to it. Let it be rather small but snug, with a good light (window), and Katie must buy & fix down a piece of carpet so that it will appear comfortable & give the old lady a happy surprise. I will depend upon you to get this done according to your own judgement & send me the bill. Wishing you a Happy New Year, I am as ever

Truly yours,

P. T. Barnum

P.S. I understand that a Waterbury co. has bought the right for State of Conn. to make those building blocks such as Bethel church is made of. They say the Danbury man was not the legal owner. If he can show he *is*, I will help him fight it, for I want the right for Bridgeport.

At the time of this letter Barnum's mother was still living in Bethel, where she died in 1868.

(125)

## TO OLIVER HENRY PERRY

Fairfield, 12 March 1866

Hon. O. H. Perry:

Yours is recd. I thank you for your kind approval of my course in the legislature last year, and if other friends in our town are of your opinion that I could be of service this year, you are at liberty to put me in nomination. . . .

Very respectfully yours,

P. T. Barnum

Barnum was indeed elected to a second consecutive term in the Connecticut legislature. Perry was one of his Fairfield neighbors.

# (126)

## TO BAYARD TAYLOR

Bridgeport, 5 June 1866

My dear Taylor,

After much tribulation I have succeeded in licking into satisfactory shape my anticipated great *free* museum. I have secured in the Conn. legislature a charter for "The Barnum & Van Amburgh Museum & Menagerie Co." with a capital of $2,000,000. The stock is real & will *only* be disposed of to earnest working *showmen* and managers of experience. I have asked my printer to send you a copy of a memorial of some of our first citizens to the President of the U.S., together with his approval of their petition & my circular to Americans & officials abroad. Only 20 copies of this document are yet printed, & my object in sending it to you is to ask you kindly to look over my circular & to make such suggestions & alterations as you think expedient.

If my life is spared, this shall become a great & good institution, worthy of the country, *free* to the public, & I hope in some degree honorable to its projector. . . .

Truly yours,

P. T. Barnum

.  .  .  .

The great "free" museum was never realized, but the Barnum and Van Amburgh Museum and Menagerie Company did go on tour, with winter stays at the "paying" new American Museum on Broadway.

## (127)

## TO GEN. N. P. BANKS

Bridgeport, 23 June 1866

My dear General,

I shall feel deeply obliged if I can receive the appointment of Commissioner to the World's Fair. I wish no money from the government, preferring to *pay my own expenses*. But I shall keep my eyes open and not only in Paris, but throughout Europe, will *freely* devote my faculties to the best interests of our noble country.

Truly yours,

P. T. Barnum

In an undated note marked "Private" that apparently accompanied this letter, Barnum writes, "It is just possible that Prest. Johnson *might* consider me too much of a *radical* to please him, but I hope he has no such feelings" (*Hertzberg Circus Collection*). Nathaniel Prentiss Banks (1816–94), politician, Massachusetts governor, and Civil War general, was a member of Congress at the time of Barnum's writing.

## (128)

## TO CHARLES HALE

Charles Hale (1831–82) was Consul-General to Egypt.

Bridgeport, 23 August 1866

Dear Sir,

I had the honor to enclose you a circular a few days since under cover of the Secretary of State.

You will have seen by this that not only the first men in our land, but also the President & heads of departments feel a deep interest in the establishment of a great free National Museum in America to which, in the evening of my life, I feel a pride in devoting my time and money.

If you could feel interested in this great project, there are doubtless numerous curiosities animate and inanimate in Egypt which could be procured without *much* effort, and which would be highly valued in the National Museum.

But my especial object in writing is to see if I cannot procure through your kindness one or two living *hippopotami*. No matter how young they may be, they grow rapidly and soon become great objects of interest here. It is difficult to procure a hippopotamus except through the kind favor of the Viceroy of Egypt. He has presented one to the zoological garden at Amsterdam, Holland (several years ago), and also I believe to the zoological garden in Regent's Park, London.

As they are brought from the Upper Nile, it is only through governmental assistance that they can well be obtained.

Several gentlemen connected with our government have suggested that the Viceroy would probably take pleasure in presenting one or two such animals to the museum and zoological garden under my charge. The expenses from Cairo of course to be borne by us, and we should engage the services of a native to attend the animal here. The spring or summer, I suppose, would be the best season for bringing it to the States. If, honored sir, you can thus be instrumental in obtaining contributions to our National Museum, you will confer a great favor upon the American public as well as

Your very obedient servant,

P. T. Barnum

*Private.* Our mutual friends Mr. & Mrs. Joseph Cushing of Dover, N.H., wish to be kindly remembered. As the Viceroy has already given hippopotami to other zoological collections, I really believe he will with pleasure procure one or two for us, upon its being suggested by you.

There are doubtless other animals & curiosities there which I would like probably to purchase if they are not contributed. If a hippopotamus should come there *for sale,* I would be glad to buy it if the Viceroy does not conclude to give us one. A portrait (photograph) of the Viceroy with *his autograph* would be very acceptable for our museum.

Truly yours,

P. T. Barnum

We want very much a giraffe or two, also rhinoceros & other animals *alive.*

{129}

## TO UNIDENTIFIED CORRESPONDENT

In early 1867 Barnum engaged in a bitter contest with William H. Barnum of Salisbury, Connecticut, for the Fourth Connecticut District seat in the U.S. Congress. Amid charges and rumors of vote-buying on behalf of his Democratic opponent, Barnum published the present letter in the Bridgeport and New York papers and later in his autobiography. His anonymous correspondent had asked if he intended to "fight fire with fire."

Bridgeport, 23 February 1867

Dear Sir,

Your kind letter of the 20th inst. has caused me painful emotions. I now wish to say, once for all, that under no conceivable circumstances will I permit a dollar of mine to be used to purchase a vote or to induce a voter to act contrary to his honest convictions.

The idea that the intelligent reading men of New England can be bought like sheep in the shambles, and that the sacred principles which have so far guided them in the terrible struggle between liberty and slavery can now, in this eventful hour of national existence, be set up at auction and knocked down to the highest bidder, seems to me as preposterous as it

[153]

is shameful and humiliating. But if it is possible that occasionally a degraded voter can thus be induced to "sell his birthright for a mess of pottage," God grant that I may be a thousand times defeated sooner than permit one grain of gold to be accursed by using it so basely!

I will not believe that American citizens can lend themselves to the contemptible meanness of sapping the very life-blood of our noble institutions, by encouraging a fatal precedent which ignores all principle and would soon prevent any honest man, however distinguished for his intelligence and loyalty, from representing his district in our national councils. None could then succeed except unprincipled vagabonds who, by the lavish expenditure of money, would debauch and degrade the freemen whose votes they coveted.

No, sir! Grateful as I am for the distinguished honor of receiving a unanimous nomination for Congress from the loyal Union party in my district, I have no aspiration for that high position if it is only to be attained by bringing into disgrace the noble privilege of the *free elective franchise*. Think for a moment what a deadly weapon is being placed in the hands of tyrants throughout the civilized world with which to destroy such apostles of liberty as John Bright and Garibaldi, if it can be said with truth that American citizens have become so corrupt and degraded, so lost to a just estimate of the value and true nobility of the ballot, that it is bought and sold for money.

My dear sir, any party that can gain a temporary ascendancy by such atrocious means not only poisons the body politic of a free and impartial government, but is also sure to bring swift destruction upon itself. And so it should be.

I am unaccustomed to political life and know but little of the manner of conducting a campaign like the present. I believe, however, it is customary for the State Central Committee to assess candidates, in order that they shall defray a proper portion of the expenses incurred for speakers and documents to *enlighten* the voters upon the political issues of the day. To that extent I am willing and anxious to be taxed;

for "light and knowledge" are always desired by the friends of human rights and of public order.

But I trust that all money used for any other purpose in the pending election will come from the pockets of those who now (as during the rebellion) are doing their utmost to aid traitors, and who, still unrepenting, are vindictively striving to secure at the ballot box what their southern allies failed to accomplish on the field of battle. If any of our friends misapprehend my true sentiments upon the subject of bribery, corruption, and fraud, I hope you will read them this letter.

Truly yours,

P. T. Barnum

P.S. The following is the law of Connecticut on the bribery of electors. . . .

## (130)

### TO EUGENE V. SMALLEY

Eugene Virgil Smalley wrote for the *New York Tribune* and other publications.

Bridgeport, 26 March 1867

My dear Mr. Smalley,

Your article on the nation in yesterday's *Tribune* has done us a world of good. We shall *save* this district if you can give us plenty of *such* help this week by exposing the *tricks* of the enemy. Here, for instance, are some of them.

They have already issued two private circulars, and two more are in type (& perhaps half a dozen more). Two of them are of the filthy Lewis S. Barnum order, and two are especial appeals to the *religious* element to scratch my name & vote for the Copperhead candidate on the ground of morality. Two or three weak *clergymen* . . . have been induced to *sign* one of these circulars, & efforts are working to get one in New Milford to do the same. The Johnson postmaster in Bridgeport is also striving to get a Methodist minister in Bridgeport to add his name, the postmaster being a supporter of that church.

The principal getters up of these things is [*sic*] a quack doctor of Bridgeport who once ran away from here for over a year to escape an indictment for murder & abortion, he having anchored the body of the dead woman in Housatonic River where it was found (his name is Dr. Jaques); and the other man is ex-congressman Wm. D. Bishop, who you know was a member of the Chicago convention—the warm political friend of Toucey, Tom Seymour, &c. and who on his way to the Chicago convention crossed into Canada at Niagara Falls and consulted with Clement C. Clay, Jake Thompson, & Geo. Saunders. He boasted of this fact in a speech on his return home. He is president of the Naugatuck R.R. and boasts that he holds the Naugatuck valley in his breeches pocket. He this week is making a pilgrimage up the valley, giving Copperhead speeches in the various towns.

Now to be *forewarned* is to be *forearmed*. If you will immediately *expose* these tricks, you will make *sure* our success in this district & help our state very much. I will guarantee & defend *the truth* of what I have here written & hope you will see the importance of ripping up these infamous plans. Much of our success in Connecticut depends upon stirring articles in the *Tribune this week.*

Truly yours,

P. T. Barnum

# ⦅131⦆

## TO EUGENE V. SMALLEY?

Bridgeport, 30 March 1867

My dear Sir,

We find at least 300 illegal votes registered for the sham democracy in 4 towns in this district. Therefore, if you find on Monday night that I am defeated by any number *less than 300,* please state in Tuesday's *Tribune* that I shall contest the election on the ground of gross frauds in the towns of Salisbury, Sharon, North Canaan, Falls Village, &c.

I hope & still expect to beat them in *spite* of the frauds, but it is not certain; & in case of defeat by less than 300 I want the *first impression right,* for I can certainly unseat my opponent for fraud.

Truly yours,

P. T. Barnum

In his autobiography Barnum writes that "when Congress met, I was surprised to see by the newspapers that the seat of my opponent was to be contested on account of alleged bribery, fraud, and corruption in securing his election. This was the first intimation that I had ever received of such an intention. . . . But, I repeat, I took no part nor lot in the matter, but concluded that if I had been defeated by fraud, mine was the real success."

# {132}

## TO J. A. WOODWARD

By the date of this letter Barnum was again traveling extensively to lecture on "Success, or The Art of Money-Getting." Woodward had invited him to address an audience in Williamsport, Pennsylvania.

New York, 22 February 1868

Dear Sir,

Receiving favorable reports regarding my mother's health, I have no doubt of being on hand to lecture for you Thursday night next, 27th inst., pursuant to my letter & telegram. . . . I shall require a *stand* on the platform for a pitcher & tumbler of water and to lay the *heads* of my lecture, although I do not really speak from notes.

And now, "although I say it who should not," I beg to observe that my lecture, although brimfull of lively mirthful anecdotes, is after all the result of considerable *thought* founded on observation and experience, and it is well calculated to *do good* and especially to the young of both sexes—those who are commencing active life and need some fixed rules to guide them. My lecture always *pleases,* and none praise it higher than the *clergy.* But often at the end of the lecture a father has told me how sorry he was that he did not bring his boy 10 or 12 years old, for it would have been a good lesson for him. Eastman of the commercial college in Pokeepsie [*sic*] gets me to lecture to his students every six months, as he says it is just what each set of scholars needs.

I give you these hints not through any spirit of egotism, but because I know there are a great many who expect simply a string of jokes and nonsense conveying no moral, & perhaps quite the reverse. This class of persons are always happily disappointed, and the more refined and intelligent an audience is, the better satisfaction do I give.

I know this is piling it on pretty thick, but experience

has taught me the truth of what I have written. Hence I am particularly anxious to address ladies & gentlemen of the highest education & morals, and especially to reach *the rising generation*. Wishing you abundant success, I am

Very truly yours,

P. T. Barnum

## {133}

## TO W. A. LEARY JR.

New York, 12 December 1868

Dear Sir,

Yours is recd. I am glad you are *advertising* liberally. There is no power like "printer's ink," judiciously applied. In my lecture I recommend *advertising* as the first, second, and third element of "success." I think your newspaper editors are aware of this, & that they will on application give favorable notices of the forthcoming lecture.

Truly yours,

P. T. Barnum

A xerox copy of this letter is in the Walter Hampden–Edwin Booth Theatre Collection and Library at The Players, New York. The location of the original is unknown.

# ⦃134⦄

## TO BAYARD TAYLOR

New York, 28 May 1869

My dear Sir,

I believe I never write you except to ask a favor. And my favors seem to run to *naming houses*.

I have built a summer residence on Seaside Park, Bridgeport. It stands so near to Long Island Sound that we can hear every wave that dashes upon the shore. A fine hickory grove forms a part of my grounds. I have thought of calling the place

Waldammeer

or

Waldameer

as signifying (in German) "woods near the sea." Is that too farfetched, & if not, would it do to spell with one "m"? I like

Waldamere

still better, but the last syllable is more French than German for "sea."

Now I want to trouble you to say which of the three foregoing you deem the least objectionable, for I expect you will hardly like either. . . .

Truly yours,

P. T. Barnum

Barnum had previously consulted Taylor on the naming of the successor to Iranistan, Lindencroft. Waldemere—as it came to be spelled—was his third Bridgeport mansion and the one he was destined to reside at the longest. The property is today part of the campus of the University of Bridgeport, which demolished Barnum's last remaining home, Marina, some years ago.

# (135)

## TO MR. THOMAS

New York, 19 March 1870

My dear Mr. Thomas,

Yours of the 13th is at hand. When you read my chapter on "No. *13*"—page 708—you will see that the *date* of your letter is propitious, for I have made up my mind that on the whole "13" is at least an *innocent* number.

Yes, I hit the Worcester train that A.M. all right, and the only things that *weighed* upon me were a hearty breakfast and the thought that the lady who "never saw an elephant" was put to the great inconvenience of providing it, with that delicious coffee, so *early* in the morning. I don't know how I can ever pay her for it, unless it may be by my succeeding in inducing you to follow my example in giving up the [?nauseous] *weed*. I reckon that would be *about* as good a present as any man could give his wife. However, I don't propose to preach to you just now.

I am glad my book arrived & feel doubly complimented in your assurance that "Mrs. T. was *buried* in it for the greater part of a stormy day." I hope it may be many years before she is "buried" in a more lonely grave! If you & she get as much fun out of the reading of the book as I enjoyed in writing it, I shall be very glad.

I should like right well to visit Plymouth Rock & vicinity in the summer, & if I do so shall hope to see you & Mrs. T. But if my poor nervous wife is well enough to spare me, I must run to California for a couple of months with 3 or 4 friends. By the way, as you have no children, why can't your wife put the cat & dog in a seminary for 60 days & you two add a couple to our California party? None of us will ever be *younger,* & if you could go & have some of your friends go at same time so as to make up a party of from 6 or 8 to any number over that, I'll bet we could do up the golden land & Brigham Young in as intelligent & *jolly* a style as it ever will be done. Then your wife would "see the elephant," and the trip would give you both food for conversation & pleasant reflection the rest of your lives. We could leave middle of April & return middle of June. I shall have several ladies in my party, & we should be delighted in having yourself & Mrs. Thomas and *any number* of your personal friends join us. If we could make up a party of 20 or more we could have a Pullman car at our own disposal to stop & lay over whenever we pleased. It will be just the season to go, and we can get back in good time to enjoy our New England summer. . . .

Truly yours,

P. T. Barnum

*Struggles and Triumphs,* a reworking and expansion of the earlier autobiography, appeared in late 1869, and the reference to "No. 13" in this letter pertains to that edition. "To see the elephant" was a phrase commonly used to describe those traveling to California around the time of the 1849 gold rush.

## (136)

## TO W. C. COUP

When his second museum was destroyed by fire in 1868, Barnum took his friend Horace Greeley's advice and retired from show business. He could not remain away long, however, and in the fall of 1870 he entered into partnership with William C. Coup and Dan Castello to form a circus company. The present letter was published by Coup in his *Sawdust & Spangles* (1901). George Wood's New York museum was advertised as the successor to Barnum's. The Cardiff Giant was a stone fake manufactured and then "discovered" by a New York farmer, who proceeded to make his fortune by exhibiting it. When he refused to sell it to Barnum, the latter had his own Cardiff Giant made and delighted in exhibiting the "hoax of a hoax." The midget Admiral Dot, whose real name was Leopold Kahn, was discovered and engaged by Barnum while on his trip to California in 1870.

Bridgeport, 8 October 1870

My dear Coup,

Yours received. I will join you in a show for next spring and will probably have Admiral Dot well trained this winter

[162]

and have him and Harrison in the show. Wood will sell all his animals right and will furnish several tip-top museum curiosities. You need to spend several months in New York arranging for curiosities, cuts, cages, bills, &c. All things got from Wood I will settle for with him and give the concern credit. We can make a stunning museum department. If you want to call it *my* museum and use my name, it may be used by allowing me the same very small percentage that Wood allows for calling himself my successor (3 percent on receipts). You can have a Cardiff Giant that won't crack, also a moving figure— Sleeping Beauty or Dying Zouave—a big gymnastic figure like that in Wood's museum, and lots of other good things—only you need time to look them up and prepare wagons &c. &c.

Yours truly,

P. T. Barnum

I will spare time to cook [*sic*] up the show in New York when you come. I think Siamese Twins would pay.

## {137}

**TO MOSES KIMBALL**

New York, 22 November 1870

My dear Kimball,

Have you got an Egyptian mummy in your museum that you will sell? If not, can you tell me where I can buy one?

Truly yours,

P. T. Barnum

## TO SAMUEL L. CLEMENS

Mark Twain was an avid reader of Barnum's autobiography and a fascinated admirer of his career. In time they became friends, visiting each other with their families in Hartford and Bridgeport. Joel Benton, a minor poet, biographer, and journalist, was a frequent guest at Waldemere.

New York, 17 December 1870

My dear Mr. Clemens,

As a forerunner of my big travelling "Museum, Menagerie, & Circus Combined" I shall publish several hundred thousand copies of *Barnum's Advance Courier,* which my advertisers will place in the houses of such towns as we are to visit.

It struck me that perhaps you would at your leisure write me a characteristic letter on the show business (or any other subject) which I could publish in my *Courier* & for which I will pay the money or reciprocate in any way you may suggest in the columns of my paper—either in advertising or noticing your *Innocents* or whatever else desired.

Our mutual friend Joel Benton, at present stopping with me, says he thinks the idea is a good one for us both, and he hopes you will see it in that light & act accordingly.

Very truly yours,

P. T. Barnum

P.S. *Pray don't* mention my paper *at present* in any public way, lest my brother showmen may steal my thunder.

P. T. B.

## (139)

## TO MOSES KIMBALL

New York, 18 February 1871

My dear Moses,

My Charity & myself will be glad to see you & yours any time you come this way—or if between 1st June & 1st Nov., at our Seaside Park house in Bridgeport, Ct.

I *thought* I had finished the show business (and all other), but just for a flyer I go it once more. I write this to ask you where I can get some living *seals* within a month. If you don't know any parties who catch them, please tell me in what part down east they catch them so that I can write a postmaster there for information.

Truly yours,

P. T. Barnum

## (140)

## TO CITY EDITOR OF THE *NEW YORK SUN*

New York, 3 February 1872

City Editor of the *Sun:*

Will you please make a note of the fact that I had a giraffe on board the steamer *Harmonia* which arrived from Hamburg. It died a day before reaching New York. It cost $10,000. I have two alive—the only ones in America.

Truly yours,

P. T. Barnum

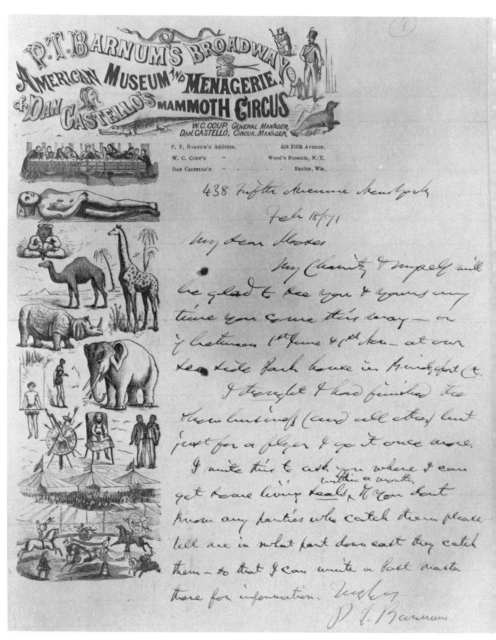

P. T. BARNUM TO MOSES KIMBALL, 18 February 1871. The "museum" department is represented by Barnum's "hoax of a hoax," the Cardiff Giant, reclining beneath a copy of *The Last Supper*.

COURTESY OF THE SHELBURNE MUSEUM.

# ⟨141⟩

## TO REV. OLYMPIA BROWN

The Rev. Olympia Brown (1835–1926) was the first American woman to be ordained a minister by full denominational authority and the founder, in 1868, of the New England Woman's Suffrage Association. At the time of her correspondence with Barnum she was pastor of the Universalist church or "society" in Bridgeport, with whose members she was sometimes at odds on account of her political and suffragette activities. Among her friends in the woman's movement were Isabella Beecher Hooker, sister of Henry Ward Beecher, and Lucy Stone, with both of whose views Barnum sympathized. Mrs. Middlebrook may have been the wife of Louis Nathaniel Middlebrook, a local lawyer and one-time editor and proprietor of the *Bridgeport Standard*. Although Barnum often claimed he did not belong to the Bridgeport society, he supported it generously and attended its services, as he did those at the church of his friend the Rev. E. H. Chapin during his winters in New York City.

New York, 6 April 1872

Miss Brown:

As you claim my attention under the head of *"animal,"* I must try to give it a few minutes.

"Common rumor is a common liar." I never heard of your presiding at Mrs. Hooker's meeting, & of course heard nothing about your being favorable to *Democrats.* I have never before heard about their proposing to hire a man or any other person than yourself, so if they so expect, and especially if they expect any $4000 man & expensive music (which I think is altogether *imaginary*), they are doing it without my knowledge or suspicion. Staples, Peck, & all the leading members of that society have heard me distinctly say & repeat that come what may, I expect only to pay $100 per year, & if they had an angel there I would not pay over $200—for the reason (if no other) that it *spoils* a society to lean upon one man.

Nobody within a year has spoken to me about your continuing another year or not, & I knew nothing of new members or their votes till I read it in your letter.

I heard long ago about your going to the polls with Mrs. Middlebrook & associating with her, but I never knew whether it was true nor cared enough about it to repeat it or think of it. When, however, I saw that atheistical statement over Middlebrook's name, I cut it out, thinking you ought to know what sort of belief these people hold.

I never belonged to the Bridgeport society & have no desire to meddle with it or to attempt to exercise influence there. I certainly shall not mix up in any *schisms* which they may have there.

Such persons as Claffin [*sic*] and Woodhull, Tilton & Middlebrook are blackening the woman's rights movement so much that I can understand that parties in the Universalist society may feel that your position & action on that question may make the Bpt. church a heavier load to carry than they can stagger under. I gave up the church several years ago & wanted it sold & the society disbanded, for it was deeply in debt & its members had no zeal or ambition & were fighting away what little religion they had on hand. But I joined them in getting it out of debt, & I think it has never held so promising a position since Moses Ballou's time as now. Yet if there is *serious* objections [*sic*] by *many* of the society to retaining you, then will arise a question of *policy* which the society must decide.

I repeat that *I* shall not be mixed up in it *either* way, for I have to pay pretty well here for Chapin's pew rents & accessories & appurtenances, & I am thankful that I don't *belong* to any ecclesiastical society.

I write by this mail to Mr. Staples that I am not opposed to you, and that if they engage the angel Gabriel I will not pay more than I have done. In great haste,

Truly yours,

P. T. Barnum

## (142)

## TO REV. GEORGE H. EMERSON

George H. Emerson, Universalist clergyman and temperance reformer, was editor of several periodicals during his career, including the *Christian Leader* newspaper, published in New York City, and the *Universalist* magazine, published by the Universalist Publishing House in Boston. His removal from New York to Boston, where he had previously lived and worked as an editor, is touched on in this letter.

New York, 14 April 1872

My dear Emerson,

Thanks for your letter & papers. I envy you the "clover" you are living in: your old home & old associates & associations, the cosy way they have of doing things at the "Hub," the freedom from cant & frippery & gewgaws that mark *our* shoddy aristocracy, the fresh cod, an occasional sip of Warren—these & a thousand other peculiar blessings pertain to Boston, especially for an old Bostonian, that must make all seem like a paradise to you. And a "pair o' dice" is about all you can deduct from the Elysium that you have attained.

As for poor me, I go about *bleating* like an unweaned calf. The invitations to lecture are all "respectfully declined" because I have lost my faithful *constant* auditor, one who knows it all by heart and can therefore conscientiously go to sleep without danger of missing a single new idea.

As for the backgammon board, it rests on the closet shelf, unprofaned by the touch of human fingers since last witnessing the defeat of a doctor of divinity or a showman—I forget which (the resemblance is so *striking*, such a lapse of memory is pardonable). I have spoken for a black ribbon with a small white edge with which I propose to "tie up" the gammon board in half-mourning, like a widow's cap. Indeed, I fancy I have discovered the peculiar sensations of an *old* widow on losing her spouse. In approaching my library & seeing no minister's hat hanging on the peg, a sort of *gone*-ness comes over me, but I rally and draw upon my immense fountains of philosophy and religion sufficiently to be able to exclaim with a sigh, "Our loss is his gain!"

There, I guess that will do for the mourner's department. The two numbers of the *Universalist* are creditable, & I easily recognize the familiar Emersonian style in some of the editorials. But I was vexed also to discover the familiar typographical errors in some of your articles. I have a horror for such inexcusable things. A close *proofreader* is a valuable adjunct to a printing office.

My big show leaves the city Monday morning, 15th. I shall see it in Phila., Baltimore, & Washington, and not again till Cleveland, 15th June. If it meets no R.R. accidents, the financial success will be *immense,* for *everybody* is going to see it.

If I find time to drop down east this summer I shall of course step into Cornhill, and if you come New York or Bridgeport way, you know where to hang your hat. I expect to be "clambaking" most of the summer.

Remember us all kindly to Mrs. Emerson & the "sissy," as well as all other friends, social & theological.  . . .

Truly yours,

P. T. Barnum

## TO MARY CLEMMER AMES

Bridgeport, 24 July 1872

Mary Clemmer Ames:

Your letter recd. I would gladly do all in my power to commemorate the noble characters of Alice & Phoebe Cary, & especially the brilliant wit of the latter, but I have no letters that would tend to do either. I fear also that my memory has not retained any of Phoebe's witty sayings & repartees that are new to you or worth recording, though she afforded me hours of rollicking laughter. The flashes were vivid, but they seem to have passed out of my mind. If I can jot down any, you can use either of them if worth preserving, but I am absorbed in various enterprises and cannot now write a *letter* that it will be worthwhile to publish (see next page).

Truly yours,

P. T. Barnum

On one of those pleasant Sunday evenings in 20th St., I tried to leave the house early, without attracting attention, and was just selecting my hat and coat from the hat stand when Phoebe & her niece came out to remonstrate.

"Now why do you follow me out?" I said laughingly. "I am not going to carry anything away."

"We wish you would," she quickly replied, throwing back her arms as if she was ready to be "carried out."

Speaking of the doctrine of endless misery, which she utterly repudiated, she said, "Well, if our creator dooms me to endless misery, I am sure He will give me a *constitution* that can bear it."

Being one day at Wood's Museum, she asked me to show her the "Infernal Regions" advertised to be represented there. I found on inquiry they were out of order, so I said, "The Infernal Regions are busted, but never mind, Phoebe, you'll see them in time."

"No, in *eternity*," was the lightning-like reply.

Phoebe entering a dry good store asked the clerk to show her a *ladies'* [sic] cap. He understood her to say *baby's* cap. "What is the child's age?" asked the clerk. "*Forty!*" exclaimed Phoebe in a voice that made the young chap shake in his shoes.

It's a shame that I can't think of a hundred finer, better things which I heard her say, & possibly my head may be

[171]

clearer before I return from Colorado, wither I go on the 1st prox.

Truly yours,

P. T. Barnum

The Cary sisters, both of whom had died in 1871, were Universalists and popular authors whose Sunday evening receptions at their New York home attracted many of the leading literary and artistic figures of the day. In a letter dated 23 May 1868, Barnum writes to a friend of taking "Phoebe Cary a riding in the park. We had a nice time & the weather was so warm we had to stop and *'take a drink'*—of lemonade *without* the stick" (*Tufts*). Mary Clemmer Ames' *Memorials of Alice and Phoebe Cary* was published in 1873.

## TO WILLIAM WINTER

The journalist and theatrical biographer William Winter often wrote flattering reviews and notices of Barnum's shows for the *Tribune*. Barnum was careful to cultivate his good will.

Greeley, Colorado, 12 October 1872

My dear Mr. Winter,

Your kind favor was forwarded to me at Chicago. I can only say in general terms that so far as *space* will admit I intend to make the 14th St. Hippotheatron the scene of the most comprehensive show in any country. We have dug down and lowered the ring 12 feet, by means of which I am enabled to add a second tier or gallery. All the seats have been taken out and comfortable chairs substituted, so that we can accommodate about 2500 persons comfortably. The building being octagon [*sic*], I have covered all the rest of the lot with rooms devoted to the most rare living wild animals; museum curiosities, including some ingen[i]ous automatons made to my order in Paris; also my usual complement of giants, dwarfs, and other human phenomena. My huge sea lions from Alaska; the only giraffes in America, 4 in number; 3 polar bears (I had 4, but one was shot in 5th Avenue); a double-horned rhinoceros, the only one ever seen in America; yaks, elands, tapirs, gnus, black leopards, Rocky Mountain sheep, ostriches, seals, African wart hogs, and other animals seldom seen; besides the finest specimens of such animals as are usually seen in menageries—lions, tigers, leopards, &c. &c.—make up the zoological department. My agent in Europe, Mr. E. W. Wolcott, is selecting the most novel and talented equestrians and gymnasts that can be found, which will be added to the best portion of my present equestrian troup[e] under the management of the popular Dan Castello. A horse-riding goat from Cairo, Egypt, more clever than the equestrian goat Alexis which I also own, will be introduced into the circus ring with performing elephants, camels, Indians, and all novelties that money can procure.

I intend opening on the evening of Monday, Nov. 11th, and afterwards give exhibitions & performances every *day* and evening. Of course, as usual there will be no bar about the premises (except *leaping* bars), and I shall as always before cater to the tastes of the moral, religious, and refined—never permitting a word or gesture that is objectionable to ladies, children, or others who desire to enjoy innocent amusement blended with instruction.

Hoping you will give us a "preliminary" that will arrest & fix public attention, I am

Very truly yours,

P. T. Barnum

## (145)

## TO REV. OLYMPIA BROWN

New York, 29 November 1872

My dear Miss Brown,

I owe you 40 apologies for not sooner answering your letter, but truth to tell, I am a *fool* to be so absorbed in business and am going to *stop* it—perhaps not till breath stops, but I hope I shall.

If I live till spring I will talk seriously with our folks about my building that S[unday] S[chool] room. Meanwhile, it will be well to examine other rooms & see what shape & size will be most convenient.

Truly yours,

P. T. Barnum

## (146)

## TO JOSEPH HENRY

Barnum's correspondence with newly founded public museums was quite extensive, particularly after the formation of his circus, whose dead animals were always wanted for mounting. In April 1873 Joseph Henry, the first Secretary of the Smithsonian Institution, sent Barnum duplicates of some "Indian curiosities," thereby beginning a long and mutually profitable relationship. Professor Spencer F. Baird, who was an authority on birds and fish and who became the second Secretary of the Smithsonian in 1878, had been acquainted with Barnum for some years prior to the date of this letter.

New York, 17 April 1873

Dear Sir,

Please accept my thanks for the Indian mementoes just recd. though not yet examined.

[174]

Whenever any of my animals die, my manager has instructions to telegraph Prof. Baird that they are at the disposal of the Smithsonian Institution.

As I often lose rare animals by death, I have no doubt your favors will be reciprocated.

Very truly yours,

P. T. Barnum

## (147)

## TO GORDON L. FORD

Gordon L. Ford was business manager of the *New York Tribune*.

New York, 24 April 1873

My dear Mr. Ford,

I don't half like to disagree with the *Tribune*. We have been friends too long, & of course we *won't* differ *seriously*. But my dear sir, although my show brings big crowds, it takes over 8000 persons rain or shine each day to pay my *daily* expenses, to say nothing of the hundreds of thousands of dollars invested in such perishable property as animals, canvas tents, &c.

The article written for the *Tribune* was of course utterly without my knowledge. It is a well written, legitimate article of public interest, and it strikes me that inasmuch as the *Tribune* would probably have published it gladly had it not been complimentary to me, the *Tribune* ought to be all the more glad to see that this purely readable and legitimate article *does* help an old friend & customer.

This is *my* view. Of course, *yours* is different, for each looks from a selfish standpoint.

I go to see my show this A.M. at New Haven, return tonight. Will you please inform the bearer, my agent Mr. Gorham, whether you conclude to publish the article—and if not, whether you will let me have a proof of it if I pay you Miss Stanton's price for writing it.

Truly yours,

P. T. Barnum

## {148}

### TO GORDON L. FORD

New York, 10 May 1873

My dear Mr. Ford,

If you will kindly see that the hippopotamus article in today's *Tribune* goes into your semi-weekly & weekly, I will thank the *Tribune* association & call it quits. The animal's *never* having been duplicated in America certainly make[s] an interesting paragraph. Mr. Gorham will get your bill and I will send check.

Truly yours,

P. T. Barnum

## {149}

### TO HENRY WHEELER

Bridgeport, 2 July 1873

Neighbor Harry Wheeler
Dear Sir,

As I originally agreed to pay you interest on my land purchase, but was cornered into paying *your taxes* by your lawyer, I prefer now to pay off my indebtedness to you and would like to have you meet me and take your money at Pequonnock Bank tomorrow at 11 o'clock and give me up the note and a quit claim deed at that time.

I have no fault to find with your following your lawyer's advice, but you know it is not my business to pay anybody else's taxes. Therefore I decide to pay you up and thus be out of debt. With friendship I am

Truly yours,

P. T. Barnum

Henry Wheeler's estate was adjacent to Barnum's at Seaside Park.

## TO JOSEPH HENRY

Bridgeport, 19 September 1873

Dear Sir,

I sail for Europe on Wednesday next, going to see about the possibility of crossing the Atlantic in a *baloon* [*sic*]—not by me, but by some aeronaut. If you think of any scientific men in any part of Europe whom I had better consult, I will thank you for a letter of introduction. . . .

I told the *N.Y. Times* reporter you thought if ever the air should be navigated, some force like guncotton must be practically applied. I see he has erred in making his report, which I regret, especially if his error should prove in the least unpleasant to you.

My manager is directed to send all animals as usual to your agt. as fast as they die.

I hope you will use enclosed ticket while my show is in

Washington. I have an extra fine collection of living wild animals.

Truly yours,

P. T. Barnum

Henry obligingly furnished the letter of introduction, in which Barnum is described as "devoting his energies to the promotion of aerial navigation" (*Smithsonian Institution Archives*). The prospect of crossing the Atlantic in a balloon—either in fact or in imagination—was at the time very much in the air.

# ⦃151⦄

## TO JOHN GREENWOOD JR.?

139 Regent St., London, 19 December 1873

My Dear G,

Fillingham recd. your letter & sent it to me.

On the 20th Nov. I recd. a cable at Hamburg saying my wife died 19th. She was paralyzed 18th, lay unconscious & died without pain next day. I was fast recovering my health, but this set me back. I have only averaged 4 hours sleep per night since, until the last 2 nights. I remain here 10 days & then go to Italy accompanied by friends. Expect to return home in March or April. It hurts my brain to write or think. Above is my permanent London address.

Truly yours,

P. T. Barnum

The recipient of this letter was probably Greenwood, but may have been Barnum's accountant and secretary J. J. Gorham, both of whom he referred to as "G" on various occasions. Robert Fillingham Jr. was employed by Barnum as one of his London agents.

## (152)

## TO REV. GEORGE H. EMERSON

Barnum had earlier spent considerable time with John Fish and his daughter Nancy while they were visiting America. He now found solace with them at their home in Southport, England.

London, 21 February 1874

My dear Emerson,

I recd. your letter sometime since, but though it gratified me much, I did not feel able to answer it, as I was so much oppressed with business & cares. . . . I expected to have been in Italy before this, but I have not yet *finished* my business in London, and as I am booked to return in *Scotia* 18th April, it is just possible I shall not go to Italy at all. I cannot enjoy sightseeing as I could before Mrs. Barnum died. Still, *time* is helping me along, & were it not for increasing years, too many cares, & rather a dizzy head, I should be all right. Indeed, I fully expect to be so very soon. . . . If you were *here* I would surely go to Italy with you, & I want to see Rome, Naples, &c. But really my pluck & courage fail me somewhat, & I may remain in London till I sail.

You asked where you could send slip of "Bunker Hill" to Miss Fish. Address: Miss Fish, 5 Portland St., Southport, Lancashire, England. I am sure she will be *glad* to hear from you.

I almost envy you. I am convinced you get more happiness in your steady, sensible way of living than I do in the dash & fire which attend my way of living. But I have *no* cause of complaint. *Nor have you!* . . .

Truly yours,

P. T. Barnum

# (153)

## TO MRS. ABEL C. THOMAS

Bridgeport, 22 May [1874]

Mrs. Thomas:

As I don't write much, you'll excuse my not before telling you what a nice time we had at the manse & how happily I was surprised at meeting so many old friends. Yours is indeed a charming retreat, & I envy you the enjoyment you get there. I look on the bright side & therefore don't fret much over my own situation, and yet I see plainly that there is more care and less true enjoyment amid tinsel, show, & vanity than in rustic & rural ways of living. But I have lived so long on excitement, pepper, & mustard that plain bread & milk don't agree with me—or rather it is *too late* to change my tastes in that direction. As the years creep on, however, I more plainly see that those are to be envied who live in a more simple, matter-of-fact way and who appreciate & enjoy glorious nature as our good Father has prepared it for us.

I send enclosed some prepared slips of paper to test your atmosphere. Keep them in the tinfoil, taking out one at a time. Hang it out of doors where there is a current of air. Let it remain 12 to 24 hours, then immerse the slip in clean water for a minute and compare the color produced with the scale of colors enclosed & let me know the result. Love to Abel.

Truly yours,

P. T. Barnum

This was written shortly after Barnum had returned from a trip to Philadelphia and a visit to his friends the Thomases in nearby Tacony. The molecular structure of ozone had recently been established, and Barnum, intrigued by the gas, liked to boast of the invigorating quantity present in the atmosphere of his beloved Bridgeport. The strips of test paper he sent to various friends around this time were no doubt treated with potassium iodide, which reacts with ozone to form iodine.

# (154)

## TO GORDON L. FORD

Bridgeport, 30 May 1874

My dear Mr. Ford,

I hope you will kindly give my thanks to Mr. Reid and the writer of the article in today's *Tribune* concerning my hippodrome. I think no other old fool in this generation will venture to expend so much in that way.

I felt a great *desire* to do a *big thing* for the public & to make it quite unobjectionable to the most refined & moral. I think I have succeeded. It is my *last* "crowning effort." Three months of the same success which I am now receiving (pecuniarily) will be required in order to reimburse the outlays made since last November. The present excitement must wane before that time, I think, but *in time* I have no doubt of getting my money back. But whether so or not is of less consequence than the fact that I have awakened a *public taste* which *will not* henceforth be satisfied with namby-pamby nonsense. Managers will be *required* hereafter to give their patrons something *better*—& therein is the public benefitted, and I am satisfied.

It is a great satisfaction to me to see that the *Tribune* appreciates my efforts to please.

Very truly yours,

P. T. Barnum

Whitelaw Reid, following Greeley's death in 1872, had become proprietor and chief editor of the *Tribune*.

## (155)

### TO SAMUEL L. CLEMENS

In the summer of 1874 Americans were treated to the spectacle of Coy Coggia, a brilliant comet. The "partnership" here alluded to involved a humorous sketch in the *New York Sun,* reprinted in the *Herald,* in which Twain and Barnum were reported to be about to "hire de comick to go a sailin' in."

Bridgeport, 16 July 1874

My dear Clemens,

I owe you a thousand thanks for taking me into partnership. I wish you would come here, take some ozone, & let me thank you in person.

Truly yours,

P. T. Barnum

P. S. Bring your wife & baby, join in clambakes, & have jolly times.

P. T. B.

## (156)

### TO SAMUEL L. CLEMENS

Barnum complained in his autobiography and elsewhere of the "bushels" of letters he regularly received from unknown correspondents—begging for handouts and jobs, offering to sell curiosities or perform miracles, proposing hare-brained business schemes, etc. Around 1874 he appears to have shown some of these "queer" letters to Twain, who for a while contemplated publishing them. Always eager to have Twain write about him and his enterprises, Barnum obligingly saved and forwarded these letters to his friend in Hartford for several years, repeatedly urging him to make use of them. Upon receiving one batch of letters, Twain wrote enthusiastically to Barnum,
> This is an admirable lot of letters. Headless mice, four-legged hens, human-handed sacred bulls, "professional" Gypsies, ditto "Sacasians," deformed human beings anxious to trade on their horrors, school-teachers who can't spell—it is a perfect feast of queer literature! Again I beseech you, don't burn a single specimen, but remember that *all* are wanted & possess value in the eyes of your

[182]

friend (*Copyright © 1983 by the Mark Twain Foundation and published with the permission of the University of California Press and the General Editor of the Mark Twain Project*).
For some unexplained reason, however, Twain never got around to publishing the letters.

Bridgeport, 31 July 1874

My dear Clemens,

Thanks for your favor of Monday. I have destroyed *bushels* of curious begging letters. Hereafter they shall all be saved for you. . . .

Yours,

P. T. Barnum

## {157}

## TO REV. HENRY WARD BEECHER

Henry Ward Beecher was an occasional guest at Waldemere, and Barnum sometimes attended his Plymouth Church in Brooklyn. This offer was made shortly after the latest of several highly publicized investigations into Beecher's conduct following charges of his having committed adultery with the wife of Theodore Tilton.

Bridgeport, 10 August 1874

Dear Sir,

I write this to say that I will be glad to pay you *ten thousand dollars* ($10,000) to lecture ten times this season, with the privilege on my part of making it fifteen or twenty times at the same rate. The lecture to be the *only* entertainment and to be delivered in the most respectable halls and churches that can be procured. I to pay all your travelling expenses, to guarantee that you shall not be absent from Brooklyn more than one sabbath altogether (perhaps none), and not to go farther west than Kansas City.

[183]

Of course, these to be the *first* lectures that you deliver the present season.

Respectfully yours,

P. T. Barnum

P.S. My dear Mr. Beecher,

The enclosed is made in the most friendly spirit and in perfect good faith. I think the great public ought to see and welcome you after this "trial by fire."

Truly yours,

P. T. Barnum

The first lecture could be given by 10th Sept. and all completed in the same month—or certainly in October.

B

## ❨158❩

## TO SAMUEL L. CLEMENS

Bridgeport, 13 August 1874

My dear Clemens,

Suppose you come down here Saturday next, stop over Sunday & remain a few days next week, have a clambake, &c.? Bring wife & babies if agreeable. I mean if agreeable to *you* & *them,* & not if they are agreeable. . . .

Truly yours,

P. T. Barnum

Am getting quite a stock of queer letters for you.

# {159}

## TO NATHANIEL P. AND EMMA BEERS

On 16 September 1874, while attending a Universalist convention in New York City, Barnum married Nancy Fish, daughter of his English friend John Fish, who was some forty years his junior. Nate Beers, cousin of Barnum's first wife Charity, and his wife Emma had deliberately been kept in the dark about these plans. Miss Ellis was Barnum's housekeeper.

Windsor House [New York], 16 September 1874

My dear Nate & Emma,

I expect Emma was a little taken aback today—but no more so than most people except my daughters & sons-in-law & Miss Ellis & my sister, Mrs. Amerman. They have known all for a couple of months.

The river *Lethe* is good to drink from sometimes. My wife has done that. The world is large—our hearts should be large. I hope & she hopes that past misunderstandings may be forgotten. I trust we may often meet pleasantly at Waldemere & elsewhere.

We go to White Mountains tomorrow morning, thence to Saratoga & home when Miss Ellis is ready—about 2d Oct.

Truly yours,

P. T. Barnum

## (160)

## TO WILLIAM EAGLE

Saratoga Springs, 21 September 1874

My dear Brother-in-Law,

"HAPPY."

Truly yours,

P. T. Barnum

Eagle appears to have been a brother-in-law on Nancy's side.

## (161)

## TO MR. CRANE

Bridgeport, 19 November 1874

My dear Crane,

Yours recd. I am dreadful *sorry* we must start so early, but it *must* be done & I will leave New York at *11* o'clock, as I see by the new timetable that reaches Rhinebeck at 2:24.

Don't let your sick mother worry about us. We are plain folks & don't want to be made *company* of. All we want is a comfortable bedroom & a moderate allowance of plain food to eat. I will try to revamp my old lecture so as to get in as little as may be of the old matter and ring in anecdotes & illustrations enough to keep people awake.

Truly yours,

P. T. Barnum

BARNUM and his "YOUNG ENLISH WIFE" NANCY FISH,
whom he married in 1874.

SMALL CARTE DE VISITE. COURTESY OF THE BARNUM MUSEUM, BRIDGEPORT.

P.S. On reflection, upon looking over the headings of my various lectures, I have concluded to talk enough about the general principles that point towards health, wealth, & happiness and then come down to a straight-out *temperance lecture*. It will be more *original* than anything else I could give them, replete with *anecdote* & *illustration* & calculated to *do good* to any who need such admonitions—& who does not, in view of the fact that strong drink is the giant evil today in our land? I hope you will get some out who specially need it.

P. T. B.

(162)

## TO SAMUEL L. CLEMENS

Barnum often urged Twain to write about him and his circus—"characteristic letters" that could be used in Barnum's "advance courier" that preceded the show each year, "funny" articles for *Harper's Weekly,* the *Atlantic Monthly,* and other publications—but with small success. Twain's reply to the present request was that he could not do something in the "show line."

Bridgeport, 19 January 1875

My dear Clemens,

Yours recd. I hope I sent you the letter from the man who was going on a lecturing *tower*!

I have heretofore destroyed a multitude of queer letters, but henceforth will save all for you.

I wonder if you have ever seen my great hippodrome. If not, I really *hope* you will have a chance to do so during the week or two that it will remain open. I enclose several "orders" to that end.

I'll not disguise that I have a small axe or hatchet to grind, though if you take hold of it, it would soon swell to an *immense* tree-chopping implement. But if you don't happen to take to it, understand I shall be *quite content*. I merely throw out the hint as one "casts his bread upon the waters." If it *don't* "return," *I'll be just as well off* as if I had not *tried* for a small harvest.

Your *comet* article in the *Herald* last year, wherein you had me for an *active* partner, of course added much to my notoriety at home and abroad. Now my "axe" is that if you should happen to be in a writing mood and could in your inimitable way hit my travelling hippodrome so that people could get an idea what is coming next spring & summer, it would help *me*—but I neither ask nor expect nor *desire* such a thing unless it so happens that in the way of your literary labors you can make the hippodrome the subject of a portion of your article. Such an article in *Harper's Weekly* would be immense and of course proportionately so in any other publication. My object is to reach *country* readers where my hippodrome will travel next summer. If you *can't* bring it into your regular work, I shall be very glad to pay you the same as you would want from any publisher, & I'll have the article inserted in some paper & then mail marked copies of it to every paper in the Union. You can't well get a good idea of hippodrome without *seeing* it, but I'll herein sketch a little about it.

My *daily* expenses in New York are nearly $5000. They will be more than that while travelling. Last August I had an immense tent made, over 800 feet long by 400 broad, and transported it to Boston, where I built seats to accommodate 11,000 persons, & I transported my entire hippodrome to Boston. There were over 1200 men, women, & children engaged by me; 750 horses, including 300 blooded race horses & ponies; camels, elephants, buffaloes, English stag and stag hounds, ostriches, &c. &c. (Don't mention menagerie of lions, tigers, & other wild beasts, for I don't take them *travelling* with hippodrome.)

Now the cost of tent, seats, and transporting the entire hippodrome & paraphernalia to Boston by rail was over $50,000. And yet though I was in Boston but 3 weeks, I was fully reimbursed and had a handsome surplus. We accommodated over 20,000 persons to our two performances each day

[189]

and frequently turned away visitors for want of room. Cheap excursion trains ran daily on all the roads leading into Boston, and thousands daily came in them.

Now by having *two* of these 800 feet tents, so as to keep one continually a day ahead, I shall next summer take the entire hippodrome on 125 railroad cars of my own to all the *larger* towns in New England and the middle & western states, frequently stopping but one day in a town. I can easily lose half a million of dollars next summer *unless* I can in advance so awaken and electrify the country as to have *everybody* join in getting up excursion trains so as to hit me where I open the hippodrome. If I *can* do this, I can *make* half a million, so it is a pretty big stake to play for—hence my anxiety. I take along *sleeping* cars wherein nearly all my 1200 employees lodge every night (I put up berths in ordinary passenger cars), and I take along cooks and cooking tents where all except 150 of my 1200 employees get every meal they eat during the travelling season. Horse tents also accommodate my horses, elephants, camels, &c. I carry blacksmiths & blacksmith tents to do all my horse-shoeing, repairing of chariots, wagons, &c. I also carry harness makers. I carry carpenters and builders who precede the show ten days to build the seats. I carry wardrobe men and women to repair and care for the wardrobe, which has cost me over $70,000 and which I use in processions and all the various plays, scenes, and the great street procession which occurs every morning. I take two immense bands of music, first-class.

My hippodromic exhibitions include the Roman chariot races and many other acts that were shown in the Roman Colosseum 1600 years ago, and on a scale that has not been witnessed in this world during the last thousand years. My Roman chariots are driven by Amazons instead of men.

But I show besides scores of thrillingly interesting scenes which Rome never saw. I give a scene called *Indian Life on the Plains* wherein scores of Indians of various tribes appear with their squaws, pappooses, ponies, and wigwams travelling as they do in the Indian territory. They encamp, erect their wigwams, engage in buffalo hunts with real buffaloes, give their

Indian war dances, their Indian pony races, snowshoe races, foot races against horses, lasso horses and other animals, and both Indians and squaws give the most amazing specimens of riding at full speed. The Indian camp is surprised by Mexicans, and then ensues such a scene of savage strife and warfare as is never seen except upon our wild western borders.

The great English stag hunt wherein 150 ladies and gentlemen appear on horseback all dressed in appropriate hunting costumes, with the English stags and a large pack of real English stag hounds, depicts a scene worth going a hundred miles to see.

Then of course we have hurdle races by ladies; Roman standing races (the riders standing on bareback horses); flat races by English, American, and French jockeys, with the best blooded race horses to be found in Europe; races by camels ridden by Arabs; elephant races; liberty races by 40 wild horses turned loose; ostrich races, monkey races, and the most remarka[ble] performances by elephants and other animals. Taken altogether, this is a colossal travelling exhibition *never* before equalled and what no other man in this generation will ever dare to wish. It involves a capital of nearly a million of dollars. My expectation is to take it all to Europe next autumn, for it will prove even a greater wonder there than here.

Truly yours,

P. T. Barnum

## (163)

## TO SAMUEL L. CLEMENS

Bridgeport, 23 March 1875

My dear Clemens,

Yours recd. It *is* a shame I have wasted so much good stuff for your collection. I hope at a proper time you will publish many of the letters. They will form almost a *new* page in the volume of human nature.

I respond to all calls for benevolence at home and abroad that I feel able to do, but cannot do *everything*. That little girl would be as delighted to have a musical instrument from anybody else as from me, so if you feel the promptings in that direction, *don't hesitate*. It will make the heart's blood warmer and move quicker, as you doubtless know from experience. . . .

You must not creep and crawl and *sneak* out of giving us at least a week's visit with your wife when the weather is warmer. I am very glad you did such a noble thing for the poor with your lecture in Hartford.

As ever truly yours,

P. T. Barnum

*If* you send your books to me, do please write the presentation on flyleaf to *Mrs.* Barnum.

P. T. B.

## (164)

### TO SAMUEL L. CLEMENS

Bridgeport, 24 March 1875

My dear Clemens,

A thousand thanks for the books which arrived today. They are duly appreciated. At present they will be used exclusively for "family instruction," but as soon as our children grow up and are capable of receiving serious impressions, your valued volumes will be used by them in sabbath school.

When my appendix is complete, I shall send you *my* religious work as a very *small* recognition of my gratitude.

My wife ardently hopes to see you place your autograph in these volumes under the roof of Waldemere. There will be a *row* if her anticipations are blasted! . . .

Your package of "queer letters" is again increasing.

With kind regards to your lady, in which my "old woman" heartily joins, I am as ever

Truly yours,

P. T. Barnum

The "appendix" referred to was the annual one Barnum wrote to bring his autobiography up to date.

(165)

## TO JOSEPH HENRY

Bridgeport, 19 June 1875

My dear Prof. Henry,

. . . I tried to prevail on Donaldson to send a captive balloon & man to Bridgeport to meet you when you come, but he has no balloon nor assistant to spare, and as he makes almost daily ascensions from my hippodrome (now in Canada), he says it is impossible to accommodate us. I regret this but hope it will not deprive me of the pleasure of a visit from you this summer. . . .

Truly yours,

P. T. Barnum

Henry, who had been a professor of physics at Princeton before becoming the Smithsonian's Secretary, had asked Barnum to assist him in obtaining the loan of a captive balloon so he could study loud sounds for use as fog signals. Shortly after this letter was written "Professor" Donaldson and his balloon were lost over Lake Michigan.

## (166)

## TO DR. OSCAR KOHN

Bridgeport, 29 August 1875

Dr. Kohn:

The sea lion is to go to Wood's Museum with the hippopotamus, and you are to take particular care of them both. Never leave them without putting a faithful man in your place to watch the people. A gentleman tells me he saw visitors cram newspapers down the throat of the hippopotamus at my old museum. Showmen or others could easily poison this one if they are not closely watched. You must be at Reiche's sometime to consult with the man who captured the hippopotamus and learn how to feed him. Not let him get *too fat*.

P. T. Barnum

Barnum had recently purchased a young hippopotamus from the New York animal dealer Charles Reiche.

## (167)

## TO H. C. WILLARD

During the fall of 1875 Barnum was lecturing for the Redpath Bureau on "The World and How to Live in It."

*Private*

Mayor's Office, Bridgeport, 1 October 1875

Dear Sir,

I go from Boston to Brattleboro morning of 7th. As my wife will be with me, we *hope* the hotel is good.

I remark in my lecture jokingly about my being *mayor—*

[194]

& hope in order to have the joke not lost, you will in noticing my coming in the papers let the public know what office I now hold.

Truly yours,

P. T. Barnum

## (168)

## TO MR. & MRS. SAMUEL L. CLEMENS

Waldemere, 2 October 1875

My dear Mr. & Mrs. Clemens,

Nothing for a long time has disappointed & vexed me (& my wife ditto) so much as being compelled to take the will for the deed in regard to your visiting us next Saturday.

The trouble is, my hippodrome closes its season on that day at Cleveland, Ohio, and although I lecture in Rutland, Vt., Friday night, I may be compelled to go from there direct to Cleveland. In any event, I shall be running to New York and my mind so absorbed with monkeys & elephants that there will be no fun where I am till my animals are placed in winter quarters. . . .

My wife is deranged on the subject of a *fernery* like yours, so our call on you the other day will be cheap if I get off for $1000 to $1500. . . .

Truly yours,

P. T. Barnum

## (169)

## TO CITY OF BRIDGEPORT AUDITOR

Bridgeport, 30 December 1875

Mr. Auditor:

Will you please send the janitor to all church commit-
tees on each side of our river & get them to have the sextons
ring every church bell ½ hour commencing at midnight Friday.

They ought to do it *free* of charge for patriotism—but
if they will not, I suppose the common council would allow
them $1.00 each. By rights that should be *understood* in ad-
vance to prevent overcharge.

Truly yours,

P. T. Barnum

Mayor

Friday was, of course, the eve of the nation's centennial.

## (170)

## TO SAMUEL L. CLEMENS

Bridgeport, 20 March 1876

My dear Clemens,

I shall send you a small package of queer letters this
week. My show this year will consist of the most extensive &
complete *menagerie* that ever traveled, also the best *circus* I ever
saw, and a curious collection of novelties which I style a mu-

seum. I am not going to exhibit Revolutionary *relics* as some suppose, nor am I going to show in Philadelphia more than a few weeks, but I am going to send the show through the country from Bangor to Kansas City, and I invest it with such patriotic features as will enable me to give a real old-fashioned Yankee-Doodle, Hail-Columbia Fourth-of-July celebration every day. I will send you the printed *details* within 8 or 10 days. I imagine they will give you an opening for a very funny article.

First we send a magnificent show R.R. car a month ahead with our advertisers; then a month later the big show follows with a hundred R.R. cars, most of which are made of *steel*—a new invention, something that can't be smashed up nor telescoped. I own all these cars, including passenger & sleeping cars. We take along a pack of *cannon*, and at the starting of the great street procession, about 9 o'clock, we fire a *salute* of 13 guns. In the procession we carry & ring a big *church bell,* and we intend to give such a patriotic demonstration that the authorities will gladly let the *public bells* join in half an hour's jubilee. The procession will abound in American flags, a chariot will be mounted with a group of living characters in the costumes of the Revolution, a large platform car drawn by 8 or 10 horses will carry on it 2 white horses on which will be mounted Genls. Washington and Lafayette, properly costumed, a live eagle will be perched aloft, an old-fashioned drummer & fifer march in procession, &c. During our circus performances we introduce a musical ovation wherein great singers lead a chorus of several hundred voices in singing national songs. While singing "The Star Spangled Banner," *cannon* will be fired by electricity & the Goddess of Liberty will wave the Stars & Stripes. This ovation to conclude with singing "America," "My Country 'Tis of Thee," at which the whole audience will rise and join. At night we give set pieces of fireworks—representing Washington, the eagle, flags, 1776, 1876—rockets, & send up fire balloons.

The other day I wrote for my advance courier, which appears in April, a little squib saying it was computed that

[197]

Barnum with his show would hear this season the firing of 3000 cannon, hear "The Star Spangled Banner" and other national songs sung 300 times, witness five thousand displays of 4th-of-July fireworks, &c. &c., and in consequence would by October become so charged, inflated, & crammed with patriotism that he would start for Europe prepared to fight every monarchical government and whip them into a love of universal liberty.

After sending off this squib, I thought what a funny thing *you* could make of this view of the case. Hence I give you these outlines of the coming show, so that when the people hear from me in April they will pop upon such a takeoff in the papers by Mark Twain. You know I had rather be laughed *at* than not to be noticed at all—showwise or perhaps *other*wise. . . .

As ever truly yours,

P. T. Barnum

## ⟨171⟩

### TO MOSES KIMBALL

Bridgeport, 14 June 1876

My dear Moses,

You don't patronize my shows, I fear, so liberally as I do yours—but I always like to give you the chance. If "good & evil" are placed before you, your "free agency" will be at fault if you neglect the opportunity of seeing my sawdust.

I hope you are well & jolly as I always am thus far.

Truly yours,

P. T. Barnum

# (172)

## TO JOSEPH HENRY

Bridgeport, 15 June 1876

Dear Sir,

I gave the usual orders to have sent to you this season any animals in my menagerie which might die, but a white bear that died ten days ago was so diseased & rotten, they cast it into some manure heap. It is awkward to send dead animals far in hot weather, for express companies reject them.

I have some Fiji cannibals in Philadelphia, and I want to obtain & put in the main building some implements of any kind: clubs, ornaments, fishing or hunting tackle, maps or pictures of those regions, or anything else appertaining to them.

I hope that you may have some such articles that you can loan me till the exhibition at Philadelphia closes 10th Nov.—and if you can *give* me any trinkets, bows & arrows, or anything to please these two fellows, I shall be glad.

Will you please look over your collection & write me what you can do for me, & oblige

Truly yours,

P. T. Barnum

In addition to his circus activities this season, Barnum was involved with the Centennial exhibition in Philadelphia. The Smithsonian, always eager to keep so prominent a donor in good humor, was happy to comply with his request.

## (173)

## TO OLIVER WENDELL HOLMES

Tremont House [Boston], 19 June 1876

My dear Dr. Holmes,

Gratitude for your kindness inspires me to assure you that I should never have presumed to *think* of placing your name on one of my "posters," as you laughingly suggested to-day.

I simply desire the public to be assured by a gentleman so widely known & honored that my tattooed man is *genuine*. If I can in any manner reciprocate your great courtesy, pray command me.

Truly yours,

P. T. Barnum

The tattooed man was the famous Captain Djordji Costentenus, completely decorated from his scalp to the soles of his feet, who first appeared with the circus this year. Barnum later published an endorsement of this phenomenon, signed by Holmes and others, in his advance couriers.

## (174)

## TELEGRAM TO RUTHERFORD B. HAYES

Bridgeport, 17 February 1877

No favors wanted, but for country's sake thank God for your election.

P. T. Barnum

## Barnum's Tattooed Nobleman.

A FULL DESCRIPTION OF THE WONDER.

[From the Bridgeport (Conn.) Daily Standard.]

"We saw at ex-Mayor Barnum's residence, this morning, a wonder of tattooing on the person of Capt. Georges Costentenus, a descendant of a noble Greek family, from the province of Albania. His statement is that while he, together with an American and a Spaniard, were mining in Chinese Tartary, in 1867, a rebellion arose, and the three joined the insurgents. Ill luck coming to their cause, they were taken prisoners, and subjected to the tattooing process for three months, as a punishment in lieu of having their heads cut off. He says that the process causes such terrible pain that it required six men to hold him while one performed the operation. After it was completed, all three escaped from prison, but the American only survived five or six months. The Spaniard lost his eyesight, and died in Morilla; but Capt. Costentenus survives and is in good health. The tattooing was done with indigo and cinnabar, producing blue and red colors; and there is not a single point on his body which is not covered with these colors, so that it is impossible to discover what was the natural color of his skin except by his ears and the soles of his feet, which are the only parts they did not tattoo. He appeared at first sight as though he was clothed with very close-fitting tights, made of a shawl or of very soft, fine drugget. Upon a close inspection, however, it is seen that he is entirely naked, and that the apparent tights are an illusion. Moreover, his whole person is found to be covered with a great variety of animal figures, with their names most ingeniously and skillfully printed into the cuticle. On the forehead are animals and inscriptions, and on the face star-like figures. On the hands are numerous red points and figures resembling sculptures, as well as long tailed panther-like shapes. On the neck, chest, abdomen, back, and extremities, the skin is a mass of symmetrically arranged and admirably exe-

## THE MIRACLE OF MORTAL MARVELS

CAPT. GEORGES COSTENTENUS, a Noble Greek Albanian,

## Tattooed from Head to Foot!

In Chinese Tartary, as punishment for engaging in rebellion against the King.

**Every Inch of his Body is Covered with 388 Beautifully-delineated Figures, in Indigo and Cinnabar, of Beasts, Birds, Fishes, Reptiles and Hieroglyphics!**

The prolonged and horrible agony of this combination of Barbaric art and vengeance necessitating

## OVER 7,000,000 BLOOD-PRODUCING PUNCTURES

Medical men pronounce him the most illustrious of human prodigies, and the Press declares him a veritable miracle among mortal marvels. Read what the celebrated Dr. Oliver Wendell Holmes and other leading Boston physicians testify of him:

"This person is remarkable as combining in one exhibition a picture gallery, a menagerie of strange animals (in their portraiture), including one not unlike the Dodo, and a proof of how much suffering man can inflict or a man can bear, the constitution accommodating itself to conditions which might seem incompatible with health and even with life. It is the most perfect specimen of genuine tattooing which any of us have ever seen.

| O. W. HOLMES, | JOSEPH S. JONES, |
| R. M. HODGES, | S. J. McDOUGAL." |
| SAMUEL A. GREEN, | |

---

## I WILL GIVE

## FIFTY THOUSAND DOLLARS

For the production of half as extensive and perfect a piece of Tattooing, or for the correct deciphering of the Hieroglyphics upon his body.

cuted figures of monkeys, tigers, lions, elephants, peacocks, storks, swans, snakes, crocodiles, lizards, mingled with bows, arrows, leaves, flowers, and fruits; on the palms of the hands are indescribable figures, and little figures on the inside of the fingers. On the back and sides of both feet to the toes are blue points, and from the toes to the nails red lines. Altogether there are 388 tattooed pictures on the entire body—on the forehead, 2; neck, 8; chest, 56; back, 37; abdomen, 52; upper extremities, 101; lower extremities, 137. He is certainly one of the greatest human curiosities ever seen. He has traveled in all countries except America, and is attracted here by the Centennial Exhibition. He spoke English, French, Spanish and Italian, this morning, and he understands the Arabic, Persian and several other languages. He is about five feet ten inches high, has a superb physique; his hair is straight, jet black and glossy. To the touch his skin has a very soft, velvety feeling; and it has so much the appearance of being clothed, that he might walk through the public streets without any one suspecting that he was not dressed in tights.

### Cheap Excursion Trains.

I employ a competent railroad man to make special arrangements for CHEAP EXCURSION TRAINS, to run at convenient hours, over all railroads, to the places where my great show exhibits.

### Free for the Orphans.

When attending in a body, and in charge of their proper guardian, the inmates of all orphan asylums will be admitted free to the afternoon exhibition of my great show. This recognition of the little ones originated with me, and I have invariably kept it up for many years.

---

BARNUM'S TATTOOED MAN, CAPTAIN COSTENTENUS, as represented in the 1879 issue of the showman's "advance courier." The endorsement of the genuineness of the Captain by Oliver Wendell Holmes and others is at lower center.

# (175)

## TO SAMUEL L. CLEMENS

Bridgeport, 10 October 1877

My dear Mark,

You *can't* well have more *begging* letters than I do, & you have, I hope, learned to say *no* pretty often. But *here* is a *peculiar* case. (I always notice that each case is singularly aggravating.)

I have promised to lecture or talk for a poor church in Bridgeport *sometime* this autumn (indefinite enough), and I want to add one or two things that will help fill our little opera house. I know you have "reformed" as to lecturing, but it struck me that perhaps in this one *horrible* case (it *is* a case of *real* charity) you would run down and *introduce* the speaker. This would be the make-weight that would fill the house & do a world of good. Of course, expenses would be paid with pleasure & a thousand thanks. Now can't you bring Mrs. Clemens & the *babies* & visit and do good at same time? This once, & I will *never*, NEVER, NEVER ask a like favor of you.

As ever yours,

P. T. Barnum

[*hand*] Take a day & night or more for *reflection* if at first you feel impelled to say "no." My little wife joins in kind regards to you & yours.

B

Twain replied that he was busy working on a book.

# (176)

## TO WHITELAW REID

*Private*

Bridgeport, 10 January 1878

My dear Mr. Reid,

As an old friend of Mr. Greeley and a swearer by the *Tribune* from the first day it started, I appeal to you *confidentially* in a matter which *may* be of import to me.

If Mr. Jewell & Genl. Hawley both fail to get the nomination for U.S. Senator, there will be half a dozen or more Republican candidates to select from. Assurances from some of my fellow members in the legislature indicate that my name will be among that number. When the fact becomes prominent, I hope and believe you will give me a fair showing and let the *Tribune* copy favorable notices which respectable papers in this state may make of me. They will be but few—if any—inasmuch as the papers are chiefly enlisted either for Hawley, Jewell, Platt, or Harrison. I only ask that my being a *showman* shall not obscure any good qualities which I may happen to be credited with.

Please excuse this intrusion upon your time & oblige

Truly yours,

P. T. Barnum

As with Barnum's earlier hopes of entering the U.S. Congress, nothing came of this scheme, either.

## {177}

## TO SAMUEL L. CLEMENS

Bridgeport, 10 January 1878

My dear Clemens,

This is a *begging letter*! *Awful*!!

I know your minutes and words are gold & diamonds, but I really *want* 5 or 10 minutes and as many lines over your fist, & I'll surely do as much for you or some other good fellow.

I think it is conceded that I generally do pretty *big* things as a manager, am audacious in my outlays and risks, give *much* for *little* money, and make my shows worthy the support of the moral & refined classes.

In my next season's traveling announcements I want a few words from distinguished gentlemen, which I shall class under the head of "Congratulatory utterances &c. &c. upon Mr. Barnum's career as an amusement manager."

Now my dear boy, I come to you for a character! I *hope* it is not in vain.

Sincerely yours,

P. T. Barnum

. . . .

## (178)

## TO SAMUEL L. CLEMENS

Bridgeport, 14 January 1878

All right, Mark. It's only a matter of taste anyhow—& I am *content*.

Of course, I did not want a quack doctor's certificate. But if "Mark" could have said as if to a third party something like what you once said in a letter to me, that the greatest wonder about Barnum's show is how it is possible to give so much for so little, or had you said the greatest wonder is to see a man who can manage & control so *big* an affair, or something else—it would have been *nice*. But really I am *quite satisfied* & don't suppose it will make any difference with the *big show*.

As ever thine,

P. T. Barnum

Barnum continued to correspond occasionally with Twain following this latest refusal, but there appears to have been a definite cooling in their relationship.

## (179)

## TO OLIVER WENDELL HOLMES

Bridgeport, 22 April 1878

My dear Dr. Holmes,

On the 27th May I shall come down on Boston like an avalanche. My horses beat the world, and I want you to share

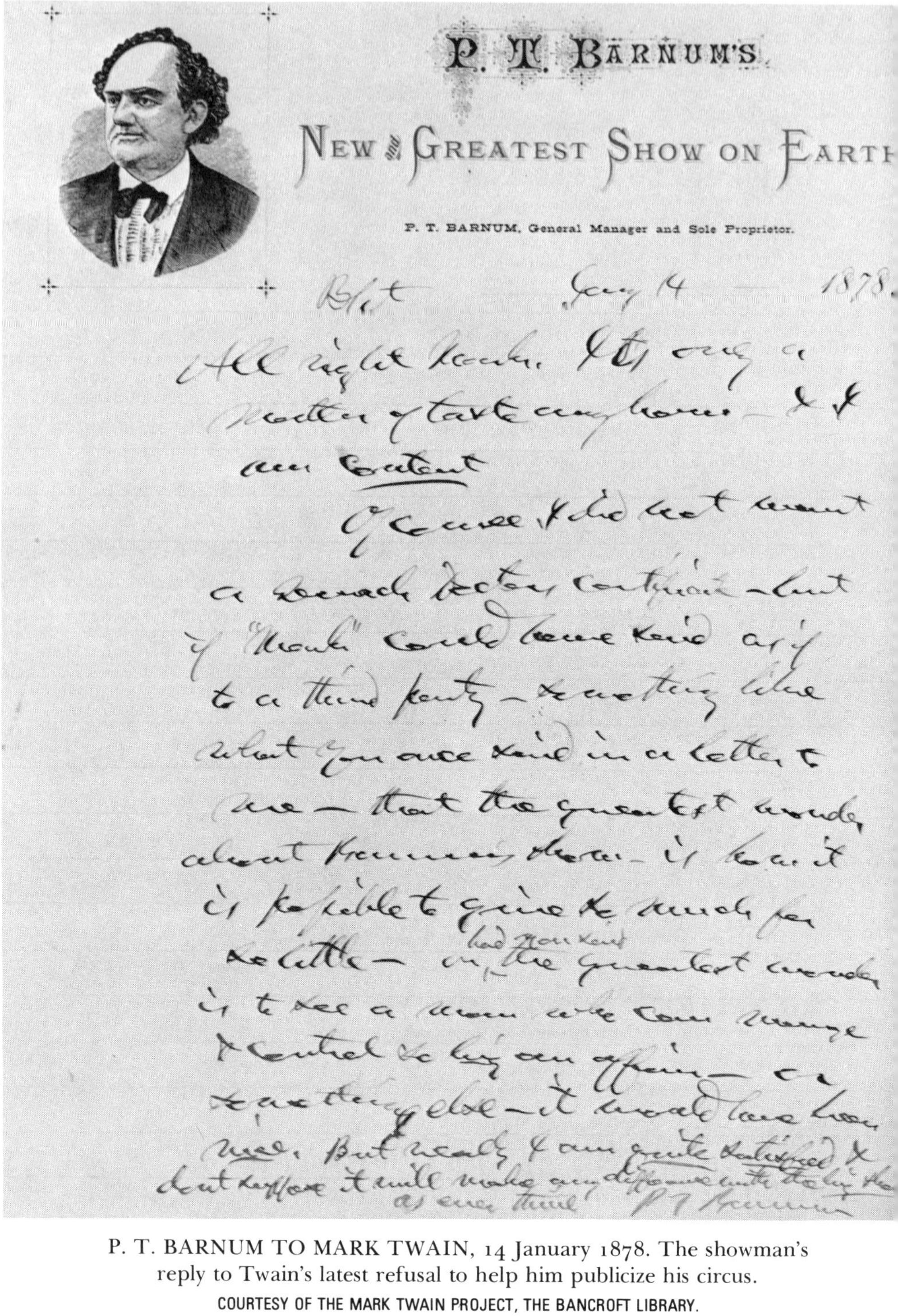

P. T. BARNUM'S

NEW & GREATEST SHOW ON EARTH

P. T. BARNUM, General Manager and Sole Proprietor.

Bpt Jany 14 — 1878.

All right Mark. It's only a matter of taste anyhow—& I am content.

Of course I did not want a regular doctor's certificate—but if "Mark" could have said as if to a third party—something like what you once said in a letter to me—that the greatest wonder about Barnum's show is how it is possible to give so much for so little—or, had you said the greatest wonder is to see a man who can manage & control so big an affair—or something else—it would have been nice. But really I am quite satisfied & dont suppose it will make any difference with the big show as ever.

P T Barnum

P. T. BARNUM TO MARK TWAIN, 14 January 1878. The showman's reply to Twain's latest refusal to help him publicize his circus.

COURTESY OF THE MARK TWAIN PROJECT, THE BANCROFT LIBRARY.

in the enjoyment which they give to all lovers of that noble animal.

Tattoo & the "Dodo" are still on hand.

Very truly yours,

P. T. Barnum

## (180)

### TO JOHN GREENLEAF WHITTIER

Especially after his marriage to Nancy Fish, who entertained a passion for American authors, Barnum improved upon every occasion to cultivate men of letters.

Bridgeport, 20 May 1878

Although probably not an ardent amusement seeker, I feel confident that so delightful a poet as John G. Whittier would be pleased to witness the marvellous intelligence exhibited by my beautiful trained stallions.

As the other features of my show are unexceptionable, I earnestly hope you will visit it in Boston next week.

Your admirer,

P. T. Barnum

## (181)

### TO HENRY WADSWORTH LONGFELLOW

Bridgeport, 21 May 1878

Dear Sir,

If there is such a thing as "poetry of motion," I think it may be found in the movements of my marvelous *trained stal-*

*lions,* and it seems meet that America's greatest poet should see them, especially as all other parts of our exhibition are unobjectionable. I hope therefore that you will kindly do me the honor to accept & use the enclosed tickets. We don't go nearer your residence than Boston, where we remain from 27 inst. till June 1st inclusive.

> Respectfully yours,
>
> P. T. Barnum

## (182)

## TO SCHUYLER COLFAX

Schuyler Colfax (1823–85) had been Vice-President under Grant. He was an admirer of freaks and circuses and appears to have been something of a connoisseur.

> Bridgeport, 3 August 1878

My dear Mr. Colfax,

Your favor recd. Thanks for your previous hints. They will be adopted. I will *never* have a pad act ridden in my ring after this season—*all bareback* riders—and I will have no double acts nor engage any performance which is not worth seeing *alone.* I *think* also I will never again permit candy & lemonade to be peddled, but furnish *free* ice water for my patrons. The truth is, I would abandon the show business if *cash* was my only reward. I want to *elevate* traveling exhibitions and *reform* them altogether, for they are an *important* power for good or evil.

I had sent my advertiser a copy of a portion of your commendatory letter, rather as a gratification to *him*—but lest he might copy from it for the press, I have sent him your letter *last* recd., with strict injunctions to *never* make use of your letters in print.

[208]

With kind regards to Mrs. Colfax & young "Schuyler,"
I am

Truly yours,

P. T. Barnum

P. S. Whenever you come here again I must claim you & yours
as guests.

P. T. B.

(183)

## TO SCHUYLER COLFAX

Bridgeport, 15 August 1878

My dear Mr. Colfax,

Your kind letter of the 8th came while I was at the White
Mountains, whence wife & I have just returned.

Your advice is *excellent,* and I almost think you ought to
have been a *showman*! But curb your aspirations—it is not for
all men to attain such dizzy heights! To be Vice-President of
the U.S. and to be able to *instruct* showmen (which *you are*) is
something.

I shall certainly adopt several & perhaps all of your hints
and suggestions. They are *all* correct. I have *seen* the woman
shot from the cannon and have been trying for a year to get
her. Hope to succeed.

I hope your "juniors" won't break their necks in their
imitations of the circus. These imitations succeed our show all
over the country, and I often fear to hear of serious accidents
thereby.

An excellent neighbor of mine is getting up a large cattle ranch company for Colorado, where he is already largely
interested, as well as myself. It is a perfectly *square, honest en-*

terprise—not a *drop* of *water* in the stock—and it is by far the best & safest investment I ever saw. A few thousand invested for each of a man's children would not only pay large *annual* dividends, but would make the children rich. If I can get one or two of my neighbor's (Sherwood) circulars, I shall mail them to you for self & friends.

My ranch & cattle are worth $140,000, but I turn them into the large co. at $100,000 and take that amount of stock, simply because a ranch of 20,000 cattle will pay much greater dividends than 6000. In haste,

Truly yours,

P. T. Barnum

The human projectile, shot from the mouth of a cannon to the arms of a partner hanging from a trapeze, was Zazel, who did indeed eventually appear with the "big show."

## {{184}}

## TO A. H. HANGER

Bridgeport, 26 April 1879

Dear Sir,

Your letter is received. You must excuse my abruptness on meeting you at my house. But when I reflected that a poor man had paid expenses to Bridgeport & remained a day or two on expense, which might all have been saved by writing a letter, I felt vexed at such unwisdom. The truth is, I receive more than a hundred letters per week from strangers asking for assistance. To respond favorably to all would take my last penny in a few months.

The drafts on my charity from persons whom I person-ally know—and for great calamities by fire, flood, yellow fever,

&c.—exhaust all I can spare. Besides sir, it is better for you to not depend upon charity from strangers. If I could furnish you a situation to earn your living, I would gladly do so. But that is *impossible*. Every place is full, & I have hundreds of applicants waiting. Try *nearer home* & depend upon your own exertions & good habits.

Truly yours,

P. T. Barnum

## (185)

## TO UNIDENTIFIED CORRESPONDENT

Bridgeport, 6 May 1879

My dear Aleck,

If it don't rain you ought to get Uncle Harry to see the procession & also to get a reserved seat & see the show. It is the *best* he will see this side of paradise.

Truly yours,

P. T. Barnum

## (186)

## CIRCULAR LETTER TO VARIOUS EDITORS

Bridgeport, 10 May 1879

Editors of the *Mercury:*

An imposter is preceding my show some ten days who represents himself as my agent, obtains advertisements (paid in advance), and falsely promises the advertisers that he will insert them in my programme and circulate them in my show tents. The scoundrel ought to be arrested for obtaining money under false pretences. If you expose him in your columns, you will protect your citizens from imposition and oblige

P. T. Barnum

This letter is in a secretary's hand, although signed and dated by Barnum.

## (187)

## TO EDITOR OF THE *ALBANY ARGUS*

Bridgeport, 8 May 1880

Dear Sir,

After spending a week in Boston, my great show will reach Albany at a single run. You have no doubt seen what marvellous success it is meeting everywhere, and how universally press & people pronounce it immensely superior to all my former efforts. As we can stay but one day in Albany, I hope you have sufficient faith in my assurances to inform your readers what an unprecedented treat they will receive on the 17th inst.

Very truly yours,

P. T. Barnum

# (188)

## TO J. A. MCGONAGLE

Bridgeport, 21 July 1880

Dear Sir,

Your letter of inquiry is received. My impression is that I am not dead.

P. T. Barnum

McGonagle, a native of Cherokee, Iowa, had written to say that in his part of the country Barnum was commonly believed to be dead. A letter from the showman would allow him to prove otherwise.

# (189)

## TO JAMES A. BAILEY

In late 1880, after a period of intense rivalry between their two circuses, Barnum entered into partnership with James A. Bailey and James L. Hutchinson, thereby forming the great combination that eventually came to be known as Barnum & Bailey. While it is popularly believed that the aging showman was more or less a "silent" partner in this enterprise, merely lending his name and money to it, there is abundant evidence that he pulled his share of the load, especially in the field of public relations. He also busily scouted and acquired various novelties for the show, kept an eye on competitors and laid plans to buy them out, eagerly sought the endorsements of prominent individuals, and visited the circus whenever he could, on which occasions he himself was always considered one of the chief attractions.

Bridgeport, 16 October 1880

Dear Sir,

I sent you to Washington copy of a rough draft I had of our agreement. Perhaps I omitted a paragraph in which it was agreed that my big show & the London should at no time come in contact or near each other &c., but the general tenor

[213]

of the agreement, locked in escrow in my lawyer's hands, is the same as I sent you.

Men who desire to do *right* have no misunderstandings or disagreements, so I guess we shall both do as we agreed.

Truly yours,

P. T. Barnum

## {{190}}

## TO JOSEPH ROSWELL HAWLEY

Joseph Roswell Hawley (1826–1905), soldier, editor, Republican governor of Connecticut, and U.S. Congressman, served in the U.S. Senate from 1881 until the time of his death. This letter, in a very deteriorated state, is in reference to Barnum's recent unsuccessful run for the Connecticut senate on the Republican ticket.

Bridgeport, 9 November [1880]

My dear General,

I don't know that I was ever more delighted with the results of an election than with the one just closed. There is no magnifying the good results which are likely to be achieved from it before 1884. My most ardent desire now is to see you in the U.S. Senate, as I have no doubt I shall if my life is spared till 4th March next. I have seen & written several of our Republican members elect and urged your election. I find thus far but *one* wish and intention, and that is surely to give you this reward for your arduous & faithful services for the right.

I never had any real taste for office, & now in my 71st year I have a real dislike for it. Our friends & neighbors the Mallorys over-urged me to run for the state senate on the ground that it was naturally democra[tic] & possibly I might carry it. As we already have a Republican legislative majority, I am *very* g[lad I] was not elected. To have spent t[he ?winter ?months] even in your pleasant city of Hartford, when my arrangements were all made to spend them among my children

[214]

and grandchildren in New York, would have been a sacrifice which neither my wife, self, or family felt willing to have made.

But I feel a deep interest in seeing you & other capable and worthy citizens *advance* in our government, & I thank God for the prospect that our country is fast getting back on the right track—South as well as North—and that on the only true plan of "conciliation": the fulfilment of the *laws by* the South exactly the same as by the North.

Sincerely yours,

P. T. Barnum

P.S. I see that the scoundrelly N.Y. St[ate] Dem. Co[mm.] are going to fight against our triumph in that stat[e. Wm.] H. Barnum, John Kelley, & ⅔ds of the Democratic [party] ought to be hung.

P. T. B.

{191}

## TO SECRETARY OF THE TESTIMONIAL ASSOCIATION FOR MRS. RUTHERFORD B. HAYES

Bridgeport, 27 January 1881

Secy. Testimonial Association:

I have mailed you today the two parchment sheets which you sent me and placed thereon, as you desired, a sentiment & my autograph.

Mrs. Hayes deserves the highest honors for the noble stand which she took in excluding wines & liquors from the White House.

Truly yours,

P. T. Barnum

[215]

SCENES FROM THE LIFE OF "THE SUN OF THE AMUSEMENT WORLD."

LARGE COLOR POSTER BY THE STROBRIDGE LITHOGRAPH CO., c. 1881.
COURTESY OF THE BARNUM MUSEUM, BRIDGEPORT.

The above letter accompanied "The Autographic Illinois State Testimonial to Mrs. President Hayes," on which form Barnum wrote and subscribed himself as follows:

We honor the brave men who have died to defend their country from material danger.

We honor no less the moral courage that has fought a bloodless battle to save the nation from moral ruin & championed a noble and unpopular cause in high places.

P. T. Barnum

Director of Moral & Refined
Exhibitions for the Amusement
& Instruction of the Public

Mrs. Hayes was popularly referred to as "Lemonade Lucy" on account of her famous nonalcoholic parties at the White House.

{192}

## TO JAMES A. GARFIELD

Bridgeport, 12 March 1881

*No office wanted!*
My dear Mr. President,

About all the favor I ask from you is, do please have the kindness to *live*, & then I know our country will be blessed.

I send by this mail a small book which I hope may edify your children.

The immediate object of this letter is to prepare Your Excellency to receive & accept in due time an invitation to your family which I shall send, to attend my truly "Greatest Show on Earth" in Washington about 17th or 18th April.

This last great crowning effort of my managerial life so far surpasses all similar exhibitions in the world that I am extremely anxious to have it visited by you and Mrs. Garfield *in*

[217]

*person* at the commencement of my traveling season. Hence I take this liberty of preparing your mind for the *great occasion*! Of course, your family will be included in the invitation and *special* arrangements will be made for your & their comfort.

Truly yours,

P. T. Barnum

Garfield was shot less than four months after this letter was written.

( 193 )

## TO PUBLISHER OF *GOLDEN DAYS* FOR *BOYS AND GIRLS*

*Private*

England, 8 June 1881

Dear Sir,

There is no subject, I think, which interests children more than accounts of wild animals—their capture, training, & performances—unless it is a *circus*. Now there *never was* so extensive & interesting a traveling menagerie or circus as mine is this year, & probably there will not be its equal again in this generation, for really it is too colossal to handle easily. If you would like to publish one or two or more chapters under the title

*A Month with Barnum*
*His Wild Beasts, Museum and Circus*

or a title equivalent to that, and choose to send a proper writer and draughtsman along with my show connected with the Great London Circus for a week or two or more, my partners, managers, & assistants will furnish them *every detail* connected with the subject of forming, creating, & conducting shows of this kind and give them a chance to witness the *system* which pervades the whole: the loading and unloading of the R.R. cars, the lightning rapidity with which our immense tents are erected and taken down, &c. &c. Your men will have free access to our show—its cook tents, stable tents, dressing rooms, sideshows, &c.—and also eat free of expense at our eating tents, where several kinds of meat & good "trimmings" are always provided, & where my managers eat. I remain in England a few weeks longer, but I have informed my managers & partners, Messrs. Bailey and Hutchinson, that I should write you this letter, and if your gentlemen call on them *with this letter,* they will be pleasantly received & provided for, including passage in our cars from town to town. . . .

Of course, I expect such articles will increase my notoriety among the juveniles in some degree—but that it will add greatly to the satisfaction & delight of your readers, you will, I think, readily comprehend. . . .

Truly yours,

P. T. Barnum

P.S. You are probably aware that my exhibitions are patronized by the religious classes—being always refined & free from vulgarity, profanity, &c.

P. T. B.

*Golden Days for Boys and Girls* was a children's magazine published in Philadelphia.

# {194}

## TO H. E. BOWSER

In early 1880 Henry E. Bowser succeeded J. J. Gorham as Barnum's accountant and secretary. He soon became one of Barnum's most trusted agents and remained in his employ until Barnum's death. "Hugh" was Hugh Brady, Barnum's coachman.

Southport [England], 20 June 1881

My dear Bowser,

. . . I am sorry that you did not know I never permit my horses, carriages, or any private property purchased for my own personal use to be used by anybody else. This rule is invariable and inflexible. Any deviation from it would demoralize Hugh and every employee of mine, besides giving me constant annoyance. The same rule applies to taking persons through my house without special permission. My private personal affairs I always have kept distinct from *business*. A moment's reflection ought, I think, to show the wisdom of this. I was always equally particular about making any *business place* or office a resort or lounging place for anybody. *Business* considerations should *never* be mixed up with other affairs. . . .

Truly yours,

P. T. Barnum

. . . .

# {195}

## TO H. E. BOWSER

Bowser was assisted in his duties by Charles R. Brothwell and Benjamin Fish. The latter was the cousin of Barnum's wife Nancy and traveled with the circus as Barnum's personal representative and bookkeeper. By the 1880s Barnum was again heavily involved in real estate speculations. He had loaned Bowser money to purchase a lot and house, and therefore felt free to regale his defenseless employee with the same homiletic advice he was wont to dispense from the lecture platform.

Mr. H. E. Bowser, I am pleased with your way of doing business—your system, promptness, and *push* which keep our matters up snug and *clear* so they can all be understood—and I am glad to believe that you have no personal favorites when conducting my business. I have directed my executors to continue you in your present position if in my employ at my decease. I intend, however, to hold on some years yet, and to that end I want to be kept clear of *care*. My study is to have you & Brothwell & Ben Fish have most of the care of details. The more confidence that I can have that you three "watchdogs" prevent all possible leaks (& cheats), the longer and the happier I shall live. I doubt whether my *net* income will be as much next year as this, for crops are short and the *furore* created by combining the two shows has somewhat abated, and my managers seem to be making great expenditures for next season. I hope & believe, however, that your cares and duties will *increase* instead of diminish. Building more houses and the general increase of details in all branches of my business will give you extra care & labor, for it is absolutely *necessary* that you become & continue *familiar* with all these details. Of course your continued *experience* makes the task easier, but "eternal vigilance" on your part is *absolutely necessary*. Every person I employ needs to be kept prompt to his work. All who owe must be made to pay promptly, and nobody be permitted to cheat, overcharge, or "play old soldier."

In consideration of these facts and in the full expectation that you will as heretofore serve me faithfully, "in season and out of season," with an eye single to my interests, I propose to pay you two thousand ($2000) for next year, beginning Jany. 1st 1882—say $38.50 per week, making $2002 per year. I only hope that you will for your own sake apply this extra salary and all the rest you can save to paying your *indebtedness*. There is more pleasure in saving than in spending, and if you begin your married life by securing all real solid *comforts,* avoiding luxuries, extravagancies, & a desire to splurge & make a show, you will find yourself gradually growing on towards independence. We can't "eat our cake & keep it." Therefore real frugality (such as few Americans know), without being mean or denying ourselves such conveniences & comforts as we can afford, result [*sic*] in the most happiness. You ought not to sink so much on a big house unless you gain it by keeping boarders. Of course I say these things for your good only.

Truly yours,

P. T. Barnum

## (196)

## TO H. B. BULT

Bridgeport, 1 December 1881

Dear Sir,

Thanks for the trouble you took to send copy of my picture. I confess that I don't like the old style as well as the modern. It is probably owing to my lack of taste.

Truly yours,

P. T. Barnum

## (197)

## TELEGRAM TO MR. LESARGE, EDITOR OF THE LONDON *DAILY TELEGRAPH*

Early in 1882, over the strenuous objections of the British public, Parliament, and Victoria herself, Barnum succeeded in purchasing the great African elephant Jumbo from the London Zoological Society. The present telegram was sent in reply to a cable from the editor of the London *Daily Telegraph*, asking Barnum to name the price for which he would cancel the sale.

[222]

New York, 23 February 1882

My compliments to editor *Daily Telegraph* and British nation. Fifty-one millions of American citizens anxiously awaiting Jumbo's arrival. My forty years' invariable practice of exhibiting the best that money could procure makes Jumbo's presence here imperative. Hundred thousand pounds would be no inducement to cancel purchase. My largest tent seats 20,000 persons and is filled twice each day. It contains four rings, in three of which three full circus companies give different performances simultaneously. In the large outer ring, or racing track, the Roman hippodrome is exhibited. In two other immense connecting tents my colossal zoological collection and museum are shown. . . . Wishing long life and prosperity to British nation and *Telegraph* and Jumbo, I am the public's obedient servant,

P. T. Barnum

## (198)

### TO UNIDENTIFIED CORRESPONDENT

New York, 7 March 1882

I send cards as you request. I am too full of elephants to command much *sentiment*. All my thoughts & cares at present are locked up in two *trunks*—one of which belongs to *Jumbo* & the other to little "Bridgeport."

If both trunks arrive in New York and our citizens possess the keys, a world of treasure will be exposed to public view.

Truly yours,

P. T. Barnum

[223]

JUMBO IN CHAINS. An example of the publicity engineered by Barnum
in advance of the great elephant's arrival in America.

"Bridgeport" or "Baby Bridgeport," the second elephant born in America, first saw the light at the Bridgeport winter quarters on 2 February. Jumbo did not arrive in New York to join the circus until 9 April.

# (199)

## TO CARRIE BAILEY

"Carrie" Bailey, who lived in Yonkers, New York, was Barnum's grand-niece through his first wife Charity Hallett's side of the family. Barnum's second wife Nancy, despite her youth, was frequently ill and was sometimes described as a "semi-invalid."

Philadelphia, 24 April 1882

My dear Carrie,

Your welcome letter found me here, where I remain alone with Jumbo & the show till Friday (unless I run to New York & back Thursday). Then on Friday I go to Washington and stay till the following Tuesday, then go to Baltimore for 2 days, & return to Sturtevant House [*New York*] 4th or 5th May and *wait there* for Nancy to get well & sail with me to England 27th May. I thought I would rather be alone in these 3 cities with the show than alone in New York with nothing to do.

I was *very sorry* when I read your letter to learn that you had been to the show and I had not seen you. I hope to see you before we sail. If you can drop a line to a *lonesome* young gentleman that will cheer him up, pray do so and say *"Personal"* on envelope, else Jumbo may get it. Love to all. . . .

Truly yours,

P. T. Barnum

## (200)

### TO NATHANIEL P. BEERS

New York, 25 May 1882

My dear Nate,

Yours recd. I have no dwarfs who can use piano. I am off for London in *City of Rome* Saturday. In haste,

Truly yours,

P. T. Barnum

## (201)

### CIRCULAR LETTER TO VARIOUS U.S. OFFICIALS &C. LIVING ABROAD

Bridgeport, 9 August 1882

Dear Sir,

I desire to carry out as far as possible an idea I have long entertained of forming a collection, in pairs or otherwise, of all the uncivilized races in existence, and my present object is to ask you kindly to render me what assistance is in your power to acquire any specimens of these uncivilized peoples.

My aim is to exhibit to the American public not only human beings of different races, but also, when practicable, those who possess extraordinary peculiarities, such as giants, dwarfs, singular disfigurements of the person, dexterity in the use of weapons, dancing, singing, juggling, unusual feats of strength or agility, &c.

With this object in view, I should be glad to receive from you descriptions of as many of such specimens as you could

[226]

obtain, and photographs as far as possible, even if it is necessary to send an agent into the interior for the purpose.

The remuneration of these people, in addition to their board and travelling expenses, is usually nominal. I shall see that they are presented with fancy articles such as are always acceptable and a small allowance monthly.

If, in any case, a group of 3 to 6 or even 10 would be specially novel, I should probably take them, but I must study economy, inasmuch as I propose to add this "Congress of Nations" to the other attractions of our great show without extra charge.

If interpreters should be absolutely necessary, please inform me what would be the cost, which must be moderate.

For yourself, I should be glad to reimburse you for any proper outlay and give you a reasonable compensation for the trouble which you may take in this matter.

If necessary, I might send a special agent to your country for any specimens which you may bring under my notice, provided they appear to me to warrant such an additional outlay.

If you should meet with any living animals or reptiles, freaks of nature or in any sense rare or unusual, I should be glad to receive and to refund to you the cost of a photograph and full description of the same, but inanimate objects I do not desire.

As it is my wish to get at least a portion of this collection together by January or February 1883, I will thank you kindly to favor me with as early a reply as convenient.

Yours faithfully,

P. T. Barnum

Several copies of this letter, in a hand other than Barnum's although signed by him, are extant. The "Congress of Nations" was a feature of the 1884 season.

## (202)

### TO MESSRS. TIFFANY & CO.

Bridgeport, 14 October 1882

Gentlemen:

I am very glad you sent your bill for eight dollars. I should never have thought of it except for your reminder.

Showmen who make their customers pay *before* they go in should never ask credit. $8 check enclosed.

Truly yours,

P. T. Barnum

## (203)

### TO SPENCER F. BAIRD

Bridgeport, 25 October 1882

My dear Professor,

Thanks for your kind letter. I did not receive your telegram nor was it necessary to send me one. I enclose you copy of letters which we have sent to every American minister & consul in any part of the world. If you will spare your valuable time to read my printed statement, you will see I am placing & sending agents to *every* part of our little ball of earth. Before the agents reach our consuls, most of them will have recd. our circular written letter. We have already engaged a party of *Nubians*—men, women, and children, twenty-five in number—& we hope to have 150 specimens of semi-civilized, or rather *uncivilized*, living specimens by spring.

Now when our agents strike *Holland* or Dutch *colonies*,

we have before found that the authorities are *reluctant* about letting their people leave the country unless they are first satisfied that the party taking them is responsible and will return them according to agreement. My managers & myself are good and responsible for several millions of dollars and don't owe a farthing in the world, but the thing will be to *convince the authorities* in New Zealand, Siam, and other distant places of *that fact.* One agent writes me from *Sydney* that he needs from me an indorsement of the U.S. Secretary of State, but I think from former experience this is impracticable. It struck me, however, that the Smithsonian Institution, with its big seal &c., might be about as effective as any document from *other* branches of the U.S. government, & therefore I hasten to trespass most unwarrantably upon your time by laying these facts before you, in the hope that you will kindly think of some manner in which you & your institution will be willing to supply some document which, when shown to these foreign governments, will convince them that our firm are *responsible* for the return of any people or animals (including, *sub rosa,* a white elephant from Siam) which we may agree to return.

Very truly yours,

P. T. Barnum

*Postscript.* Of course I don't want the Smithsonian nor any institution or person to guarantee us in the remotest manner, but we need that some prominent public authority should state the facts about our great & successful show and that we are regarded by our best citizens as gentlemen of honor & responsibility &c. &c. *Something* that will *show* to these governments that we are solid, honorable, & reliable.

Yours &c.,

P. T. B.

Baird had become Secretary of the Smithsonian in 1878. The donation of dead animals to the Smithsonian was continuing apace, and around this time, too, Barnum was sending Baird suggestions for the creation of a national zoological garden, eventually realized in 1891. That he was also once more thinking of a permanent museum is established by a letter from Baird dated 9 May 1882: "If you start a museum in New York with first-class aquaria &c., I shall be happy to place the vessels &c. under my charge at your service in supplying the stock. I can promise almost anything that is to be found in the North Atlantic" (*Smithsonian Institution Archives*). The "printed statement" referred to was an article published in the *New York Clipper*. Needless to say, Barnum got his letter of endorsement.

**(204)**

## TO REV. DIXON SPAIN

By his own admission Barnum was a liberal imbiber of spirits and a mighty smoker of "segars" in his youth. After realizing the effect his drinking was having on himself and others, he poured the contents of his wine cellar onto his lawn, begged his friend the Rev. E. H. Chapin for a copy of the "pledge," and thereafter became one of the most popular and persistent platform lecturers in the temperance movement. The smoking habit he also eventually conquered, and he was proud of having never succumbed to that other peculiarly American vice so wasteful of time: baseball. The present letter was expressly written for use by the English branch of the temperance crusade, and was edited and altered by another hand, presumably that of the Rev. Dixon Spain. The original writing is here restored.

Bridgeport, 18 November 1882

My dear Mr. Spain,

I have been both sides of the fence in this liquor-drinking custom, and I *know* whereof I speak. From 1840 to 1848 I was a pretty free drinker and prouder of my "wine cellar" than any of my other possessions. Thirty-two years ago I became a total abstainer. Had I not done so, I should doubtless have been in my grave long since, for I had gone so far in the miserable and ruinous habit of "treating," being treated, and "liquoring up" that this unnatural appetite would soon have become stronger than resolution, and I should have succumbed as thousands do every year.

If men would fill their pockets with cold boiled potatoes every morning, and whenever they met a friend would draw out a potato, take a bite, and say, "Here is your good health, my boy," it might appear ludicrous, but it would be a thousand times more sensible than drinking one's "health" in poison, as all intoxicants are. No man has a right to expect good health, a happy home, or financial prosperity who disorders his system, muddles his brain, and wastes time and money in imbibing intoxicating drinks as a beverage. An acquired taste like drinking or using tobacco not only, like all habits, becomes a "second nature," but these particular habits are stronger than nature, because they continually require *increased* quantities to produce the same effects—which is not true of natural appetites.

I am nearly seventy-three years old, have always been actively engaged in business, and still am. I enjoy robust health, am always in good spirits, inclined to hilarity, and enjoy social life exceedingly—but I see no fun in the imbecile mirth caused by strong drink. Most of my numerous employees are total abstainers. Such men make fewer mistakes, can accomplish more bodily or mental labor, and are therefore more reliable than even the best of man who takes the risks of "putting an enemy in his mouth to steal away his brains."

Pure water is the natural drink for man and beast. My lions, tigers, and even the great Jumbo himself drink nothing stronger than water. Their natural strength is enormous, but a constant use of rum, brandy, beer, or "half and half" would disturb their digestive powers, weaken their muscles, poison their blood, and cause suffering, disease, and death—the same as it does in the case of human beings.

There is no more sense in our drinking wine, beer, or any intoxicant when in good health than there is in the Chinaman losing his senses, time, money, and health in smoking opium. It is all a delusion and snare. It is an unmitigated evil, causing more misery and crime than all other evils combined. Indeed, this pernicious habit is the *cause* of by far the greatest portion of the poverty, crime, and suffering found in any country where it exists.

Without this habit, and with the Christian religion, the inhabitants of any country would be clear-headed, intelligent, healthy, prosperous, joyful, and contented.

Truly yours,

P. T. Barnum

## (205)

## TO REV. DIXON SPAIN

Bridgeport, 20 November 1882

My dear Mr. Spain,

I have not the time to *copy* this enclosed hastily written scrawl, but if you can decipher it & find it worth printing (with any verbal alterations which you think proper to make), I will thank you to mail me several copies to above address. In my *Struggles & Triumphs,* published recently by Ward, Lock & Co. of London, you will find several paragraphs relating to intoxicating drinks, in my message as mayor of this city, on page 326—& you may or may not make use of them. The cause of total abstinence is fast gaining ground in the U.S., and as liquor drinking as a beverage is the parent of nearly all the crime, poverty, & misery of Great Britain, I cannot but earnestly wish & pray that it may in a great degree cease in your country as well as the world over.

Truly yours,

P. T. Barnum

# (206)

## TO SPENCER F. BAIRD

Bridgeport, 11 April 1883

My dear Professor Baird,

I am *very* sorry if you could have used our rhinoceros & elephant, for it cost us hundreds of dollars to cut them up & have them carted away. My managers thought you did not want such big things. When these things die they are anxious to get them out of the way *immediately,* & I am sorry they did not have the thoughtfulness to telegraph you.

P.S. I find on inquiry that they sent for the veterinary surgeon Prof. Leotard to cut open the rhinoceros to find cause of death, & then he laid claim to his skeleton for his collection. I try hard to beat it into my partners' heads that your institution *must* have all you want that dies on our hands, & I will *keep trying*—but they are *showmen,* intent only on *pushing* the show to a profit.

We shall have another ostrich & giraffe die this season. Now do you want either if they die as near you as New York?

Truly yours,

P. T. Barnum

*Mum.* The elephant was cut up soon as possible to prevent Bergh's men from looking for wounds.

---

"Bergh" was Henry Bergh, president of the ASPCA, with whom Barnum and his managers had several run-ins. On 13 April Baird wrote in reply that the Smithsonian curators were distressed at not getting the rhinoceros and elephant, but that as "we have our eye on Jumbo, perhaps our not getting the late lamented deceased will not make so much difference" (*Smithsonian Institution Archives*).

## TO REV. E. H. CAPEN

The Rev. Elmer Hewitt Capen (1838–1905) had in 1875 become president of Tufts College, the Universalist school on whose board Barnum had served until the time of his bankruptcy. During his administration the college flourished, with many new buildings being constructed on its Medford campus, among them the Barnum Museum of Natural History, built and endowed by Barnum. Until its destruction by fire in 1975, a notable feature of the museum was its "Barnum Room," in which the mounted hide of Jumbo (who became the school mascot) and other Barnum memorabilia were prominently displayed. The structure has since been rebuilt, although not on so imposing a scale as formerly, and continues as a center for research in the biological sciences.

Bridgeport, 21 April 1883

My dear Mr. Capen,

It is not *likely* that I can do as you suggest, for I have but a short time to stay here, being nearly 73, & am not prepared at present to expend more than I have already arranged for.

Meanwhile, if you have the time to learn what amount of money would accomplish the thing proposed, & let me know *at your leisure,* I will see if there is any chance for it. But I tell you candidly that the chance is so *remote* that I hope you will not hurry in making figures, nor *mention* such a thing to *anybody.*

Truly yours,

P. T. Barnum

## TO REV. E. H. CAPEN

New York, 28 April 1883

Dear Sir,

I *would like* to see you at Bridgeport on your return to Boston for an hour or two's talk, though upon a pinch half an hour *might* do it. . . .

I *think* on reflection there is a *chance* for an *immediate* advancement of the first sum you named, but am not *sure* yet. Meanwhile, please give details your *earnest thought* & keep *mum*.

Truly yours,

P. T. Barnum

## AGREEMENT FOR THE BARNUM MUSEUM OF NATURAL HISTORY

Bridgeport, 3 May 1883

I hereby agree to give to Tufts College in Medford, Mass., the sum of thirty thousand dollars for the erection of a museum of natural history, the same to be erected under the direction of Rev. E. H. Capen, president of the college. This gift is made on the condition and with the understanding that if I add twenty thousand dollars as a fund for the maintenance of the same, the museum shall be forever called The Barnum Museum of Natural History. In case the trustees of Tufts College shall refuse to accept this gift on the foregoing condition, then they shall return to me all sums which they shall have received by virtue of this promise on demand without interest. Said Rev. E. H. Capen affixes his assent to this agreement.

P. T. Barnum

I hereby assent in behalf of Tufts College to the foregoing conditions.

E. H. Capen

(210)

## TO REV. E. H. CAPEN

Bridgeport, 4 May 1883

Dear Sir,

I returned plans to Mr. Rinn by express.

If *stone* will last the longest, perhaps that may be best. If brick are used, would it not be well to make it a little *ornamental* by introducing light-colored brick over windows, doors, & in other parts? The *name* might also be built into the wall with the modern ornamental letters made of terra-cotta, or into the arch over main entrance. Indeed, nice & inexpensive terra-cotta ornamental work is made at Perth Amboy, N.J., now to use on brick buildings effectively. They have an office in New York.

If a niche for a full-length statue or bust could be introduced over the door, it might come in use someday for somebody. You see the passion for *display* is "strong in death," but *you* have the power & *my full permission* to use *your own* judgement and discretion in the matter & let any suggestions which I may offer go for what they are worth *only*.

I shall today write to you a private letter, seal it & address it to you, then place it in an envelope addressed to my

[236]

chief executor, H. E. Bowser, with directions for him to mail it to you immediately after my decease. That letter is written to you to meet the emergency if I should have a sudden "taking off," and in it I bind myself & executors for value received to make the whole gift $50,000. If I get poor I can destroy the letter, but I hope to *live* to hand over the amount in cash & thus make the letter inoperative & unnecessary.

Truly yours,

P. T. Barnum

P.S. In lower corner of all envelopes addressed to me, always please write *"strictly personal."*

P. T. B.

P.S. No. 2. May 5th—My telegrams from Phila. show that my exhibition there is drawing larger audiences than ever before anywhere—so I guess the $50,000 is sure & the $30,000 is *ready* now just as fast as you can use it in the building, and the quicker you get at it and the faster you drive it, the better I shall like it. *Life is short.*

P. T. Barnum

. . . .

## ⟨211⟩

### TO BENJAMIN FISH

Bridgeport, 8 May 1883

My dear Ben,

Last year when I was in Washington I sat for my *bust* to Clark Mills, the artist, who had orders from the Smithsonian

Institution to take it. I want you to call at that institution, see it, & tell me how it looks.

Truly yours,

P. T. Barnum

Mills had actually made a living face mask of Barnum at Spencer Baird's request, in preparation for a bust "to be placed in our series of representations of men who have distinguished themselves for what they have done as promoters of the natural sciences" (Baird to Barnum, 1 May 1882, *Smithsonian Institution Archives*). Unfortunately, the artist died before completing his work, and the bust that eventually went to the Smithsonian was a plaster copy of a later work executed in marble by Thomas Ball. Ball's original bust was destroyed in the 1975 fire at Tufts.

(212)

## TO REV. E. H. CAPEN

Bridgeport, 16 May 1883

Dear Sir,

I have followed your advice and engaged Mr. Thomas Ball to make my bust. I am to visit him in Boston about 10th or 16th June, and as I shall have to remain there several days, I will when there make an appointment to meet you at the college. We *must* keep all *mum*. . . . I prefer to furnish funds along as they may be wanted—not less than $1000 at a time & not faster than they will be needed, as I always keep my bank account close-down. But just as fast as you can make use of it, it shall be forthcoming. You shall have bank drafts in which my name shall not appear.

Truly yours,

P. T. Barnum

# (213)

## TO REV. E. H. CAPEN

Home [Bridgeport], Saturday [16 June 1883]

Dear Sir,

Yours of 13th recd. Sorry to say I must be in Boston with Prof. Thomas Ball next Tuesday & probably remain till Friday. . . . I had better not go to the college, & hereafter I hope you will address me in a *plain envelope,* as it will be quite a triumph if we can escape all suspicion and throw them on the *wrong track.*

On or before Thursday, 21st, the Nassau Bank of New York will place to your credit in the Lincoln Bank at Boston $5000, & the same thing will be done as often as needed till the sum amounts to $30,000. . . .

I told, *privately* & *confidentially,* one of my managers, Mr. Hutchinson, I was going to endow a scientific institution to be called Barnum Museum of Natural History, & I would like to have *Jumbo* mounted & placed there whenever he dies. He replied, "It shall be so, by all means," and as I *also* agree to this, I see no difficulty in securing that immense and unapproachable specimen when he dies, which I hope will be at least fifty years hence.

Truly yours,

P. T. Barnum

Barnum and various institutions, among them the Smithsonian, had been contemplating the final disposition of Jumbo almost since the moment Barnum acquired him.

# (214)

## TO REV. E. H. CAPEN

Crawford House [New Hampshire], 8 July 1883

My dear Dr.,

Yours of 6th recd. I dare not *promise* more than the $50,000 altogether. If I drop off soon & the show don't have better luck, that will be the *maximum*. But if I live a few years longer & prosper financially, I may think it expedient to cheat my grandchildren out of a few thousands more. "A thing of beauty is a joy forever," and we are apt to regret doing a thing cheaply or in an inferior manner. "I came to time" because you thought $25,000 would do for *each* branch upon a pinch, but when you said $30M & $20M, I said O.K. When you again thought $32M would be needed to make the building all that is desirable, I said instead of your waiting *possibly* (but not *probably*) till my death for the $20M, I would furnish $5000 of it in cash as fast as needed—thus leaving $15,000 for the codicil to take care of—though I *think* next season I should, if the building pleased me, hand it over in money.

I shall see my managers both in Montreal—Messrs. Hutchinson & Bailey. They each own ¼ & I ½ of the whole show. Hutchinson gladly consented to let his ¼ of the dead Jumbo go where I want my ½ to go. I expect to get Bailey's consent next week to the same, and so in regard to *all* animals which in future die on our hands. . . .

By the way, you ought to call in the P.M. at Thomas Ball's studio, 6 Bedford St., 3d or 4th story, & see his *Paul Revere* & tell him I desired you to ask him to let you see my bust in its present unfinished state. But if he knows *who* you are, he will smell a rat, for already he suspects it is for a public institution. Thermometer here 65 at noon! Glorious!

Truly yours,

P. T. Barnum

[240]

## (215)

### TO HENRY A. WARD

Prof. Henry A. Ward (1834–1906), the distinguished naturalist and founder of Ward's Natural Science Establishment in Rochester, had dealt with Barnum in the past. With this letter he became one of the principals in a reciprocal and at times rather complex relationship involving Tufts, the Smithsonian, and the circus, whose dead animals were the basis for numerous donations, exchanges, and "credits." This letter is in a hand other than Barnum's, signed by him.

Block Island, R.I., 22 July 1883

Dear Sir,

I want hereafter during this season or longer to have my managers forward to you all specimens which die in our menagerie, and wish you to preserve the skins for me, ready for mounting, including everything from a monkey to an elephant. . . .

Truly yours,

P. T. Barnum

## (216)

### TO HENRY A. WARD

Bridgeport, 9 October 1883

Dear Sir,

. . . I shall have my managers understand that if we lose *Jumbo* (which heaven forbid!) you must be telegraphed to immediately, & hope you will lose no time in saving his skin & skeleton. . . .

Truly yours,

P. T. Barnum

JUMBO WITH HIS KEEPER MATTHEW SCOTT.
COURTESY OF THE BRIDGEPORT PUBLIC LIBRARY

## (217)

## TO REV. E. H. CAPEN

*Private*

Bridgeport, 9 October 1883

My dear Mr. Capen,

On my return last week I found nearly a peck of begging letters, some dozen of which were for assistance in building or repairing churches or helping to pay church debts.

Now I *tremble* for the consequences, not only in the above direction, but in some degree to a possible hard feeling among *heirs & "poor relations."* If, therefore, it were possible to *keep dark* during my life (even if it should be a dozen years) without affecting the pecuniary interests of the institution, it would be a great favor to me. But perhaps you may not be *able* to keep it secret—in fact, I half fear that it has leaked out already & perhaps inspired some of the begging letters above mentioned. Rev. Mr. Gunnison wrote me from Brooklyn asking if his brother might come & talk to me about St. Lawrence University. My secy. Bowser answered that I could not help nor talk about it.

We shall probably send you the remaining $10M *this week* for fear if I don't, I shall be *short* after next week when the show returns & the animals begin to eat their heads off. . . .

Truly yours,

P. T. Barnum

Notations on the back of the 3 May 1883 agreement indicate that Barnum paid the initial $30,000 pledged to Tufts by 31 October of the same year. In addition, he had already sent Capen $250 so that the museum's vestibule might be paved with a superior kind of brick—the first in a series of donations that was to go far beyond the original amount promised.

# (218)

## TO HENRY A. WARD

Bridgeport, 22 October 1883

My dear Professor Ward,

Thanks for your letter. I have sent copy of it to Bailey & Hutchinson. I suppose they would not want you to publish any hint that Jumbo can *ever die,* but I will agree to your using it as an advertisement provided Bailey & Hutchinson consent. If I live another year, I shall want to procure on reasonable terms as possible specimens of natural history for a museum connected with a college in the West.

Truly yours,

P. T. Barnum

Barnum's uncharacteristic fear of publicity in the Tufts business, and his almost pathologic concern over what his heirs and others might do once the word got out, is again evidenced in this letter. Ward himself had not yet been let in on the secret, and the reference to the "college in the West" is a deliberate misdirection. He was finally informed of Barnum's true plans a few weeks later, "under *solemn promise* of never divulging it while I live" (Barnum to Capen, 11 November 1883, *Ward Papers*).

# (219)

## TO GEORGE C. WALDO

Bridgeport, 17 November 1883

My dear Waldo,

Don't for the world *lose* enclosed 51-year-old pamphlet which has just been presented to me.

In 1830 to 34 there was a great rage of fanaticism, 4-day protracted meetings, rantings and curses to hell fire of unbelievers. Many victims ran mad—I published a list of 113 well authenticated cases of insanity, suicide, & murder resulting *directly* from these raving, crazy, fanatical meetings. The pretended libel was on Deacon Seth Seeley of Bethel, *father* to Prof. Seeley, president of Andover. I proved the truth of my charge of note-shaving, which I called "usury," but under a strong charge by Judge David Daggett, who had just been *converted* to orthodoxy, the jury, being told that the "greater the truth, the greater the libel," found me guilty, expecting I might & would only be fined 6d without costs, as they themselves told me. But Judge Daggett sentenced me to imprisonment 60 days and a fine of $100, both of which penalties I paid.

You will see the pamphlet speaks of me as a *young* man (I was then but 22). At that time Universalists were not permitted to testify in a court of justice. I thought that perhaps you might be interested in *reading* this pamphlet. Do as you like about alluding to it in *Standard*—it is of no consequence to me—but pray *return* it to me unscathed.

Truly yours,

P. T. Barnum

George C. Waldo was a close friend of Barnum and editor of the *Bridgeport Standard*. The pamphlet enclosed was no doubt Theophilus Fisk's *The Nation's Bulwark: An Oration on the Freedom of the Press*, delivered on the occasion of Barnum's release from the Danbury jail in 1832.

{220}

## TO EDITOR OF *GOLDEN DAYS* FOR *BOYS AND GIRLS*

Bridgeport, 20 December 1883

Editor of *Golden Days*:

I beg to inform you *confidentially* that another party who publishes a children's paper of considerable popularity is about to send their artist to sketch interesting features of "The Greatest Show on Earth" at its winter quarters here. If you wish to do the same, your artist can go to the Sterling Hotel in Bridgeport as my guest during his stay here. We have a baby sea lion and its mother; a dwarf elephant 12 years old, half size of baby elephant; besides about 40 elephants, horse training, &c. &c.

As juveniles are more fond of reading of wild animals & circuses than anything else, I take the liberty to give you this hint, without attempting to disguise the fact that all such notices are pleasant & probably profitable reading to me as well as the publishers.

Truly yours,

P. T. Barnum

In a hand other than Barnum's, although signed by him.

## (221)

## TO EDITOR OF YOUTH'S COMPANION

Bridgeport, 20 December 1883

Editor of *Youth's Companion*:

I beg to inform you *confidentially* that another party who publishes a children's paper of considerable popularity is about to send their artist to sketch interesting features of "The Greatest Show on Earth" at its winter quarters here. . . .

Truly yours,

P. T. Barnum

I am anxiously awaiting news of the sacred white elephant.

P. T. B.

Also in a secretary's hand, although the signature and appended note are in Barnum's.

[246]

## {222}

## TO PROPRIETORS OF THE *MAINE FARMER*

Bridgeport, 21 December 1883

Proprietors of the *Maine Farmer*:

This is written to thank you for your notice of the sacred white elephant and to assure you that although your editor seems a little dubious in regard to the statement published concerning him, it is *terribly true*! If the "crittur" lives to reach this continent, everybody will be convinced that it is an achievement unparalleled in the history of public shows.

Truly yours,

P. T. Barnum

Barnum's "Royal Sacred White Elephant," Toung Taloung, procured at great trouble and expense in Siam, arrived in America in 1884. Except for a few pink patches, it was anything but "white."

## {223}

## TO JAMES F. ROGERS

The following is apparently a reply to one of the "begging letters" Barnum regularly received.

Bridgeport, 28 December 1883

James F. Rogers:

Your letter is recd. I sympathise with you in being a cripple, but trust you will bear it with fortitude. All afflictions are intended to accomplish good ends. Many an infirm person has made the world better & happier for his having lived in it. Our heavenly Father does all things well. His will be done.

Truly yours,

P. T. Barnum

## (224)

## TO NATHANIEL P. BEERS

Bridgeport, 1 January 1884

My dear Nate,

. . . My show managers, in booming the white elephant, made numerous enormously fictitious statements, but I
let it go. I owe $200,000 on Broadway & Houston St. property
& am liable to lose $100,000 or more any show season. My will
& codicil occupy about 20 pages instead of 700—but don't
please deny the statements made.

Truly yours,

P. T. Barnum

## (225)

## TO HENRY A. WARD

Bridgeport, 9 January 1884

My dear Professor,

I learn that we have lost ½ dozen monkeys this season,
besides a monster babboon [*sic*] or monkey for which we paid
$1000. All their dead bodies have been *thrown away,* notwith-
standing previous orders to send all to you. It seems the order
did not get down to the *monkey keeper.* So after blowing them
all sky-high, I hope I have fixed it so that all dead animals will
hereafter be sent to you. Such as you can't utilize for my one

*special* object you can perhaps exchange with Smithsonian for curiosities, duplicates, models, &c. for the *new* establishment.

Truly yours,

P. T. Barnum

At the bottom of this letter is a note by Frank A. Ward, who was assisting his father at the time: "I shut my eyes when I came to this."

## (226)

## TO MRS. MARY A. LIVERMORE

Mary Ashton Livermore (1820–1905), a Universalist, was another leading light in the abolitionist, temperance, and woman's rights movements.

Bridgeport, 12 January 1884

My dear Mrs. Livermore,

Our church people beg me to ask if you *can* squeeze out a night on which you will lecture for them for $50 & expenses. This is not to be expected unless you happen to have a night entirely disengaged. They have hard pulling here, although I pay ¼ of all expenses & often give them hundreds extra. But the church *does good* here & must be kept going. If you come, we shall be glad to have you stop with us. I will show Jumbo & 40 other elephants.

Truly yours,

P. T. Barnum

# (227)

## TO REV. E. H. CAPEN

It was finally decided, at Capen's urging, to reveal the extent of Barnum's donations to Tufts during the college's 1884 commencement exercises. The initial plan was to have Barnum address the faculty and trustees on this occasion, which took place on 18 June.

*Private*

Bridgeport, 28 May 1884

My dear Mr. Capen,

. . . I think you are probably *right* in your suggestions, & therefore I will consent to your making the announcement at the dinner, as you suggest. I will be present if possible, & have no special reason for doubting it—but Emperor William says, "Men at my age have no plans." I am not quite of His Majesty's age, but I can't stand much knocking about. If you announce me as going to be there, I hope it won't be done in such a way as *possibly* to arouse suspicion. I don't intend my wife or *anybody* not now in the secret shall have a *hint* till they read it in the papers. I can't say much in way of a speech, for I have quit public speaking. It tires me to stand or talk much.

If you have any hints to give me as regards the tenor of my remarks, let me have them, please. Of course, if the thing is to be *done,* let us have good reporters present & a good agt. of Associated Press. . . .

Truly yours,

B

## (228)

**TO REV. E. H. CAPEN**

Bridgeport, 10 June 1884

Dear Mr. Capen,

. . . I shall get to Boston by Tuesday next (D.V.) & stop at Vendome Hotel. . . . I cannot say *much,* as I am feeling my age some, & shall not occupy more than 5 or 6 minutes. But I hope *you* will be sure to state how *far back* I promised to do this thing & that I have paid for the building—so that if it can be got into print, my folks will see that it is no new & sudden idea & that the money is already mostly *paid.*

Truly yours,

P. T. Barnum

I don't leave here *before* Monday P.M.

"D.V.," or "Deo Volente," was one of Barnum's favorite expressions around this time.

## (229)

**TO REV. E. H. CAPEN**

This strange "postscript" was very likely an addendum to Barnum's letter of 10 June.

Bridgeport, 12 June 1884

*Postscript No. 2*! Hurrah! I am up & dressed—have eaten my breakfast! It is now 9 A.M. & in the broad *daylight* things look brighter than when one is nervous in bed alone under gas-light!

[251]

Go ahead as you please. Proclaim as loud as you please—
only let it be known that much is *paid in.* I *cannot & dare not*
go next week to Boston, but will send you a letter to read at
dinner if you like it.

This will open the flood-gate of begging letters from all
parts of the earth, but I must stand that.

Truly yours,

P. T. Barnum

Heirs may as well know I do what I like with my own. Hope
you will send me your speech & the doings.

I am *awful* sorry to disappoint you about going myself,
but I really dare not. I should sleep less & less every night till
the 18th & then would be sick in bed. Please send me several
copies of paper containing the doings.

B

I will come & see the museum if able before 1st July.

(230)

## LETTER TO REV. E. H. CAPEN,
## READ AT TUFTS COLLEGE ON 18 JUNE 1884

Bridgeport, 13 June 1884

My dear Mr. President,

It is with unfeigned regret that I find it impossible to
attend the commencement exercises at Tufts as promised.
Often have I wished to be with you on these annual occasions,
if for no other reason than to mark by my presence the deep
interest I take and have always taken in an institution the
prosperity of which I have watched with no small degree of
satisfaction and pride. But a busy life has invariably brought
with it duties which have deferred from time to time the re-

alization of my desire to visit College Hill in June. Planning with more than usual foresight (as I had imagined) to be with you this year, and believing the time had come when I could in person extend my congratulations to the faculty and my best wishes to the students, I find I must forego even this visit. But if absent in the flesh, I am with you in spirit, and my thoughts will wander to you in your rejoicings of commencement on the 18th inst.

Deprived in my own youth of rare educational advantages, I have learned to appreciate their worth and to take solid delight in every evidence of greater enlightenment and progress. I never see an urchin plodding his way unwillingly to school but I contrast the meagre facilities of sixty years ago with the present wealth of instrumentalities within the reach of every American boy and girl. And so when I hear the common-school bell ring, I bless the day which no longer sees any valid reason for ignorance in this country. I have always declared that I took more pleasure in paying my school taxes than any other, for education often tends to lessen vice and crime, as well as to secure to its recipients reputation, honor, and success.

I may be pardoned, Mr. President, if on this occasion I assert that my interest in the higher education of the day has ever been constant and profound. Had my earlier advantages been greater, I might have achieved more; but looking back on a long and eventful career, I confess in no boasting vein that I have conscientiously labored to elevate and ennoble public amusements, which play no small part among the educational agencies of the times. How successful I have been in blending healthful and moral instruction with recreation, it is not for me to state, but the satisfaction experienced in my life-work has been in itself a reward altogether apart from and superior to any golden harvest I may have reaped. Not that I am insensible to the latter, for it is because of it that I am able, under the Providence of a good Father who has blessed me all my life, to do somewhat for Tufts in the foundation of the Barnum Museum of Natural History.

I am happy in the thought that this museum will be another factor in the work of the college, helping it on its high career of usefulness. I have for many years past decided to do something for an institution the growing excellence and thoroughness of which must commend it to lovers of knowledge everywhere. And now that the decision has been made, and the museum building erected, I hope the college may possess for many decades to come facilities sufficient to inspire its students to investigations in a branch of science which so wonderfully reveals in varied form the infinite wisdom and power of the Creator.

But I am afraid this letter exceeds all bounds, and should it be read on commencement day, it will be considered irksome. And yet I cannot close without assuring you, Mr. President, the officers, teachers, patrons, and students of the college, of my strong faith in the brilliant future of Tufts. I believe from what I know of the sacrificing spirit and intellectual standing of its faculty that the possibilities within its reach will be attained, and that it will become an educational centre fostered and nourished not only by men of brain, but also by men of fortune. It augurs well for the future of any cause when people of means are ready to give generously in its behalf. The history of most denominations today reveals the fact that there is more giving than formerly, and with it corresponding prosperity. Whilst feeding the churches, let us not neglect to foster the colleges, but endeavor to give them such prestige and position as shall enable them to exercise the most salutary influence and do *the very best work*.

Hoping that others may do much more than I have, and that all will feel a pleasure in contributing according to their means, I am, my dear Mr. President,

Respectfully yours,

P. T. Barnum

# (231)

## TO REV. E. H. CAPEN

Bridgeport, 15 June 1884

My dear Dr. Capen,

Yours with the *scraps* recd. Also yours of yesterday saying my letter is the next thing to my being with you. I am glad the reporter will get the copy of your speech, but can hardly expect that both will be published in full. Shall be mighty glad if an intelligent agent of the Associated Press will send a pretty extensive account of it by telegraph. I guess if a sharp reliable reporter can get the speech & letter in type Wednesday evening for morning papers, *he* could get an Associated Press agt. to send it over the wires same night for Thursday morning papers.

Truly yours,

P. T. Barnum

It will be a great relief to both of us to get rid of this *secret*. The marble bust will arrive soon, but you will probably not care for it at present.

B

P.S. It is *possible* I may leave home by Friday next & am very anxious for my wife & daughters to know & read all they can about it without first getting a hint from me—& before I get away—so I can face the music here. Hence I would be glad if you could get mailed if possible Wednesday night or Thursday morning *early* as full report as any paper may publish:

3 copies mailed to me

| | | | |
|---|---|---|---|
| 1 | d[itt]o Edt. | *Standard,* | Bridgeport, Conn. |
| 1 | " " | *Farmer,* | " |
| 1 | " " | *Morning News,* | d[itt]o |

Truly yours,

P. T. Barnum

## (232)

### TO REV. E. H. CAPEN

Bridgeport, 20 June 1884

Dear Professor,

Thanks for your letter & the masterly manner in which you managed the affair. . . . My marble bust will arrive in N.Y. from Italy in a week or ten days. . . . So when you get ready for placing it in museum, you may follow Mr. Ball's directions by getting a plain marble pedestal (at reasonable price) 3 ft. 6 inches high and send bill of pedestal to me & I will pay it. . . .

I hope by 1st September the museum building will be complete & the birds & animals placed, so that Mrs. Barnum can see it all in order, if this can be *conveniently* done. Let title be put in *plain* readable letters, please, over the entrance.

Truly yours,

P. T. Barnum

## (233)

### TO SPENCER F. BAIRD

Bridgeport, 21 June 1884

Dear Prof. Baird,

I neglected to say in my last letter that my managers & self think Jumbo's skin or skeleton should go to your institution—you taking your choice, & then the "Barnum" Museum at Tufts College take the other. That seems under the circumstances to be the way to do the most good & to best hand down our names.

Truly yours,

P. T. Barnum

P.S. We hope, however, that Jumbo may yet live many years, but think it as well to decide now as ever where he shall be *distributed* when he ceases to breathe.

P. T. Barnum

The confusion over the final disposition of the "double Jumbo"—mounted hide and skeleton—was to grow over the next several years. On 25 June Baird wrote to Barnum that "we much prefer his skeleton to his skin!" (*Smithsonian Institution Archives*), an arrangement to which Barnum assented.

(234)

## TO EDITOR OF THE *NEW YORK TRIBUNE*

Bridgeport, 2 November 1884

Sir:

I own about 200 houses, besides several costly public buildings and considerable real estate in this flourishing manufacturing city. I pledge myself to sell all I possess here for one quarter less than its present acknowledged value if the Democrats elect their President. Every taxpayer and every workingman and woman will see business permanently palsied if the South gets into the saddle. It will establish free trade, get pay for its slaves, and obtain pensions for all rebel soldiers.

P. T. Barnum

Published in the 3 November issue of the *Tribune*. Cleveland won the election, and Barnum, instead of selling for one quarter less or even full value all he possessed, invited the President and his family to the circus.

[257]

# (235)

## TO SPENCER F. BAIRD

Bridgeport, 9 December 1884

My dear Prof. Baird,

I hope you looked at pages 349 & 50 of the book which I mailed you last week, & thus learn that you are in due time to have the skeleton of Jumbo & the skin of the sacred white elephant under the roof of the Smithsonian.

Several years since you did me the honor of sending an artist to me to take a cast of my face for a bust which you kindly offered to place in your institution. As the artist died without completing the bust, I have now directed my agent in Boston to send you the cast from the marble bust which Thomas Ball of Florence (formerly from Boston) made from life for the Barnum Museum of Natural History at Tufts College. . . .

Truly yours,

P. T. Barnum

The book referred to was the latest edition of Barnum's autobiography.

# (236)

## TO ULYSSES S. GRANT

New York, 12 January 1885

Honored Sir:

The whole world honors and respects you. All are anxious that you should live happy and free from care. While they admire your manliness in declining the large sum recently tendered you by friends, they still desire to see you achieve financial independence in an honorable manner. Of the unique and valuable trophies with which you have been honored, we all have read; and all have a laudable desire to see these evidences of love and respect bestowed upon you by monarchs, princes, and people throughout the globe. While you would confer a great and enduring favor on your fellow men and women by permitting them to see these trophies, you could also remove existing embarrassments in a most satisfactory and honorable manner. I will give you one hundred thousand dollars cash, besides a proportion of the profits, if I may be permitted to exhibit these relics to a grateful and appreciative public, and I will give satisfactory bonds of half a million dollars for their safekeeping and return.

These precious trophies, of which all your friends are so proud, would be placed before the eyes of your millions of admirers in a manner and style at once pleasing to yourself and satisfactory to the best elements of the entire community. Remembering that the mementoes of Washington, Wellington, Napoleon, Frederick the Great, and many other distinguished men have given immense pleasure to millions who have been permitted to see them, I trust you will, in the honorable manner proposed, gratify the public and thus inculcate the lesson of honesty, perseverence [sic], and true patriotism so admirably illustrated in your career.

I have the honor to be truly your friend and admirer,

P. T. Barnum

Grant had recently become bankrupt and had only six months to live when Barnum wrote this letter. Since he had made over all his trophies to W. H. Vanderbilt, he declined the offer.

# (237)

## TO JOHN GREENLEAF WHITTIER

Bridgeport, 11 March 1885

Dear Friend,

It is seldom that one gets more of a favor than he asks for, but there was a pleasant exception in my case when I received your esteemed letter of Jany. 16th. I did not "ask for bread and receive a stone." I asked for your name written by your honored hand, and I received a precious autograph letter which will be handed down to my posterity as a kind remembrance of your good nature in doing more than I could have presumed to ask for. I am glad to be reminded by you that we hold some sentiments in common. My chief pleasure at 74½ years, as it has been for some years past, is to give the public and especially the youth of our nation instruction & pleasure, with the poison left out. This you have always done, and the world, including my humble self, love you for it.

Your devoted friend,

P. T. Barnum

P.S. Nearly a million of copies of my autobiography, to which I annually add an appendix, have been disposed of under my show tents. As we furnish them to our patrons at 50 cts. per copy—*about cost*—they are necessarily printed on inferior paper and altogether are a cheap affair. As I have none of better paper or binding, I take the liberty of mailing you a copy (poor & rough as it is), not with the expectation that you will read it, but with the hope that its last 50 or 60 pages may at some time receive a glance from your eyes.

My young English wife has thumbed over and over all of your published writings with great delight & reverence. She takes pleasure in reading them to me, and I as great pleasure

in hearing them—perhaps the greater because I have read &
re-read them *alone* and received higher hopes & aspirations
therein years before I saw my English bride.

As ever thine,

P. T. Barnum

Whittier's letter of 16 January, in which he writes of Barnum and himself both catering to the public in their own ways, is at Swarthmore College.

【238】

## TO SPENCER F. BAIRD

On 14 April 1885 Baird wrote to Barnum to express his concern over the cessation
of dead animals donated by the circus. Knowing Barnum's interest in supplying the
new museum at Tufts, he pleaded for at least duplicate material, in return for which
he promised to send Tufts "more than an equivalent" of the Smithsonian's duplicates
(*Smithsonian Institution Archives*).

Bridgeport, 20 April 1885

Dear Prof. Baird,

Your favor of 14th recd. I by no means intend to divert
any large portion of our dead animals from the Smithsonian
& shall never *sell* a duplicate nor send one to my museum at
Tufts College, but I desire all duplicates, triplicates, & all sorts
of "cates" to go to our great *National* Museum—if you really
*want* duplicates, which I suppose you do for exchange.

When Prof. Henry was alive and my first museum was
burned, he told me that he recognized mine as a *scientific* establishment, & therefore he said he would send me for my
new museum one of each and all specimens of *impressions* or
*casts* taken. He showed me a number of casts which had been
taken there from real inanimate curious objects, and which he
said he sent to various scientific institutions throughout this
country & I think also Europe. Now one each of all such arti-

cles would be valuable to my little pet museum at Tufts, and I am glad to read your very liberal proposition to supply Tufts with duplicate specimens from the animal kingdom, as well as fossil remains &c. and ethnological material in the way of pottery, reproductions of ancient towns, villages, &c. These considerations will serve to stimulate my efforts more than ever to have every spare hide, hoof, horn, skin, & skeleton which our menagerie produces placed in the Smithsonian. I shall send your letter to Prof. E. H. Capen, president of Tufts College, and also send him this letter (which he will remail to you), and I hope thus to have a perfect understanding between us all which will be mutually beneficial for many years. . . .

Truly yours,

P. T. Barnum

. . . .


## (239)

## TO JAMES L. HUTCHINSON

*Private*

[Bridgeport], 29 June 1885

Dear Hutch,

I met Seth B. Howes the other day, & he began asking about Bailey's health. He spoke of the shows & mentioned Cole's. Said Cole's was doing better than any other show except ours. But he did not believe Cole's or any of the other shows outside of ours would make a cent this year. I told him ours was making 12 to 15 per ct. better than last year. He asked what we should do in case Bailey broke down. I said probably take another in his place & asked if *he* wanted to buy in case of an opening. He said, "I am 70, and my income is

$30,000 per year for rents, besides my interest on bonds &c., and I would not touch any business. But," he said, "there is a world of money to be made in England with your show & your name, and more in France than Great Britain, for the French are rich, love circuses, & show *Sundays* (7 days each week)." But he said nobody could get along by just running through the country & inquiring. He said a good man was needed who knows *England* & *France* & their ways of doing business. I said I guessed & hoped Bailey would recover, but if we should need another partner, I asked who was the best. He replied Cole, if he would buy, but Cole is worth nearly a million & his mother governs him & might oppose it. "I suppose you own each one third. But you receive each year $25,000 bonus, I know," said Howe. "Well," I replied, "I should waive my bonus to all the partners if we make a change." Howe replied, "Cole is a *strictly honest* man, and I am sure if he joined your show he would suit all hands. I have heard him say if he had the name of Barnum attached to a show, he would be surer of continued success and a pile would be made in foreign parts—France, England, Scotland, & Ireland." "Well," I answered, "if you happen to see Cole, you might *confidentially, never to be repeated,* ask his views if occasion should offer." I told him I would never sell out my name, living or dead. I write you these particulars so you won't clash in case you should see Cole. If Bailey keeps quiet and can stop *thinking,* I think he will recover. At least, we all hope so.

P. T. Barnum

Howe said the London Show would never have been seen in America if the war had not broken out between France & Germany, and he says that the first year we should never charge in England less than $1.25 to 1. and 50 cts. Those high prices, he says, would fill our tents with royalty, nobility, & gentry— whereas if we charged *less,* those classes would not attend at all & mix with the rabble. The 2d year we might charge less & the 3d year go to France, and then return to America and raise the devil, but possibly we might need to remain 4 years.

[263]

Seth Howe could give us lots of points if we should go, whether Cole joined or not.

I suppose if we really go to California next year, we can charter steamers to take us to Australia if we like.

Truly yours,

P. T. Barnum

Barnum had joined Seth B. Howes in sending out the Great Asiatic Caravan, Museum, and Menagerie in 1851, and his meeting with his erstwhile partner seems to have first set him thinking about the possibility of taking the show to Europe. As this and other letters written around the same time also indicate, James A. Bailey (1845–1906) sometimes suffered from mental distress and was a source of anxiety to his partners. W. W. Cole and James E. Cooper were to replace him in the concern at the end of the 1885 season.

**(240)**

## TO MRS. JAMES A. BAILEY

Bridgeport, 5 July 1885

Mrs. Bailey:

This is my 75th anniversary of my birth. I have worked hard during my life and sometimes I have overworked my *brain*. I found the only sure cure was a season of *brain-rest* and *not thinking*.

Hearing that your husband is still ill and knowing that it comes from too much *thinking,* I beg you and him to remember that our business *will not suffer* this season in his absence. It is all moving like good machinery. Hutchinson, Young, & Fish, as well as our head men in all departments, are keeping everything straight. Mr. Bailey need not *think* of the show for six months to come. I assure him it will be well managed and will make money. Give him my best wishes and the same to yourself. I am standing heat better than for five years. Keep quiet in a cool place—don't fret, but look on the bright side.

Truly yours,

P. T. Barnum

Merritt Young was treasurer with the show.

## (241)

### TELEGRAM TO HENRY A. WARD

On 15 September 1885, while the circus was playing at St. Thomas, Ontario, Jumbo was struck and killed by a speeding freight train. Professor Ward was shortly on the scene with his assistants, while Barnum immediately began laying plans to turn this latest disaster to the show's advantage. Hutchinson himself, in a telegram to Bailey the following day, tells of getting Barnum's consent to keep both the mounted hide and skeleton with the circus—a double spectacle that would "make him draw more than ever"—and of the necessity of talking it "strong" in order to convince rivals and the public that the loss of Jumbo would not "materially affect the drawing power of the show" (*Bridgeport Public Library, Historical Collections*).

Bridgeport, 17 September 1885

Go ahead, save skin and skeleton. I will pay you justly and honorably. Have not [*sic*] doubt you will finish both for exhibition. I meet Hutchinson in Buffalo Saturday. Cannot arrange details with him by telegraph. We shall do everything honorably with you.

P. T. Barnum

## (242)

## TO MESSRS. HARPER BROS. & CO.

*Private*

Bridgeport, 18 September 1885

Gentlemen:

Millions of children and adults (myself included) are mourning the death of *Jumbo.*

Would you like to publish for the holidays *The Life, History, and Death of Jumbo, with Many Incidents & Anecdotes not heretofore Published*

by P. T. Barnum

profusely illustrated? The title can of course be changed from the above. Probably numerous *cuts* now extant can be used. If properly gotten up, would it not be an interesting Christmas children's book—perhaps on *both* sides of the Atlantic?

Truly yours,

P. T. Barnum

## (243)

## TO MORRIS K. JESUP

Among the contenders for the remains of Jumbo, the American Museum of Natural History now entered the picture, and eventually succeeded in easing out the Smithsonian for the prize of the skeleton. The banker and philanthropist Morris K. Jesup, one of the museum's incorporators in 1868, had become its president in 1881.

Bridgeport, 21 September 1885

Dear Sir,

My partners are with the show traveling west. *They* expect to exhibit the Jumbo skeleton for some years in the traveling show. So far as *I* am concerned, there is a tacit understanding that the Smithsonian, or rather the National Museum at Washington, should have the skeleton. But my partners have never assented to this, and offers for it are already cabled us from England. At present it is worth $100,000 or more *per year* for exhibition in our show.

Truly yours,

P. T. Barnum

# (244)

## TO REV. E. H. CAPEN

Bridgeport, 24 September 1885

Dear Mr. Capen,

I am too much overworked to write. I will, however, say to you *confidentially* that the day before I recd. your letter I made a codicil bequeathing $20,000 over and above all I had done to that date to the Barnum Museum of Nat. His. at Tufts College, *provided* my estate should be valued by the appraisers worth a *certain sum,* which I estimate is $200,000 or $300,000 *less* than I am now worth. The *interest only* for the first fifty years to be used.

I have a new partner, Mr. Bailey being compelled by ill health to sell out. *I fully intend* that Jumbo's stuffed skin shall be given forever to the Barnum Museum & *hope* before next May to get consent of my partners to so dispose of it. But at present all is chaos & bother. We intend to have Jumbo's skin stuffed & exhibited *with our show* for some years. Excuse brevity.

Truly yours,

P. T. Barnum

"My wife & I" fully intend to see you & the college & museum within a month—probably less. But poor woman, she is now confined to her bed again.

P. T. B.

Tufts College & the museum there are getting & have got since Jumbo's death much more free newspaper advertising in American & European journals than ever before. "It is an ill wind &c."

P. T. B.

## (245)

### TO HENRY A. WARD

The following letter is not in Barnum's hand, but is a copy apparently made by Ward before returning, as requested, the original letter to Barnum. Baird had written to Barnum from Woods Hole on the same date to offer advice and to express the Smithsonian's disappointment at not getting the skeleton to mount.

*Confidential*

Bridgeport, 26 September 1885

Prof. Ward:

I have advices from Smithsonian as follows: "We think that it will be absolutely impossible to have the skeleton properly prepared under a year or two, and that if set up at once the exuding oil and grease would catch the dust of travel and of exhibition so as to be more disagreeable than otherwise. . . . In stuffing the skin, *it could be made considerably larger than in nature*! . . .If the skull is broken into a great many pieces (as we understand), it will need a *very nice* operation to mend it."

Now my dear Ward, I think if above statements are correct, it is much better for you to take one or two years to prepare the skeleton, for we want it in *best state possible* for per-man[en]cy. I don't think it would help us much for a year or two to show anything but the *skin* stuffed, and by all means let that *show* as *large as possible.* It will be a *grand* thing to take all advantage possible in *this* direction! Let him show like a mountain! If we don't show skeleton for a year or two, then we had better have *ivory* tusks exactly like the original. Please *return me this letter* with your ideas.

Yours truly,

P. T. Barnum

## (246)

### TO SPENCER F. BAIRD

Bridgeport, 27 September 1885

Dear Prof. Baird,

. . . It is my *full intention* that the Smithsonian shall receive Jumbo's skeleton in due time as a *gift.* I may not perhaps be able to carry it out, for I don't own *quite half* of the show & I shall have one or two *new* partners. But I hope when their minds get settled down to accept our *great* loss, I may be able to get their *written consent* to this arrangement. If I fail, it will be no fault of mine. . . . There is a great pressure on us to allow skeleton to go to *Am. Museum, Central Park, New York*— but I tell you *confidentially* (*strictly so*) that *I* shall *not* consent to it & shall continue to send you our dead animals. We have been cabled from London for a *price* for skin & skeleton by a naturalist there. My partners think it is for British Museum, & they evidently have some idea that the skeleton *may* be sold for a large price when its public exhibition is finished in our show. The skull is badly cracked, & therefore after Prof. Ward has done his best in patching it, its value as a scientific specimen will, I suppose, be trifling. If it is but a few hundred dollars, I shall pay my partners for their share if they desire pay, & shall then freely give the skeleton to the Smithsonian, where I think it *ought* to be. I am glad to do all I can for your institution, & my zeal in that direction is not lessened by the fact that *you now have the means of reciprocating generously* by contributing such duplicate birds, animals, casts, &c. as you can spare to help my pet "Barnum Museum of Natural History" at Tufts College.

As ever truly yours,

P. T. Barnum

## (247)

## TO JAMES A. BAILEY

Among the many absurd rumors surrounding Jumbo's death—rumors that have been repeated and elaborated upon to the present day—was a story that Barnum and his partners, knowing Jumbo was ill, planned and executed his death. The present letter is in reference to one such report (perhaps the inspiration for all the others) by a journalist who resided in Bridgeport and had attempted to extort money from Barnum on a previous occasion. The newspaper proprietor, after traveling to Bridgeport to meet with Barnum and conduct an investigation, published a handsome retraction and full explanation of the affair in a subsequent issue, and the venal correspondent was discharged.

Home [Bridgeport], 4 October 1885

Dear Bailey,

Last Sunday a correspondent of the *Hartford Sunday Globe* charged us with getting Jumbo killed on purpose for an *advertisement,* as Jumbo was sick, had consumption, & we knew he could not live till spring. The lie was so circumstantial, many believed it, & I sued the proprietor next day for $50,000. He was stubborn, but when he got convinced, he paid all law costs & our lawyer—so his correspondent is *squelched* at no cost to us. Hope you are getting better.

Truly yours,

P. T. Barnum

# (248)

## TO JAMES A. BAILEY

Bridgeport, 12 October 1885

Dear Bailey,

Your telegram recd. I am as glad as you are that things are fixed *as they are.*

I shall never cease to admire many traits in your character, your manliness & integrity, nor your marvellous perceptions of how to hit public taste & to do it in the best way, expending liberally where & when it is judicious. I have for nearly two years been worried over your wakefulness, knowing that unless cured, serious results must follow. I only hope you will regain your health *fully,* and that what you mentioned Saturday may occur.

Truly yours,

P. T. Barnum

Barnum and Hutchinson had agreed to buy out the ailing Bailey's share in the show and to take on W. W. Cole and James E. Cooper as their new partners at the end of the 1885 season. The death of Jumbo before the show reached winter quarters, however, considerably decreased the value of the circus (according to one report, by as much as one half); consequently, adjustments had to be made in the original sums agreed upon. At the time of their final settlement Bailey apparently expressed the hope that he might one day become Barnum's partner again.

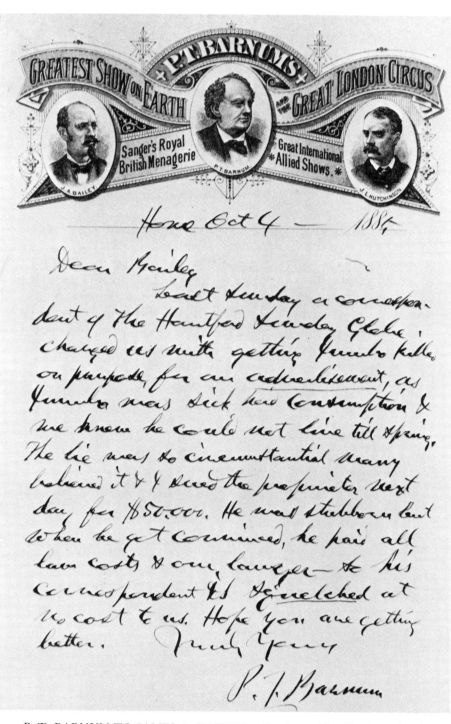

Home Oct 4 — 1885

Dear Bailey

Last Tuesday a correspondent of the Hartford Tuesday Globe charged us with getting Jumbo killed on purpose, for an *advertisement*, as Jumbo was sick with Consumption & we knew he could not live till spring. The lie was so circumstantial many believed it & I sued the proprietor next day for $50,000. He was stubborn but when he got convinced, he paid all law costs & our lawyer — to his correspondent I *squelched* at no cost to us. Hope you are getting better.

Truly Yours

P. T. Barnum

P. T. BARNUM TO JAMES A. BAILEY, 4 October 1885. The letterhead depicts Barnum and his partners Bailey and James L. Hutchinson.

## TO WILLIAM A. CROFFUT

William A. Croffut, editor, journalist, and travel writer, was associated with many newspapers during his career.

Bridgeport, 20 October 1885

Dear Croffut,

It is proved beyond question—not only by Jumbo's keeper Scott & four of our reliable showfolks, but also by several others who witnessed Jumbo's death—that when the great, noble beast first saw the deadly train approaching, he immediately seized the trick elephant Tom Thumb, threw him over the track to a place of safety, then instantly pushed Scott out of danger, and it being too late for Jumbo to retreat & save himself, he charged the locomotive and was crushed to death in 3 minutes by being pressed between a heavily loaded freight train standing still on a sidetrack & the incoming freight train.

Now my dear C, you are a *poet* & can probably beat the enclosed, but the writer so neatly touches the peculiar & noble points in good old Jumbo's character that I am anxious to see it in print & go the rounds of the American & English press. If you can ring it into your letters or get it into some newspaper, & send me a copy or *two*, I shall feel very much obliged. The N.Y. City newspapers are too full of politics at present—indeed, so are all N.Y. State papers—to find room for poetry. I prefer it to *start* anywhere except in Bridgeport & then our papers here will copy it.

My poor wife has been growing weaker for a month, & within 2 or 3 days we must move her temporarily to an institution where she can have administered the proper treatment—but pray don't make an *item* of this, for she & I both have a horror of reading that she is ill. She will be well, our doctors say, in 2 or 3 weeks.

As ever truly yours,

P. T. Barnum

[273]

# (250)

## TO HENRY A. WARD

At Hutchinson's insistence it was decided to exhibit both the skeleton and mounted hide of Jumbo with the show, and Ward was instructed to rush their preparation so as to have both Jumbos "strong as thunder" in time for the 1886 season.

Home [Bridgeport], 24 October 1885

Dear Prof. Ward,

Let this & all our doings be strictly *private,* please. I have an idea here that will help *you* & help the show if carried out successfully. I propose that you write a *private* letter to Harper Brothers, Franklin Square, New York, entirely in your name, without a hint that either I or anybody else know of it.

In that letter, written on your *business* sheets, you describe your occupation & your position as you like, say how much you have traveled, what you have done for Agazzis [*sic*]— or *not,* just as you please—& send, if you like, pictures of your antedeluvian specimens &c. & perhaps photo of yourself. But the *main object* of your letter should be to tell them that if they like when the skeleton & stuffed Jumbo are ready to publish their pictures in *Harper's Magazine,* you will send *them exclusively* the photos, as well as exact description of dimensions, weight, & all scientific particulars. But say you prefer to have them publish with the above the view of your museum & specimens &c. just as it is, including your own portrait, showing your taxidermists at work &c.—thus furnishing a chapter of 3 or 4 pages, more or less, of most interesting historical & statistical matter. And if they agree to this, *nobody else* shall photo any part of the whole subject till it appears in their *Magazine.* Say you will have the photos taken, or if they prefer to send an artist to sketch, you will tell them when to do it. Ask an *answer,* saying that if they decline, you desire to make the proposition to *The Century.*

They may write you that they prefer to publish it in

*Harper's Weekly,* but their magazine has 3 times the circulation which their weekly has, & before accepting the *Weekly* I would try *The Century.* Both magazines circulate largely in Europe, & I am anxious for you to get a worldwide reputation through this Jumbo affair.

You see the idea, & you know best what to write. We intend to make a big splurge over Jumbo's skeleton & hide & will ring you in to the best advantage in our handbills & advance couriers & have a placard, which you may prepare, to be placed in our show alongside of the specimens. Pray make specimens very strong to stand wear & tear of several years' travel.

Yours &c.,

P. T. Barnum

## (251)

## TO REV. E. H. CAPEN

On several occasions Barnum had expressed his intention—provided he could get his partners' consent—to donate the skeleton of Jumbo to the Smithsonian. Meanwhile, he continued to send to the Smithsonian the remains of other dead animals in exchange for exhibition materials for his "pet" project, the Barnum Museum of Natural History at Tufts College. In the fall of 1885 Professor John P. Marshall, the curator in charge of the Tufts museum, paid a visit to the Smithsonian, with instructions from Barnum to "smell out" all the "queer things" and ask for duplicates (Barnum to Capen, 30 October 1885, *Tufts*). The trip was not as productive as Barnum had hoped it would be, and from then on his relations with the National Museum were strained.

Bridgeport, 20 November 1885

Dear Dr. Capen,

Yours & Prof. Marshall's letters indicate that Prof. Baird cannot or *will not* carry out his promises—so hereafter I will (unless my partners object) have all our dead animals sent to Prof. Ward to use for museum in exchange or otherwise. . . . I am disappointed in Smithsonian's meanness, & now I want this matter simplified so that *I* need not hereafter be often bothered with details of skins & bones. I am constantly overworked, & now Prof. Marshall must decide to somehow accept or reject such dead animals as we may have, without setting my poor head a whizzing any oftener than is absolutely necessary.

My three partners own much more than half the show. They care more for dollars than for science or for the museum, & it is only because they don't happen to see *dollars* in our dead animals that they don't as yet interfere with my giving them for benefit of museum. I am as ever

Truly yours,

P. T. Barnum

## (252)

### TO HENRY A. WARD

*Private*

Bridgeport, 28 November 1885

Dear Prof. Ward,

You need not try *The Century* nor any other magazine or paper, because we have decided on a *better* way to give you a genuine & almost unlimited celebrity if you follow our suggestions *strictly* & *not otherwise.*

We propose (*confidentially*) that when the two specimens are *ready,* on or before 1st March, you "set your house in order" so as to show all *your* affairs to best advantage. We will bring to your place, at our own expense, a parlor car & sleeper containing editors or reporters from all N.Y. City papers & from the principal newspapers on the route, & also invite at our own expense editors from Buffalo & western cities & Boston & Springfield, perhaps, who, all combined, will make a *spread* of the news all over this country & Europe. But in order to make our *very expensive* scheme a *success,* it is of the *utmost importance* that you do not allow anybody to *photograph* the specimens, nor even to allow anybody to *see* the specimens as they begin to approach an advanced state, for if any person thus seeing them should get anything about it into a newspaper, it would *spoil* all *novelty* of the affair, & other newspapers would neither let us take their reporters to Rochester nor publish a word about it. So please *exclude everybody,* including Rochester reporters (they will come in with the others when we arrive with them from New York). So look out for photographers, sketchers, & reporters—& the only way to do that effectually is to *exclude everybody* from the Jumbo specimens.

Truly yours,

P. T. Barnum

## {253}

## TO HENRY A. WARD

New York [1 March 1886]

P.S. I was very sorry to receive your statement regarding the pecuniary result of your preparing the two specimens. There will be no use in my showing your letter to my partners. They will be sure to say, as I do, that "this is a matter of *business.*" Your offer of $1200 was submitted to my partners & accepted. Now I cannot go to them and say *you miscalculated* the expenses, for they would reply, "That is not *our* affair. If he had miscalculated the other way, so that he made hundreds of dollars more than he expected, would he have given it to us?" They & I would no doubt regret that *you* made a mistake, but it is *no fault of ours,* and you will surely gain thousands of dollars through the celebrity which the affair will give to you & your business. I am, dear sir,

Your friend,

P. T. Barnum

This appears to be a "postscript" to a telegram sent to Ward on the same date: "Let all friends see Jumbo without doing injury" (*Ward Papers*). The reporters had been admitted to see Ward's work a few days earlier. Ward had agreed, the previous September, to mount both the skeleton and hide of Jumbo for $1200, a figure 30 percent less than he would normally charge in return for the "advertisement" he hoped to receive. But the expense, in terms of both time and money, required to achieve this great undertaking was more than he had calculated.

## {254}

## TO JOHN P. MARSHALL

Bridgeport, 31 May 1886

Dear Sir,

. . . Mrs. Barnum, although weak & sick herself & unable to go to Boston, says if I excuse myself on account of "old age," I shall never be younger, & that she thinks I ought to go to Boston Tuesday, 15, stay at college part of Wednesday, & return home Thursday A.M. She reasoneth well, & if I drop in to the college on the 16th by 10:30 or before, you need not be surprised, for I *want* to be present on commencement day, as I never attended a "commencement" of any college. . . .

Truly yours,

P. T. Barnum

Barnum did indeed make it to commencement on the 16th, and even made a speech at the college dinner that day.

## (255)

## TO MRS. LUCY A. THOMAS

Lucy Thomas was the wife of Abner C. Thomas, the son of Barnum's friend the Rev.
Abel C. Thomas, and a niece of Alice and Phoebe Cary.

Bridgeport, 10 July 1886

Dear Lucy,
Thanks for congratulations of those nice little girls. . . .
My health continues robust, for which I am grateful & astonished. 76, after all I have gone through & put through [*sic*],
with no aches or pains of old age, is at least lucky. I wish my
poor wife was half so fortunate. She has her ups & downs, the
latter being twice as numerous as the former. It gives me pain
& regret to see & think of, for she really suffers much. . . .

Truly yours,

P. T. Barnum

## (256)

## TO EDITOR OF THE *BOSTON JOURNAL*

Bridgeport, 6 August 1886

Sir:
Your valued paper of Thursday, July 29th, contains an
account of an enormous sea serpent, which according to the
testimony of eight or more intelligent & respectable witnesses
was plainly seen near the shore at Rockport, Maine, on Saturday, July 24th. There really seems to be no reasonable doubt
that this reptile did make his appearance on the coast as represented. Equally strong evidence of the existence of sea ser-

pents has frequently been given by various witnesses in different parts of the world.

Our modern improvements in firearms seem to render it possible to kill and secure such a hitherto uncaptured specimen of natural history. In order to stimulate seamen and others in any part of the world to attempt its capture, dead or alive, I will pay twenty thousand dollars for such a specimen as is described in your paper. If it should be only half or two thirds the estimated length of the Rockport sea serpent, I will pay pro rata, the reptile to be delivered to me preserved in a fit state for stuffing and mounting. If captured, it will, of course, be added to my Greatest Show on Earth and eventually be permanently placed in the Barnum Museum of Natural History at Tufts College, Mass.

Truly yours,

P. T. Barnum

During the summer of 1886 newspapers published several circumstantial descriptions of a great sea serpent seen swimming off the New England coast. Barnum's offer was published in the *Boston Journal* and subsequently in other papers around the nation. The serpent had actually been sighted off Rockport, Massachusetts.

## {257}

## TO HENRY A. WARD

Bridgeport, 28 August 1886

My dear Prof. Ward,

. . . Suppose those down east sailors & others who are scattered along New England coast, armed & watching for the sea serpent & my $20,000 reward, should really kill him. What shall be my first move to secure its skin properly *till* your man could get there & properly preserve it?

Truly yours,

P. T. Barnum

"Preserve sea serpent in ice or if not attainable use salt," was Ward's reply.

## (258)

## TO REV. ALEX MCMILLAN

Bridgeport, 4 September 1886

Rev. Alex McMillan:

Your letter just recd. Am very sorry to say that our big-head (or man) is with the show in Iowa, & I have not the least idea where a similar thing can be procured.

Wishing you success in teaching your people and children the propriety of innocent amusements & recreation—for I believe in a *cheerful* Christianity—I am

Truly yours,

P. T. Barnum

## (259)

## TO WILLIAM T. HORNADAY

William Temple Hornaday (1854–1937), the distinguished naturalist and zoological park director, was at this time chief taxidermist at the Smithsonian's National Museum. From 1886 on he often attempted to mediate and clear up "misunderstandings" between Barnum, the Smithsonian, and the museum at Tufts, but finally, after he became convinced the Smithsonian would never get Jumbo's skeleton, threw it up as a hopeless job.

[281]

Bridgeport, 4 September 1886

Dear Mr. Hornaday,

Thanks for the photo. It is very suggestive. You seem to have plenty of subjects for mounting & plenty of work to do. I only wish your large establishment afforded duplicates to a greater extent than I supposed it would. I had thought that Americans would send you from the West all sorts of American animal skins, and also from foreign parts where they might be traveling. But everybody seems intent on *his own* interests—so I suppose the Natl. Museum is not often remembered by those who are away from it. My partners cannot raise courage at present to start a zoological garden at Washington. *Nous verron* [*sic*]. I am not sure about the middle letter to your name. I loaned your book to my grandson in N.Y. & your signature makes your middle letter a little obscure, but I guess this letter will reach you.

Truly yours,

P. T. Barnum

## (260)

## TO REV. E. H. CAPEN

Bridgeport, 27 January 1887

Dear Dr. Capen,

Yours recd. You have probably seen by my letters to Prof. Marshall that I have got a new partner (Cooper) who is more *illiberal* than my other two partners, Hutchinson & Cole— and as Cooper has charge of the animal department, he takes pride in cutting me off from obtaining our dead animals free. When I get my three partners together in March next, I shall endeavor to remedy this, especially so far as small animals are concerned. I own but ⅜ths of the entire show, and not being *personally* with it, I can't do so much in this way. But I shall do my best. . . .

Truly yours,

P. T. Barnum

. . . .

## {261}

## TO REV. E. H. CAPEN

*Private*

Bridgeport, 5 February 1887

Dear Mr. Capen,

. . . Don't encourage false hopes regarding my doing more than I have already provided for in my will—$20,000— for I think that my duty to other objects, as well as to my children, grand- and great-grandchildren, will preclude my going farther. Yet as a matter of curiosity, if nothing more, I will thank you to tell me the estimated costs of those 2 *wings* which you surprised me by kindly flapping in my face while at my house! In haste,

Truly yours,

P. T. Barnum

## {262}

## TO HENRY RENNELL

Barnum doted over his grandchildren and great-grandchildren, referring to the latter as his "baby double-grands." Among his favorites in the second category was Henry Hurd Rennell—"Old Harry" or "P. T.," as Barnum sometimes addressed him—born in 1884 and descended through Barnum's daughter Helen. The Rennells made their home in Harlem, but customarily spent the summers in Bridgeport, living in a house near Barnum's Waldemere, abutting on Seaside Park and Long Island Sound. In this pleasant locale "Old Harry" was thoroughly spoiled by "Grandpop" Barnum, who loved to take him riding in his carriage, dressed him in a favorite sailor suit, and provided him with a succession of iron dogs and live goats and donkeys to ride and drive. Henry Rennell went on to graduate from Yale and to become an engineer and owner of a wire company in Southport, Connecticut. He died in 1958.

Bridgeport, 1 March 1887

Dear Harry,

I thank you for your nice letter. I think about you and would like to see you every day. I am sorry you have a cold and hope you will get well right away. I mean to go to New York next week, Saturday, and shall try to see you Sunday. You must come to the circus always when you like and see lots of horses and riders, elephants and monkeys. They are all funny. Besides, we have men and ladies who swim under the water and men covered all over with hair and little ponies. You will like to see them, and I will be with you. I send you my love and a hundred kisses. Duke sends his love to Harry. Grandma Barnum sends her love and 105 kisses.

Grandpa Barnum

【263】

## TO MORRIS K. JESUP

Bridgeport, 28 April 1887

Dear Sir,

. . . As you are aware, perhaps, I gave a museum building to Tufts College and continually purchase from my partners such dead animals as are needed in that museum. I have purchased the two-horned rhinoceros for that institution. If we should have another and he should die, myself and

[284]

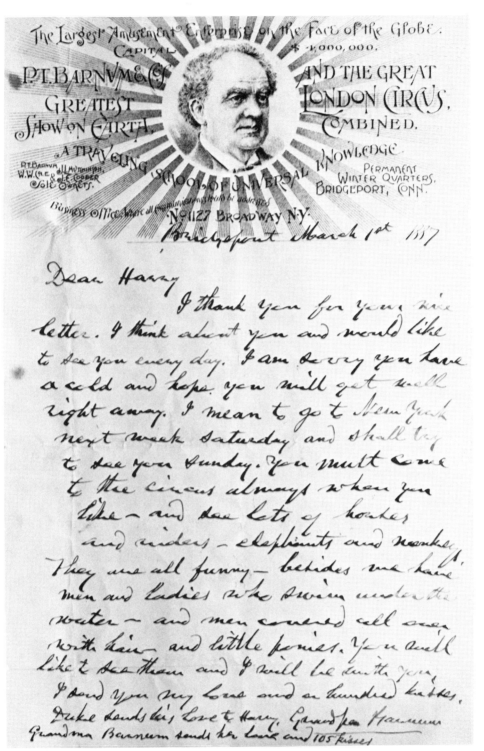

The Largest Amusement Enterprise on the Face of the Globe.
CAPITAL $1,000,000.

P.T.BARNVM&C°
GREATEST
SHOW ON EARTH.

AND THE GREAT
LONDON CIRCUS,
COMBINED.

A TRAVELING
SCHOOL OF UNIVERSAL KNOWLEDGE

PERMANENT
WINTER QUARTERS,
BRIDGEPORT, CONN.

Business Office where all communications should be addressed
N° 1127 BROADWAY N.Y.

*Bridgeport March 1st 1887*

*Dear Harry*

*I thank you for your nice letter. I think about you and would like to see you every day. I am sorry you have a cold and hope you will get well right away. I mean to go to New York next week saturday and shall try to see you sunday. You must come to the circus always when you like — and see lots of horses and riders — elephants and monkeys. They are all funny — besides we have men and ladies who swim under the water — and men covered all over with hair — and little ponies. You will like to see them and I will be with you. I send you my love and a hundred kisses. Duke sends his love to Harry. Grandpa Barnum. Grandma Barnum sends her love and 105 kisses*

P. T. BARNUM TO his great-grandson "HARRY" RENNELL, 1 March 1887. The impression made on a young child by the representation of Barnum in this letterhead may readily be imagined.

partners will try to have your establishment secure it. We have already a tacit understanding that you shall have the first chance for Jumbo skeleton, if you should desire it, after we cease exhibiting it. Jumbo's mounted skin will go to Tufts College.

Respectfully yours,

P. T. Barnum

In a hand other than Barnum's, signed by him. In a letter to Professor Marshall dated 6 May, Barnum writes, *"entre nous,* the Smithsonian has behaved so shabbily, I hope Jumbo's skeleton will go to the N.Y. institution eventually" *(Tufts).*

## ⦃264⦄

## TO REV. E. H. CAPEN

Bridgeport, 13 May 1887

Dear Mr. Capen,

   . . . In order to keep things *secret* about the museum & me, I destroy your letters after reading them & therefore have to ask you confidentially to confirm my recollections or quicken my memory:

   1st—Please repeat what is the estimated *sum* required to make the two additional wings to the main building.

   2d—Is the sum $20,000 which the institution has on hand, recd. from me to help support it, above the $55,000 previously given by me?

Truly yours,

P. T. Barnum

P.S. If the wings are ever built from bequest by me, it will be done under your supervision.

B

# (265)

## TO JOHN P. MARSHALL

*Private*

Bridgeport, 10 July 1887

Dear Sir,

. . . I write this as *confidential* for you & Prof. Capen. I know that Prof. Ward always gets *too high prices* if he can, but I also know that for *cash* he can be *bargained down* to low prices by shrewd Yankees. Perhaps neither you nor Prof. Capen can even for the time being squeeze in under that head. Ward's 1st letter (which I sent you) led me to believe that he had a *valuable* & to our museum a *very important* collection which he would sell *cheap*. He also urged the importance to the museum of a catalogue. I reluctantly half agreed with him to advance a sum not exceeding perhaps $2000 to apply on legacy in my will *if you* thought it a *necessary* & *much needed* expenditure and a really *cheap purchase*. His scenting of money started him up, & he wrote me he had seen you (sick as you were) and that you approved of purchasing most of his collection, & he wanted to supply *cases* enough to make up the $2000 cash outlay & he would call on me Friday, 8th, which he did. I was not well—was preparing for the Adirondacks where I go tomorrow with my wife for a few weeks—& I told him I did not feel able nor willing to advance money in that direction at present. This settled all his expectations of *money* at present. I don't think we should *humor* him in that way. If he has especially important specimens which the museum can't buy *reasonably* after I am deceased, and if he can be *screwed down* to *low prices,* I will advance on future legacy a few hundred dollars for that purpose. But I think that catalogue & cases should not be got until you get my legacy, or until you can get the money from other sources. I know that neither of you gentlemen desire to bother me, & yet I myself am anxious to advance a little & to pay Prof. Marshall's expenses to Rochester & back *if* there is reasonable hope of expending anything less than $1000, & that for almost *indispensable* specimens worth double the price asked for them. Letters will reach me if addressed Bridgeport—but we all need rest & quiet this hot weather.

Truly yours,

P. T. Barnum

Ward had offered a collection of invertebrates to the museum.

## (266)

## TO HENRY RENNELL

Paul Smith's, N.Y., 27 July 1887

My dear Great-Grandson Harry,

It is such a long time since I last saw you, I expect you have grown so large I shall hardly know you. Your sailor's suit will soon be too small for you, I suppose. I am glad to hear you have kept watch of the pumping of muddy water. I should have to hurry home if I did not know that you are watching the people who work for me. You must keep your eyes open and see that they all behave well. You can ride my iron dog when you like, but be careful he don't fall over on you, nor bite you. If you want any more sand before I come home, tell Mr. Pat, my gardener, to cart it for you. When you want any new whips or brooms, you know Grandpa Barnum has got plenty of money to buy them for you. You and I must ride together and see the pigs and other nice things when I get home, and we must ride every day. Goodbye, my dear Harry.

[288]

BARNUM and his FAVORITE GREAT-GRANDSON "HARRY"
RENNELL, wearing the sailor suit Barnum refers to in his letter of 27 July
1887.

PRIVATE COLLECTION.

[289]

Grandma Barnum sends you her love with mine. We hope you are a nice good boy.

Your loving grandpop,

Phineas Taylor Barnum

Paul Smith's in the Adirondacks was one of Barnum's favorite summer retreats. Here he customarily worked on the appendices to his autobiography and wrote articles for various magazines and newspapers.

## {267}

## TO HENRY A. WARD

St. Albans, Vt., 2 August 1887

Dear Prof. Ward,

The people in this region are half crazy about the sea serpent. A hundred respectable persons testify to having seen him in Lake Champlain this season. Clubs are formed in different parts for killing him, & I have assured them I will give $20,000 on conditions offered last year, but a statement will appear in Associated Press papers within 3 days stating that I insist that any persons capturing the monster shall immediately telegraph Prof. Ward, Naturalist, Rochester, N.Y., & he will despatch a force of men at once to preserve him. Now as soon as you see your name thus used in the newspapers, I advise you to take the notice to agent of Associated Press in Rochester & give him a despatch saying over your name that if this monster is captured, the captors must *do so & so* in order to preserve him till you get there. Look out & not get caught by a bogus telegram. If you get a telegram saying a sea serpent is captured, you telegraph immediately to telegraph office in that place asking if it is *really a fact*. Also telegraph if you like to the postmaster & say answer is paid. I will pay all these expenses. If the serpent is not 50 feet long, he is under my mark—but take him if he is only 15 or 20 feet long & leave the captors to agree with me about price. I shall be at Crawford House, White Mountains, for a week and perhaps much longer.

Truly yours,

P. T. Barnum

# (268)

## TO HENRY A. WARD

White Mountains, 9 August 1887

Dear Prof. Ward,

I am too old to bother with turtles in *detail*. . . . The turtle would be so large as to occupy a big cage & I think would not draw enough extra to make it pay unless we could get the report afloat that the capturers thought they had secured the sea serpent. Indeed, *Boston Herald* of today says this *is* what has been seen & supposed to be the S.S. till it was captured. Meanwhile, you might answer . . . & see what it weighs & measures & what will buy it. I can't bother with it *alive* as I could have done 20 years ago.

Truly yours,

P. T. Barnum

## (269)

## TO HENRY RENNELL

Bridgeport, 12 September 1887, 3½ P.M.

My dear Baby Double-Grand, P. T. Rennell,
the Young Sailor,

You can't think how much I miss you and how I look towards your house up here very often each day, thinking I may see you and your dear Duke. But you are gone and Duke is getting fat on grass, the idle, lazy fellow. I would like much to see you now, but we can't help it. We hope you & your papa will come with cousin Fannie & her mamma and "lunch" with us next Friday and have a *nice* time. Grandma Barnum & I send you our love. My iron dog almost wags his tail because he wants to see you. The merry-go-round man is sorry you have gone, & so is Gladdis and everybody else. One thing I am afraid you will *forget*—that is your goat & harness & carriage next summer. Do please *try to remember* it. Now I am going out *alone* in my buggy. If you were here I should drive you awful fast. Hope I shall do it next summer.

From your loving grandpa,

P. T. Barnum

# (270)

## TO JAMES A. BAILEY

At the end of the 1887 season Bailey, restored to health, became Barnum's equal partner in the "Greatest Show on Earth." The winter quarters burned in November of the same year, destroying most of the menagerie and the sacred "white" elephant.

Bridgeport, 5 June 1888

Dear Bailey,

. . . An Italian went through Bridgeport 2 days ago, exhibiting in the streets a couple of boxing monkeys on a little table he carried along. Those who saw them say they boxed splendidly and were a tremendous attraction. He would not let them box till the spectators made a generous contribution. He has gone towards Boston. I could get a friend there to get his address (for another year) or perhaps hire him next winter to train some monkeys for us. Or possibly our pig & monkey trainer would do it for us in same way. I have no doubt it would show *well* & tickle the people in our ring or on the stage next season. Brothwell is busy drawing plans for winter quarters. Success to you & the show.

Truly yours,

P. T. Barnum

# (271)

## TO JAMES A. BAILEY

The circus of Adam Forepaugh (1831–90), with headquarters in Philadelphia, was at this time the greatest rival of the Barnum & Bailey show. Competition between the two establishments was often bitter, and sometimes ludicrous, as when Forepaugh, following the arrival of Barnum's white elephant Toung Taloung in 1884, exhibited a "white" elephant of his own—whitewashed to the complexion of driven snow. At other times an uneasy truce prevailed between the two circuses, with each of them exhibiting in the other's home town and agreeing not to confront each other on their summer routes.

[293]

Dear Bailey,

Forepaugh's show was crammed yesterday afternoon & night. Less than ¼ of the seats were *reserved.* He says they took $8000 in Ansonia. He don't cater for the genteel & refined class & *he don't get them,* but he pleases the masses. His expenses are trifling compared with ours. But we can't afford such dirty & cheap paraphernalia & performers. We can, however, next year have *much less* performances & no museum in big tent.

His big horse is not over 17½ hands high. If you wrote the man from whom we buy horses in N.Y. (Dalman) to let one of his buyers visit when in that vicinity the 19-hands 4-year-old horse described in letter I sent you, he might as a common horse buyer get *refusal* of the big horse at lowest price & then send you or me the particulars. He would be good in sideshow this year or next. Forepaugh seemed friendly. He will immediately stop the bills calling his "The Greatest Show on Earth," & he says if we ever see anything wrong, he will stop it if we let him know it. [*written in margin*] Forepaugh gets his bills printed in Hartford cheaper, he says, and all cuts large or small are *free.*

Truly yours,

P. T. Barnum

P.S. 1 o'clock P.M. I have just returned from downtown. The people who attended Forepaugh's last night were not satisfied. All the shooting by Dr. Carver and the hundreds of shots by Indians and cowboys take place at *opening of the show,* so the tent is so full of smoke for first half hour that persons can't see from one ring to the other. Everybody says it is a *common show* as compared with ours. But he draws large crowds of working and the business class of people. Bowser & Brothwell think he must have taken $9000 yesterday, including privileges.

Forepaugh said when I first saw him yesterday A.M. he

had directed in his will to have the show sold out when he dies. In the afternoon he said, "You & Bailey can get a million and a half of dollars or more by making the two shows into a stock company of $3,000,000 capital." He says by running the 2 shows under one name as a stock company and putting the shares at $100 each, half of the stock or more can be sold at par in Phila. & New York—and when the two shows make a dividend of 15 or 20 percent, the stock will be above par. Forepaugh would like to help engage performers & make contracts, but will never touch a cent of money. He says one R.R. contractor could do it for both shows, that performers would have to take less salaries by half, that the printing would be cheaper, &c. &c. I replied you would decide that. He says he likes you, knows you are an honest man, & he will come over & see us in the winter & thought I had not better mention it to you till then.

P. T. B.

## (272)

## TO JAMES A. BAILEY

Bridgeport, 10 June 1888

Dear Bailey,

I hope you did not think because I wrote you about 4 PAW'S desire to form a stock company that I favored such an idea. Far from it.

I met Mr. Childs yesterday who mentioned his trying to bargain with owner of that Broadway & 6th Ave. & 35th St. triangular building for a museum for us. My dear boy, we must make haste *slowly* till our treasury is vastly improved. Of course you will not commit me for any outside enterprise till we consult personally, for I should require time to *think* before

[295]

"THE FROG AND THE OX," a humorous comment on the rivalry between Barnum's circus and that of Adam Forepaugh, whose establishment was absorbed by Barnum & Bailey in 1890.

COLOR POSTER BY THE STROBRIDGE LITHOGRAPH CO., 1880S.
COURTESY OF THE BRIDGEPORT PUBLIC LIBRARY.

agreeing to bind ourselves to a lease or any large outlay within the next year. In haste,

Truly yours,

P. T. Barnum

## (273)

## TO JAMES A. BAILEY

Home [Bridgeport], 5 July 1888

Dear Bailey,

From last week's returns, according to my figuring, while we are taking more money, there is more expended in proportion and consequently paying less dividends. No doubt you are too busy to examine *figures*, while I have more leisure and study them out. Of course, what hurts me hurts you just as much, & therefore you are as much interested in *economy* as I am. But if you get Merritt to look into it, you will see, I think, that we are expending more than we can afford. I find no fault with this, for I don't know as it can be helped. If it can, then when you consider the figures of expenses, I know you will cut them down if it is possible to do so *without hurting us* more than it will help. The trouble is, everybody thinks we are rich and making fortunes, so they raise prices of everything—railroads, lots, licenses, posting, &c. &c. I hear they charge us $1000 per day license in Minneapolis. If we pay it, then next time St. Pauls [*sic*] will charge us the same & it will run like wildfire to all large towns. I saw it so stated in a newspaper, but I don't believe it as I have not heard it from anywhere else.

On this birthday bringing me to 78 years, my health is better than it was several years ago. But a man of my age cannot stand much worry or work, and he cannot reasonably ex-

[297]

pect to live much longer. I try to impress on the public that we are prepared to keep the show at the *top of the heap* for *generations* to come, & I hope it will be so. . . . You manage it ten times better than I could do it, & I have no fault to find, but a man looking on a game of checkers will sometimes see a move that the players don't observe, & so I give you a friendly hint if I think it is worth anything—& perhaps it is not. . . .

Truly yours,

P. T. Barnum

## (274)

## TO JAMES A. BAILEY

[No place or date, but probably c. July 1888]

Dear Bailey,

Pray don't think of buying museum curiosities *yet.* There are hundreds of thousands of them the world over & in the U.S., but we want *first* to try one year with big show, & I will provide [*sic*] that the big show has *all* the chances at museums when I think it is prudent to start them & before anyone else has a chance at my name. We must have a stock co.:

*Capital One Million Dollars*
P. T. Barnum, President
James A. Bailey, Vice-President & Manager
Merrit Young, Treasurer
——————————, Secy.
*Directors*

| P. T. Barnum | James A. Bailey |
| --- | --- |
| Merrit Young | H. E. Bowser |
| —————— | —————— |

. . . .

# (275)

## TO DAVID PELL SECOR

David Pell Secor was a well-known artist and art critic in New York circles. He eventually resided in Bridgeport, where he died in 1909.

Paul Smith's, N.Y., 10 August 1888

Dear Sir,

I recd. your esteemed letters, & though I am too old to write much or to have "plans," I hasten to scribble a few lines lest you may be entertaining wrong notions of a possible museum in the dim hereafter by my partner & self. *First,* we are not sure of having one *at all. Second,* we could not attempt to compete with the N.Y. Museum of Natural History.

Hence ours would *not* be a natural history museum at all. We should perhaps have some rare specimens of stuffed beasts & birds, but should also have wax figures, automatons, working models of machinery, &c. &c. Groups of animals with artistic effects, such as lions attacking camel &c., I have seen numerous specimens of in Europe, & we are offered them there cheap. But we would not think of arranging with any party about purchasing any specimens in natural history nor indeed any other articles at present. My age (78 last month) makes it uncertain whether I shall live long enough to carry out such plans as we may hereafter make. If you happen to see any *living* curiosity very rare—biped or quadruped—I shall be glad to hear from you and to procure it if feasible.

Yours truly,

Phineas T. Barnum

I return to Bridgeport 1st Sept.

## TO HENRY RENNELL

Paul Smith's, N.Y., 10 August 1888

Dear "Old Harry,"

I hope Ginger and the *other* donkey are well & enjoying themselves. As both donkeys are fond of music, I hope they go to the park concerts. The policemen know you are a *good* boy and always obey your papa and mamma, so they will not put you in jail, but will take good care that you don't get hurt in the crowd.

I expect to be home in 3 weeks, but while we are away I expect you will boss my new house and the new winter quarters. I wanted you also to boss the men who are digging in the park, but Grandma Barnum says that is too much for you to do, so you need not do that. . . . If you don't look out sharp and be a very nice boy, your little brother Frank Junior will put your nose out of joint. He is a beautiful big-eyed jolly little chap. Give him a kiss for me, and mamma may kiss you for me. I hope when I get home we shall have a ride behind my "awful fast" black pony, and you must not go to sleep again when we ride out together. I suppose you drive Duke sometimes and that you once in a while ride the elephant in the merry-go-round. I am sure you are having lots of fun and getting strength and health to last you in New York all winter. I expect to live in New York in the winter and take you riding around Harlem sometimes. Goodbye John—don't stay long—good BOY.

Your grandpop,

P. T. Barnum

# (277)

## TO HENRY RENNELL

[Paul Smith's], 15 August 1888

Dear Harry,

I am glad to hear that Ginger backs and will stand still when you wish him to. Yes, I was a naughty boy, had my mouth washed with soap, and was sent to jail and locked up for 2 months. So you look out and not do as I did. I am glad you can boss the park workmen as well as those at my house and winter quarters. I can't ride camels & elephants here, for there is no merry-go-round. So Grandma Barnum and I go out in a rowboat on the lake. . . . We are all well & send love to all and these 3 [*three circles*] kisses.

Your grandpop,

P. T. Barnum

P.S. Let Frank Junior knock off your hat for me.

P. T. B.

Young Harry, it would seem, had been regaled with stories of "Grandpop" Barnum's youthful escapades, no doubt inspired by Barnum's reference to "jail" in the preceding letter.

# (278)

## TO JAMES A. BAILEY

*Private*

Paul Smith's, N.Y., 27 August 1888

Dear Bailey,

You notice Park & Tilford have *numerous* stores. One only advertises the other—all succeed *because all are* equally *good.* Caswell & Massey, the good druggists, do the same thing with the same success. I continually feel that *somehow* we ought to have 2 shows, one east & the other west, & this can only be done successfully by absorbing Forepaugh's show. He is really getting more public recognition and making more and more money each year, and there is constant danger that Cole & Hutchinson may join him & thus *strengthen* his name and compel us to keep up a too expensive show. Forepaugh's wife is young & wants him to stop traveling personally. He dare not trust it to his son, but he would like to stop traveling and join us in a stock co. of 2 millions, he retaining stock enough to keep young Forepaugh teaching animals & traveling *under our management.*

Now perhaps if we give Forepaugh to understand that we intend to start 2 shows, he may be induced to put his son, his name, & his show property into a stock company with ours, he taking say one quarter and we 3 quarters of the whole stock. A still better way, perhaps, would be for it to go to the public that Forepaugh has retired from business, that the Barnum & Bailey have bought him out and *absorbed* it, and will make a new show equal to the other & thus run 2 shows. Under such an announcement we give Forepaugh ¼ of the stock or such share as we may agree on & take from him & his son a private obligation & bond that they will never again let their names be used, that they will not sell out their stock & that Adam Jr. shall devote himself to the interests of the co., that we shall

[302]

manage the whole & that the Forepaughs may have an accountant travel with the show to look after their interests, that old Adam shall privately advise, consult, aid in buying horses or in any manner that might benefit the co., but shall not travel with it.

  *Some sort* of plan of this kind would fortify us against all opposition, give us a full sweep of the country and the world, enable us to hire attractions cheaper, make it unnecessary to have quite so big shows, and get our printing and all other work done cheaper, pay less salaries to advance agents, &c. &c.—because we should have a complete *monopoly* which nobody would ever *dare* to assail. *Then* the new company could gradually establish museums and do anything else to give it strength & profit for generations. If you privately and seriously think this matter over, I am sure you will see some such plan to remove all opposition will *pay best in the long run.*

P. T. B.

I don't like Forepaugh any better than you do, but he is a stubborn old chap with considerable horse sense, and his show is a continual annoyance and injury to us—and also a *menace,* for in his anxiety to stop traveling personally he is almost sure to get showmen of capital to buy a share of his show cheap and relieve him of the trouble of managing it. His son, Adam Jr., of course has his faults, but if he is managed by us he can be useful as a trainer of animals & a performer. Old Adam is determined to keep his son in the business, so if we can keep his claws cut and have him *interested* in making the show attractive & successful, we thus "chain" the young tiger. You & I or my estate would always hold majority of stock and would have an agreement & bond signed that we should always have an *equal* voting power, and the outside stock should never be voted on, either by its owners nor by you nor me. Other parties desirable might become small owners of stock occasionally so as to keep good coming men in training, but your estate & mine, which now own the whole, must always retain the controlling power. Let us get Forepaugh out of our path *someway* & we sweep the board for all time.

P. T. B.

In this, one of the most remarkable, prescient letters he ever wrote, Barnum charted the course of the American circus to the present day. In 1890, following Forepaugh's death, his show was absorbed by Barnum & Bailey; on the eve of the Depression the Ringlings, successors to Barnum & Bailey, nearly succeeded in establishing a monopoly on circus entertainment with their purchase of the American Circus Corporation, a syndicate consisting of five separate shows; and today the combined Ringling Bros. and Barnum & Bailey Circus annually fields two complete circuses or "units," the Red and the Blue. Even a museum of sorts has been established at the show's permanent Circus World attraction in "Barnum City," Florida.

{279}

## TO HENRY RENNELL

Paul Smith's, N.Y., 28 August 1888

Dear "Old Harry,"

When I made you "Boss" of the new Waldemere, I did not expect you would pull down that big hickory tree in front of the house. You must put it up again immediately so I can see it in its old place Friday when I get home. I am glad "Ginger" *backs*. Give him my love and tell him not to back off the park wall and drown my Harry. I hear that Frank Junior almost begins to walk. Ask him to please not walk away to New York before Thursday, for I want him to pull off my spectacles & hat. Also ask him to please not put Harry's nose out of joint, for it is a pretty nose and would not "blow" nicely if a joint was broken. Don't get married before Grandma Barnum and I get home. Tell Hugh to wind up the coach horses and black pony so they will go "awful fast." Tell Duke to cock his tail up high and look proud. Get ready to ride downtown with

[304]

BARNUM'S LAST TWO MANSIONS, WALDEMERE and MARINA, at Seaside Park. Waldemere (on the left) was dismantled once the new residence was completed in 1888.

me and go to sleep as usual in the carriage. Goodbye, good
b.o.y.

Grandpop,

P. T. Barnum

Give love to papa and mamma and the broken-legged people.

## (280)

## TO WILLIAM F. VILAS

In 1883 the first of the independent Wild West entertainments was launched by "Buffalo Bill" Cody, who succeeded in adding to his show the "killer of Custer," Chief
Sitting Bull, during the 1885 season. The idea evidently appealed to Barnum. Vilas
was Secretary of the Interior.

Bridgeport, 25 September 1888

Dear Sir,

I am about to ask a favor of you which I think you will
wish to grant if I can set the matter clearly before you and
show you what I believe to be true—that any personal profit
coming to me will be small as compared to the benefit to the
government.

Fifty years ago (in January 1837) I had an interview
with President Jackson in the White House on the subject of
Indians. He was at that time transferring the Seminoles from
Florida to a reservation east of the Mississippi.

In the course of his remarks he said that a very effec-
tual and practicable way of impressing the Indians with the
numerical strength of the whites would be to take their chiefs
through the country, and especially to show them our largest
and most thickly populated cities. Also, he said, the sight of
buildings, manufactures, industries, schools, &c. might inspire
some degree of awe and respect in the savage mind. Several

[306]

times since that interview I have tested the wisdom of General Jackson's suggestion. I have, by aid of the government, induced prominent Indian chiefs who were in Washington to see their great Father to visit New York—have taken them through the city, the public schools, the courts of justice, the city prison, and finally into my museum, where I introduced them to the multitude.

I never asked of them any performance, and they felt that they were holding friendly receptions. I never continued this longer than three days, but it was long enough to prove the correctness of President Andrew Jackson's prediction. The savages were amazed, awed, and impressed by the superior numbers and achievements of the white man.

My great traveling show gathers under its canvas each week on an average one hundred thousand persons, and the street pageant attracts fully three hundred thousand per week. The strict moral discipline under which my seven hundred employes are kept is, I am sure, well known to you by reputation and the indorsement of the clergy and distinguished men and women wherever we go.

Now I very much desire the permission and approval of the government to induce *Sitting Bull* and his family to travel through New England and the middle states next year with my exhibition.

If the government has no objection to my project, I shall be much obliged to you for information as to Sitting Bull's whereabouts and the best way to reach him.

Respectfully yours,

P. T. Barnum

THE BARNUM MUSEUM of NATURAL HISTORY at TUFTS
COLLEGE with the mounted hide of Jumbo about to be moved inside,
1889. This photograph shows the original appearance of the building,
before the wings were added.

COURTESY OF TUFTS UNIVERSITY ARCHIVES AND SPECIAL COLLECTIONS.

[308]

## (281)

## TO CHARLES H. STEVENS

Charles Henry Stevens was editor and publisher of the *Homer* (N.Y.) *Republican*. The "malicious report" referred to in this letter was the creation of a journalist who wrote for the New York City newspapers.

Bridgeport, 21 December 1888

Dear Sir,

Permit me to thank you, which I cordially do, for your kindness in contradicting in your paper of 20th inst. the malicious report that I shall retire from "The Greatest Show on Earth." No sir! I shall die in harness, beloved, as I hope, by at least all of the *children*.

Truly yours,

P. T. Barnum

## (282)

## TO JOHN P. MARSHALL

New York, 18 March 1889

Prof. Marshall:

If you & Prest. Capen think that the mounted skin of Jumbo put in Barnum Museum *now*—to remain till wanted, perhaps not *for years* & possibly never—will *help* the college, I will send it to you at my own expense for freight within a few days, if you will place it at once on exhibition in museum, get it into Boston newspapers, and keep it clean & safe.

Truly yours,

P. T. Barnum

. . . .

[309]

# (283)

## TO MORRIS K. JESUP

New York, 18 March 1889

Dear Sir,

   We propose to loan to your establishment, free of charge, the skeleton of our great elephant Jumbo, on condition that you keep it in good order, clean, free from chance of being handled or injured, and held by you at all times subject to our order.

P. T. Barnum

Jumbo's skeleton, minus a few toe bones but otherwise in good condition, is presently stored in the "whale room" of the American Museum of Natural History. Around 1907 it was declared the "type specimen" of a subspecies of African elephant, and as such has particular value for taxonomic science. Both the skeleton and mounted hide of Jumbo were taken to England with the circus during the winter of 1889–90, but were then returned to the same institutions.

# (284)

## TO H. E. BOWSER

Barnum was determined that his name should continue actively with the circus after his death, and to this end he bequeathed $25,000 to his grandson Clinton Hallett Seeley, son of his deceased daughter Pauline, on condition he legally change his middle name to Barnum and habitually use this name "so that the name Barnum shall always be known as his name." It was also Barnum's wish that "Clinte" should travel with and assist in the management of the show. C. Barnum Seeley had little interest in circus matters, however, and did not live up to his grandfather's expectations.

*Private*

New York, 12 April 1889

Dear Bowser,

   Lest your mind might not be quite at ease after seeing the announcements about C. *Barnum* Seeley, I simply want to say what I have often told you—that I am *perfectly satisfied* with the manner in which you fill, & have filled from the first day you joined me, the responsible position you hold in my affairs.

This splurge about Clinte is simply to give him a *boom* in public estimation & to show that my *name* is to be continued. I have not given him, nor do I expect to give him, any power whatever in regard to my affairs. He felt modest & half frightened about taking my name, lest some of my progeny should be jealous. But they need not be, though I think him more capable than any & all of them of doing business properly, and I hope he will by & bye quit the brokers' board & attend to his own building & get posted as much as he can about the show business & my real estate. Neither he nor my wife or *any* of my progeny know anything about the *footings* of my estate, nor do I wish them to know. . . .

Truly yours,

P. T. Barnum

# (285)

## TO JAMES A. BAILEY

[New York, 14 April 1889]

Dear Bailey,

I hope your mind is at rest about my eldest grandson, C. Barnum Seeley. It was necessary for Hurd, Rennell, & Thompson to know that young Barnum will be the one to look after my estate's interest after I am gone, although *he* will have only $1/9$th interest in my estate—that being his share as divided among my children & grandchildren. It is better for you & me that my successor be named Barnum. He thinks everything of you and your management, and every way he is the *best* representative of my estate that can be found. But while I live *he has nothing to say*—only the more & better he gets posted about all my affairs, the better it is for you & me. Nobody but him (and my executors) can have a word to say after I am gone. But I have no right to go this ten or fifteen years, & I shall certainly stick to life & *to you* as long as I can. *You suit me exactly* as a partner and as a friend.

Truly yours,

P. T. Barnum

. . . .

## (286)

### TO OLIVER WENDELL HOLMES

Bridgeport, 5 June 1889

Dear Dr. Holmes,

The last time I had the pleasure of meeting you I asked and recd. the favor of your written opinion concerning the Tattooed Greek, for which I was thankful.

*I ask no favor now,* except that you will use enclosed tickets and if convenient see by far the most amazing traveling show that I ever dreamed of sometime during week after next. I expect to be in Boston during that week with my 40-year-old English wife. Her highest aspiration is to see the author of the "Autocrat," whose writings delighted her beyond measure before she ever saw the U.S.

Admiringly yours,

P. T. Barnum

# (287)

## TO OLIVER WENDELL HOLMES

Boston, 20 June 1889

My dear Dr. Holmes,

The fates seem surely to be against me as well as my wife. I ran to Tufts College commencement for a couple of hours yesterday, pursuant to a previous engagement, and got back to the big show only ten minutes after you had left. Unfortunately, "a miss is as good (or bad) as a mile," so I had to grin & bear it. I mailed to my wife your very *promising* letter, in case she called on you. She replies that when she read it she cried. Of course, that's women's first resort & relief—but she begged me, as she was not to blame for being sick, to try & get you to send her to Bridgeport, Conn., at *any* convenient time, your valued photo & autograph. I know it is asking *much,* but the English are so desirous of obtaining such *mementoes,* it is difficult to shake them off.

I called at your house yesterday & begged my way to your library, so that I can make my wife more miserable by telling her what she has missed. Pray excuse this *long* rigamarole & believe me ever

Your admirer & friend,

P. T. Barnum

# (288)

## TO JAMES A. BAILEY

Paul Smith's, N.Y., 26 August 1889

Dear Bailey,

. . . My stomach bothers me here with indigestion. It is getting worn out, but I am gaining strength for the London tour, I hope.

Now my dear fellow, if our horses get to Bridgeport before *2d* Oct. they will not only be *taxed*—also R.R. cars—but it will establish a *precedent* which will cost us hundreds if not a thousand dollars per year every year, & *we ought not to do it.* If you let off our horses at Port Chester, N.Y., & let them *travel* to Bridgeport, it would help us some if they don't cross Conn. line till *2d* Oct., but none of our movable property ought to be in *Conn.* till after *1st* day of Oct., as that is the day fixed to tax property. Do try to avoid it *somehow.*

Why can't Gardner or somebody go & see Forepaugh & arrange with him to let us show in Philadelphia a week? He might do it by getting a good price for his lot—& perhaps by our threatening not to let him have a lot in Bridgeport next year and by making other threats, or possibly by coaxing. I suppose our bill posters have *finished* & been discharged. Still, you *can* fix it for Philadelphia *somehow* if you see that it is best, & it really seems to me it will be thousands in our pocket now & hereafter. Pray *try* to fix it.

Truly yours,

P. T. Barnum

. . . .

Horses, mules, poultry, and a multitude of asses are still subject to property taxes in Connecticut.

## TO JAMES A. BAILEY

Paul Smith's, N.Y., 26 August 1889

Dear Bailey,

I am dreadful sorry for our railway accident and the trouble it must have given you. It ought at least to show us the importance of making our show into a *stock company.* Neither of us have a right to jeopardize all we are worth in any single enterprise. If we should somehow kill 50 persons instead of 30 horses it might cost us ¼ million dollars. We can form a *stock company* with a small comparative capital—say two or three hundred thousand dollars, you continuing to own half the stock & I half—& then whatever happens we are liable only for what property the *show* owns. Please send this to Mr. Hull or any other attorney you please & let us fix it good & strong for our own safety.

Truly yours,

P. T. Barnum

## TO ISAAC T. ROGERS?

In October 1889 Barnum sailed for England and what he termed "the closing act of my eventful life"—a season of the "Greatest Show on Earth" at London's great exhibition hall Olympia, where Barnum himself, driven daily around the hippodrome track, was accounted one of the prime attractions. Isaac T. Rogers, variously addressed in other letters written around this time as "old friend" and "beloved old gentleman," had served with Barnum in the Connecticut legislature in 1865, at which time their friendship commenced.

London, 10 January 1890

Dear Antique,

It's a queer episode & perhaps finis for Phineas at the age of 80 or thereabouts to enjoy, but I could not have chosen a more tempting nor pleasant way of winding up a long, active, and enjoyable life. You are right about the London *Times* column. Money could not have purchased it. The lesser branches of the press & all shades of the people from crown to cabin are unanimous in praise of the pluck & enterprise which have given them the *really* "Greatest Show on Earth" that was ever gotten up by two persons. The hospitalities extended to Mrs. Barnum, my grandson Barnum Seeley, & myself are beyond all my expectations, especially from the class of dignitaries who do it. I am obliged to decline $^9/_{10}$ths of them. I never allowed any person to patronize me—neither did my wife ever permit it to her, she says—but it has not been attempted here in a single instance. We all meet as friends & on *equal* ground, & much pleasure is thereby mutually enjoyed. . . .

Our healths have thus far been surprisingly robust, but yesterday my Nancy began running at the nose, and an hour ago Dr. Playfair pronounced it influenza & tells her to keep her bed a few days, partake of no solid food, & not let her husband catch it. It is milder here than in N.Y.

If we live through & have no accidents, the big show (which is daily *full*) will close about 15th Feb. & reach Bridgeport about 5th to 10 March. *I* shall not start for New York *before* 1st March, & we may be wise enough to go to Nice & perhaps Italy to spend the whole of that terrible month. But "man proposes &c." May good health & happiness attend on you & yours—& if not, may we always receive as blessings whatever the good Father sends us. Wife joins in love to you & yours.

As ever thine,

P. T. Barnum

# {291}

## TO WHITELAW REID

London, 8 February 1890

My dear Mr. Reid,

We close our successful show season here next Saturday night, 15th inst. On that eventful night my wife and I shall be in the royal box at Olympia. Lord Chief Justice and Lady Coleridge assure me that they will be there, and we fully expect our U.S. Minister, Mr. Lincoln, in the same box (as he says he hopes his son will be much improved by that time). Also the Earl of [and] Countess of Rosebury, the Lord Mayor of London and the Lady Mayoress, with other distinguished persons. Also in the royal box or my private box adjoining we have the promise of their presence from U.S. Consul-Genl. John C. New & wife, Mr. Oliver R. Johnson, Vice-Consul, &c. Now my dear friend, I beg the *great favor* of your presence in the royal box on that farewell night and if possible that of Mrs. Reid.

You perfectly understand the great éclat that your name will give and the consequent benefit it will be to me and my marvelous show on our return to America, & I sincerely hope & trust that you will even strain a point if necessary in order to serve an old friend of 80 who has accomplished such an unprecedented success with all classes in England from the princes and peers to the peasants. Expecting a favorable reply, I am now as always

Yours sincerely,

P. T. Barnum

By the date of this letter Reid was U.S. Minister to France.

[317]

## (292)

## TO REV. DIXON SPAIN

London, 13 February 1890

Dear Sir,

Your letter recd. We have already shipped all blocks & electros of me to the U.S. I send you a *good* photo from which a block could be made by what is called the "process" for I think a small expense. . . . As I have no recollection of what you call my "marvellous testimony," I shall feel obliged if you will kindly send me a copy of your leaflet.

I have now been an abstainer forty-three years. I am robust, hale, & hearty. I do not have an ache nor a pain. I awaken after 7 hours sleep with a feeling of gratitude and some surprise that I, who am within 5 months of 80 years old, am in such *capital health.* Had I continued to drink intoxicants, I should have been in my grave thirty or more years ago. . . .

Very truly yours,

P. T. Barnum

The "marvellous testimony" was that contained in Barnum's letter to Spain dated 18 November 1882.

# (293)

## TO JAMES A. BAILEY

London, 22 February 1890

Dear Bailey,

I am anxious to know whether or not the Philadelphia business is to be completed, & you might cable

> Barnum
> Hotel Victoria
> London
> *Yes*

if it is done—or *No* if it is not. Indeed, you can write also if you have anything special to say, for Mrs. Barnum's doctor, Playfair, decides that we *must not* leave here before 21st March. But in any event I shall, if I live, get to New York *before the show opens,* even if I have to leave my wife behind to come a few weeks after I do. But it is almost a case of life and death with my wife. The doctor tells her she is getting much better—making blood & good blood, of which she had but little—& that a very few weeks more will *cure* her. She feels and knows she is gaining, and therefore it is very important that she don't give it up. Please let me know *when* we shall open & where, and if life & health are spared me I shall be on hand days & probably *weeks* before we open. . . . Hope you get home all right & that the animals will be equally lucky.

Truly yours,

P. T. Barnum

. . . .

Bailey and the circus were en route for America when this letter was written. The "Philadelphia business" was the purchase of Forepaugh's circus, made by Barnum, Bailey, and James E. Cooper and managed by the last.

## TO JAMES A. BAILEY

London, 26 February 1890

Dear Bailey,

That lion, horse, & man which showed at Covent Garden are now with Hengler for a few weeks, & I understand that they are booked with other circuses & gardens in Great Britain for *big prices* a year in advance. Of course it is a *sell* in part, & yet many who see it think it wonderful—& the *posters* are very *taking*. I hear that Hagenbeck's brother has a similar set for sale. I don't propose that *we* shall buy it, but would it not be a big feature for *C*? By the way, I depend on you to see that some good accountant shall be with C in my interest, & I suppose you will also be represented there. All we want is to have everything done *on the square* & to *know* through our own representatives just *how* things are conducted. C is honest & smart, & yet he may not be so particular about forming and preserving a good reputation for the concern as we should. I have no person in particular in view for the place, but Benj. Fish or Bowser must know of a suitable man who will be an honest *worker* at fair wages.

I am very sorry we have such a great number of my Life on hand. In that book it is stated that they may be purchased at *Low's Exchange,* 44 Charing Cross, London. Since we closed Olympia, Low's people have recd. orders for a dozen or more books with P.O. orders to pay for them. I don't suppose they will sell many, but they ought to keep them *on hand,* and as we want to get rid of them so as sometime to add an appendix about London season, I hope you will let Low have *at cost* whatever books he may offer to take, & I should not mind trusting him for them if he wishes it & give him the privilege of returning fifty volumes in good order if he can't sell them. . . .

Quite likely Mrs. Barnum will remain here a month after I leave, but if I am alive & half well I shall be *surely* in New York some days before show opens—even if you open April 14th, which I fear will be a week or two too early for canvas tent. You know how it was last year in Brooklyn from April 22d to 27th. I am strong & *well* & hope you are ditto.

Truly yours,

P. T. Barnum

. . . .

The horse-riding lion act was new at this time. Carl and Wilhelm Hagenbeck—in addition to their circus activities—were renowned as animal dealers and for their training of animals. "C" was James E. Cooper.

## (295)

## TO JAMES E. COOPER

Bridgeport, 9 April 1890

Dear Cooper,

As Mr. Bailey informed you, I have engaged a man to represent my interests in the show and to work faithfully for the benefit of *all* of us. It is absurd to think of my putting money into anything of this sort without having a representative with it. Everybody does this. Mr. Bailey & I understood this before I engaged Mr. Evans. He is a perfect bookkeeper, a good businessman, strong, sensible, and just the man of business we want. You certainly are not justified in engaging men for *all* the responsible positions, & you must *keep open* this bookkeeper's place for my man. I know you are *honest,* or else I would never have joined you. But business is business, & it must be done *right.* You & Mr. Bailey & I must pull together *harmoniously*—play into each other's hands—and we can make a heap of money without fail all the time. . . . Success to *you* & *us*.

Truly yours,

P. T. Barnum

. . . .

## TO WILLIAM T. HORNADAY

Still trying to placate Barnum, Hornaday had recently forwarded a large collection of specimens to the museum at Tufts. "During the last week I have been much disquieted," he wrote to Barnum on 29 March, "by a rumor that has reached us from New York to the effect that Jumbo's skeleton, which you promised us some years ago, is 'positively to go to the American Museum of Natural History' at New York, to remain permanently, when the great show returns from Europe. *Surely* this is not true. What says the King of Showmen?" (*Smithsonian Institution Archives*). Upon receiving the present reply from Barnum, Hornaday sent it to George Brown Goode, Assistant Secretary of the Smithsonian in charge of the National Museum, with the following memorandum:
   This letter convinces me of three things as follows:
   1. That the Barnum Museum of Tufts College is utterly insatiable.
   2. That the National Museum will never get Jumbo's skeleton.
   3. Having now fully squared accounts with Mr. Barnum, that we should *call* it square and quit! . . .
Goode apparently agreed with his assessment, for the memorandum bears the notation "File all *Barnum*" and, at its top enclosed in a heavily drawn box, the valedictory "R.I.P." (*Smithsonian Institution Archives*).

New York, 16 April 1890

Dear Sir,

I recd. your letter at Bridgeport, forwarded it to Prof. Marshall, & asked him to give me his report on the articles you sent so I could write you. He writes that the specimens have not yet arrived.

At the age of 80 I have not too much strength to expend in correspondence, but in order that we (I mean Prof. Goode, you, & the Smithsonian Institution) should have a clear understanding of my feelings, I will state a few things.

Long before my New York museum was burned, I was personally acquainted with Prof. Henry & we were good friends. Whenever I could be of service to the Smithsonian, I gladly did so. Prof. Henry appreciated this & said he recognized my museum as a *public institution,* entitled to receive—& I should receive—casts of everything that other public institutions recd. from the Smithsonian, as well as duplicates of any curiosities which could be spared. As my wild animals died, they were invariably sent to the Smithsonian, and I was glad to have it so. When later on I built a *museum* building for Tufts College, I began to care more about getting contributions for it than I ever did for my N.Y. museum & so expressed myself to you—& also said I intended that Jumbo's skeleton [*sic*] should find its last resting place there. I felt *and still do* that a great *national* museum situated in the nation's capital is the most proper place for Jumbo's skeleton. Hence whenever I have said this to any of my *partners* who owned a share in Jumbo, as well as in the whole show, it has been conceded that my idea is correct. But Jumbo is still occasionally an attraction at various times in our show. He has been a big *drawing* curiosity during our late visit in London. Anticipating that such occasions may occur (for instance, if we should send a show to the continent of Europe or perhaps to Australia), we merely loaned the *skeleton* to the N.Y. Museum of Nat. His., had it *labelled* "loaned by P. T. Barnum," and took from its president a receipt with a written statement that the skeleton was *loaned* by Barnum & Bailey & *held subject to their order.* The same thing is done by the Barnum Museum at Tufts College in regard to Jumbo's stuffed hide which we took also to London, though we hope that college will finally own it, as we hope the Smithsonian will finally own the skeleton.

I confess that I have felt that the National Museum did not contribute as much as she easily could, and *ought,* toward the Tufts museum, but this feeling has not extinguished my paramount desire to do what I reasonably can for this great *national* museum, as well as for its zoological garden when it starts. Having thus thrown a small ray of light on this subject,

I will say no more at present, but let the *future* declare whether the proper thing will be done by me and also by the Smithsonian & National Museum.

Our great show will be in Washington, I think, next month. . . .

Truly yours,

P. T. Barnum

## (297)

## TO FRANK PARSONS

Frank Parsons (1854–1908), educator, lecturer, political and social scientist, was the author of numerous books and articles. The present letter was evidently solicited for one of these publications.

Bridgeport, 20 May 1890

Dear Sir,

I will snatch a few busy moments to reply to your two questions.

1st. The child's training in literature and life begins with the stories told him at his mother's knee. These should be told him in plain, pure, grammatical English, and he should be taught at the first to pronounce words correctly. Too much "pootsy-tootsy," namby-pamby baby talk is undesirable. Stories for children should be so chosen as to develop imagination and observation, and to cultivate courage, tenderness, generosity, and cheerfulness. No poor or ignoble book should enter the house. As the child grows older, he should have read to him passages of literature which, while fairly within his comprehension, are models of literary style. The great world of history, biography, and travel, selected from "the best thoughts and best words" extant, should be gradually & pleasantly opened to him, and he should be talked with about these readings, in an informal way, while walking or playing with his preceptor—be it mother, sister, or other relative.

Learning thus the natural bent of the child's mind, it should be sacredly respected—for as one has an inclination, taste, & genius for one branch of study and pursuit, and another for another, we should be careful to not put them on the wrong track at their first start in life. Those who do not follow where their natural genius leads will be apt to find it uphill work as long as they live. Round pegs will not fit square holes.

As the true end of culture is to make people as unselfish as possible, and hence easier to live with, children should be taught courtesy and toleration by being invariably courteous and tolerant ourselves.

I should, above almost everything else, try to cultivate in the child a certain kindly sense of humor. Whenever a pure, hearty laugh rings through literature, the child should be permitted & taught to enjoy it. It should also be taught to accept the inevitable cheerfully.

2d. The reading which I enjoy most comprises history, travels, biography, and such works as *the Spectator,* the writings of Shakespeare, Irving, Whittier, Franklin, with occasional dips into Holmes, Dickens, Lowell, Stowe, Twain, and others of that ilk. A skimming of the best newspapers and foreign and domestic magazines seem to me indispensable to rational enjoyment.

P. T. Barnum

As I write in great haste, without revision, please make verbal or other corrections wherever you find them needful.

P. T. Barnum

## (298)

## TO REV. E. H. CAPEN

Bridgeport, 22 May 1890

Dear Prof, Capen,

I am *extremely sorry* to have disturbed you when you are so busy & then to have it turn out as it has, of no immediate advantage to anybody. But such is life. Disappointments turn up at every hour, & though vexing, they are all right in the end.

I have been unexpectedly called on for the expenditure of a hundred thousand dollars for the extension of the show business & therefore cannot spare a dollar this year for the museum. Any expense incurred with the architect I will gladly pay when you send me the bill.

Those "wings" are *sure* things in the future, but at present you & Prof. Marshall must take the "will for the deed." The "will" has it, all right, & the "deed" will be.

I shall not be able to attend commencement because I am a foolish old man of 80 and have agreed to visit the big show at Chicago at that time.

Truly yours,

P. T. Barnum

## (299)

## TO JOHN P. MARSHALL

Bridgeport, 22 May 1890

Dear Prof. Marshall,

I think I am as *sorry* as you can be that I felt obliged to write President Capen by this mail, giving him the reason why I *cannot* this year carry out my earnest intentions in regard to those "wings," but so it is, & there's no use in crying. "It's all for the best," as we Universalists must believe, & so we must continue to hope & expect to fly with that pair of "wings" when the proper time comes.

Truly yours,

P. T. Barnum

The wings were indeed added, the second as late as 1934, through money Barnum bequeathed to Tufts.

## (300)

## TO JAMES A. BAILEY

Paul Smith's, N.Y., 12 August 1890

Dear Bailey,

We intend to leave Paul Smith's next week, Thursday 21st, & get home 22d. If Mad[ison] Sqr. Garden is in good condition & its seating need not be made new for us, perhaps you may think it best to use it a few weeks during Christmas holidays, when all the children return to their New York parents. If this could be done and a little *pantomime*—Bluebeard or Cinderella—could be introduced in the ring, or the lions on horseback or in harness can be bought by Starr and used there instead of Kiralfy's show, it seems to me it would be worth our while, besides giving a show there with some different features in the spring. But I only suggest this idea as it happened to cross my mind.

Truly yours,

P. T. Barnum

George O. Starr was one of Barnum's London agents.

(301)

## TO JAMES A. BAILEY

Bridgeport, 24 August 1890

*Suggestions*—good, bad, & indifferent

The writer of this enclosed Alabama letter I never saw, but I have seen so many of his *cute* writings that I opened a correspondence with him. I wrote him that it was possible but *not very probable* that we might sometime want to engage a bright, smart *press agent,* and if he liked, he might send me a description of himself. He has done so in enclosed letter. He is evidently a good scholar and a sharp writer with original ideas. If we should have to part with Stow or any other *press agent,* I think he could be able to more than fill the place of the best of them. . . .

2d. Hope you will print under my portrait next season

*The Children's Friend*

It pleases parents & children.

3d. How would it do to let Cooper advertise next year

[328]

as *"former partner* of P. T. *Barnum* and *J. A. Bailey"*? Would it not help his show & not hurt us?

3½. Hope you will engage Madison Sqr. Garden for a few weeks next spring.

4th. We are doing well so far this season, except Oakland Gardens. Now I hope we won't spend too much for wintering and in fitting up for next season. The same advance couriers which we print this year & same lithographs are just the thing for next season & will save us much in drawing pictures & setting type.

*Private.* Here is what Fish wrote me from Muskegon Aug. 21st (don't mention it to him). He writes, "I feel tired and weary, low-spirited. We have had a pretty hard season and now going to be a long one, Nov. 8th (and no more salary for it), and next season will be the same. At the moment I feel I have had enough of show business when I have completed this season. But being out of sorts and as all things look gloomy then, I will write no further."

I have written Fish that he knows I am paying him about $1000 per season for auditing Bowser's accounts, although he don't do it thoroughly because the show takes the time I expected he would devote to my Bridgeport interests, and if his letter means that he ought to have more salary from the show, he must mention it to you. If he does so, you can do what you think best. We know he is honest and correct in accounts & has got used to show business, and a new man in his place would not probably be half as satisfactory. But nobody must think we cannot do without them. If he *ought* to have an increase of $200 or $300, I am agreed.

P. T. B.

The Alabama writer was possibly M. M. Brannan.

## (302)

### TO HELEN HURD RENNELL

Barnum spent the month of October 1890 in Denver, visiting his daughter Helen and enjoying, as his wife later wrote in *The Last Chapter,* "a month of flawless happiness." The present letter was written to his granddaughter. Petrel's Nest was one of the cottages Barnum had built for family and friends at the Bridgeport "compound."

Denver, 10 October 1890

Dear Helen,

We sincerely hope that in this mellow October the country is pleasant to you all, & that you are all enjoying the healthful breezes of Bridgeport in general & Seaside Park in particular. As I miss you all & think of you many times daily, I shall not be surprised if we are somewhat missed, & especially as all of us, including the residents of Petrel's Nest, left you almost at the same time. But these changes, & others harder to bear, *must* frequently occur in this life, & "the wind is tempered to the shorn lamb" where such a lovely disposition as yours is the guiding star. I hope Harry, Frank Jr., & Mildred are well & happy, & that you & Frank Senior enjoy the evenings better than when I was calling him to California Jack. Aunt Nancy is out riding. She agreed before we left home that what writing was done should mostly be with her hand, as mine needs a rest, as well as my head. We are both well & enjoying new scenes daily. We shall *not* go to *Japan,* as the Denver papers have it, but it is *possible* that since we are halfway to California, we *may* go there. Hope Frank's business is good. I watch money market reports daily, & as "what is one man's meat is another's poison," I smile at every increase of interest rates, seeing that they promise him a little profit besides the reputation of being a millionaire. . . . With best love to all, I am

Your affectionate grandpop,

P. T. Barnum

[330]

THOMAS BALL'S MONUMENTAL BRONZE STATUE OF BARNUM in
Seaside Park, unveiled on 4 July 1893.

# (303)

## TO JAMES A. BAILEY

Upon returning to Bridgeport in the fall of 1890, Barnum was felled by a stroke in early November and remained confined to his home until his death the following April. This, his final letter to his partner Bailey, was written five days before his death. From a typed transcription in the McCaddon Papers of the Princeton University Library Theatre Collection. Location of original letter unknown.

Bridgeport, 2 April 1891

My dear Bailey,

Although I would not pain my family by expressing such an opinion openly to them, yet I cannot but feel that my present sickness must necessarily have a fatal termination. If such should be the case, I know you will not consider a few words of advice from me as an impertinence, but will heed them and treasure them up as a legacy.

Although all arrangements for the continuance of our show are now completed and I have made further directions for its management in my will, still, a few words from one who has been more than ordinarily successful in the journey of life will not come amiss in the control of your future movements. I fully believe that if you faithfully follow my methods you cannot fail.

It has been my universal plan, as you well know, to make the public aware of what I was about to offer it, to get the best of everything and the most of it, and then to advertise freely and without fear. Never attempt to catch a whale with a minnow.

I am indebted to the press of the United States for almost every dollar which I possess and for every success as an amusement manager which I have ever achieved. The very great popularity which I have attained both at home and abroad I ascribe almost entirely to the liberal and persistent use of the public journals of this country.

But it is of no advantage to advertise unless you intend

THE BARNUM INSTITUTE of SCIENCE and HISTORY, today the
Barnum Museum, whose land and building were donated by Barnum.

[333]

to honestly fulfil the promises made in this manner. You must—I repeat it, *must*—have always a great and progressive show and also one which is clean, pure, moral, and instructive. Never cater to the baser instincts of humanity, strive as I have always done to elevate the moral tone of amusements, and always remember that the children have ever been our best patrons. I would rather hear the pleased laugh of a child over some feature of my exhibition than receive as I did the flattering compliments of the Prince of Wales. I am prouder of my title "The Children's Friend" than if I were to be called "The King of the World."

I regret exceedingly that my bodily weakness prevents my being present at the exhibition in New York, for I veritably believe that if I could again see the rows of bright-faced children at our matinees and observe their eyes grow round with wonder or hear their hearty laughter, it would do me more good than all the medicine in the world.

I am too weak to write more now, but let me entreat you to never allow the honorable and honestly acquired title of "The Greatest Show on Earth" to be in any way disgraced or lessened in fame. Go on as you have begun and I know you will continue to prosper.

Should this be, as perhaps it may, my last communication to you, I wish to assure you of my unalterable esteem, affection, and trust in you, and to bestow a fatherly blessing upon one who is in every way so worthy to become my successor.

Fraternally yours,

P. T. Barnum

# ❦APPENDIX❦

## "I Thus Address the World"

The following is a transcription of a cylinder recording of Barnum's voice made toward the end of his trip to London during the winter of 1889–90. Around 1940 it was issued on a 78 rpm National Vocarium disc with a spoken introduction by Yale University's legendary "Billy" Phelps; and in 1970 it was again issued, this time on a 33⅓ rpm disc, in Argo's *The Wonder of the Age: Mr. Edison's New Talking Phonograph.*

I wish to give my parting thanks to the British public and to assure them that I shall ever gratefully cherish most pleasant memories of their kindness and hospitality, even higher than the pecuniary success with which they have crowned my efforts to please them.

I thus address the world through the medium of the latest wonderful invention, Edison's phonograph, so that my voice, like my great show, will reach future generations and be heard centuries after I have joined the great and, as I believe, happy majority.

P. T. Barnum

[335]

# ❦LOCATIONS OF LETTERS❦

**THE NUMBERS IN** the following list correspond to those of the letters in this edition. "Autobiography," followed by dates, refers to the three key editions of Barnum's own story. "Location Unknown" refers to letters whose originals, if still extant, have not been found. "Private Collections" is used to designate letters whose owners wish to remain anonymous.

American Antiquarian Society, Worcester, Massachusetts (Miscellaneous Manuscripts): 30
American Museum of Natural History Archives: 243, 263, 283
Autobiography: (1855) 28; (1869) 35, 76, 129; (1889) 197, 236
Barnum Museum, Bridgeport, Connecticut: 140
Boston Athenaeum Library: 8, 9, 10, 11, 12, 13, 14, 15, 16, 17, 19, 20, 21, 22, 23
Boston Public Library, Department of Rare Books and Manuscripts: 116
Bridgeport Public Library, Historical Collections: 1, 44, 66, 70, 98, 159, 169, 186, 200, 224, 247, 273, 275, 285, 293, 294, 295
British Library, Department of Manuscripts: 85, 204, 205, 292

# ❧A NOTE ON SOURCES❧

**AS STATED IN** the introduction, the impetus for this publication came from the editor's perusal of Barnum's letters over the course of many years and his belief that others would take an equal interest, even delight, in reading them. While beginning to assemble his materials, he was pleasantly surprised to discover that Barnum had taken his place alongside such luminaries as Emerson, Holmes, and Longfellow in *American Literary Manuscripts* (2d ed.; Athens: University of Georgia Press, 1977), a work that, besides furnishing additional justification for the present volume, has been an invaluable guide. The *National Union Catalogue of Manuscript Collections* lists the locations of a few manuscripts not included in *American Literary Manuscripts*. There do not appear to be many letters or manuscripts in libraries abroad.

Barnum himself, in the various editions of his autobiography, published a fair number of letters both by and to him—together with speeches, written agreements, proclamations, etc.—and virtually all of these may be found in George S. Bryan's superb two-volume edition, *Struggles and Triumphs: or, The Life of P. T. Barnum, Written by Himself* (New York: Knopf, 1927). Based on the 1855, 1869, and 1889 editions of the autobiography, and including Nancy Barnum's separately published *The Last Chapter,* this is as complete an edition as one could desire, omitting very little that is in the three earlier editions and covering the entire span of Barnum's life. In making use of any letters in the autobiography whose originals could not be located, the present editor has quoted directly from the three earlier key editions, depending on when the letters first appeared in them.

Barnum's twentieth-century biographers—among whom the most noteworthy to date are M. R. Werner, *Barnum* (New York: Harcourt, Brace, 1923), Harvey W. Root, *The Unknown Barnum* (New York: Harper, 1927), and Irving Wallace, *The Fabulous Showman: The Life and Times of P. T. Barnum* (New York: Knopf, 1959)—occasionally quote from his letters, but these are nearly all taken from the autobiography. More scholarly and original is the work of Neil Harris, whose *Humbug: The Art of P. T. Barnum* (Boston: Little, Brown, 1973) is an outstanding contribution to our knowledge of Barnum's operational methods and public career. It was Harris, for instance, who first made use of the uninhibited Barnum-Kimball correspondence preserved in the Boston Athenaeum, besides a great many other previously untapped primary sources, although none of the letters he cites are quoted in their entirety.

Among other publications, stray letters and documents are scattered throughout an almost bewildering variety of books, periodicals, and contemporary newspapers. Otis Skinner, for example, at the very beginning of his autobiography *Footlights and Spotlights* (Indianapolis: Bobbs-Merrill, 1924), proudly quotes, and even reproduces as an illustration, the letter of recommendation from Barnum that secured him his first acting job in Philadelphia; and the autograph dealer Charles Hamilton, in an article entitled "P. T. Barnum, Genius of Humbug" (*Hobbies,* March 1953), transcribes several Barnum letters that were then in his possession.

A great many letters unlisted in both *American Literary Manuscripts* and the *National Union Catalogue of Manuscript Collections* are preserved in smaller libraries and historical societies. Even more, the editor suspects, remain in private hands. A number of circus collectors—in particular Mr. Fred Pfening III, who recently acquired the collection once the property of Granville Wood—have amassed considerable holdings of Barnum manuscripts. Then, too, there are the archives of the various municipalities, businesses, educational institutions, societies, churches, etc. Barnum was associated with, many of which are still in existence and possess letters and other documents pertaining to the showman's career.

Doubtless much remains to be discovered, and from time to time one runs across a tantalizing clue—to the diary on which the first edition of the autobiography was based; to a "long box" in which Barnum's secretary Bowser placed numerous letters, papers, contracts, and other memorabilia with the deliberate object of preserving them for posterity—although there is no way of knowing precisely how much was lost in the many fires Barnum suffered. Barnum himself was in the habit of destroying letters whose contents he wished to keep secret and in his own letters was generally guarded about his personal affairs. He only rarely retained copies of his letters (these were usually of a contractual nature), and he regularly weeded out ("overhauled" is his own term for the process) correspondence he did not deem worth keeping. Apparently his letters to his wives were not greatly prized, for they are at a premium, although a fair number to his daughters, grandchildren, great-grandchildren, and other relatives are extant.

Finally, as the editor may well decide, depending on the reception of the present work, to prepare a second volume of Barnum's letters and papers, he would appreciate hearing from individuals and institutions possessing manuscript materials of which he is currently unaware.

# ❦INDEX OF PERSONS❦

Lowercase roman numerals refer to the pages of introductory material.
Arabic numerals refer to the *numbers of the letters* and their commentaries.
Boldface arabic numerals indicate that the individuals are also the addressees.

[347]

[349]

## About the Editor

A. H. Saxon holds the Ph.D. in the History of Theatre from Yale University and is a fellow of the John Simon Guggenheim Memorial Foundation and the American Council of Learned Societies. In 1980 he became the first American to be designated an honorary lifetime member of the Club du Cirque; and in the same year, in recognition of his work on Barnum, he was presented with the medal of the Barnum Festival Society of Bridgeport, Conn. Other works by him include *Enter Foot and Horse: A History of Hippodrama in England and France*; *The Life and Art of Andrew Ducrow & The Romantic Age of the English Circus*; and (as editor) *The Autobiography of Mrs. Tom Thumb*. He is presently at work on a biography of Barnum.